Visions of Marriage

Asian Anthropologies

General Editors:
Hans Steinmüller, London School of Economics
Dolores Martinez, SOAS, University of London

Founding Editors:
Shinji Yamashita, The University of Tokyo
J.S. Eades, Emeritus Professor, Ritsumeikan Asia Pacific University

Recent volumes:

Volume 15
Visions of Marriage: Politics and Family on Kinmen, 1920–2020
Hsiao-Chiao Chiu

Volume 14
The Art of Fate Calculation: Practicing Divination in Taipei, Beijing, and Kaifeng
Stéphanie Homola

Volume 13
Cosmic Coherence: A Cognitive Anthropology through Chinese Divination
William Matthews

Volume 12
Stories from an Ancient Land: Perspectives on Wa History and Culture
Magnus Fiskesjö

Volume 11
Aspirations of Young Adults in Urban Asia: Values, Family, and Identity
Edited by Mariske Westendorp, Désirée Remmert, and Kenneth Finis

Volume 10
Tides of Empire: Religion, Development, and Environment in Cambodia
Courtney Work

Volume 9
Fate Calculation Experts: Diviners Seeking Legitimation in Contemporary China
Geng Li

Volume 8
Soup, Love, and a Helping Hand: Social Relations and Support in Guangzhou, China
Friederike Fleischer

Volume 7
Ogata-Mura: Sowing Dissent and Reclaiming Identity in a Japanese Farming Village
Donald C. Wood

Volume 6
Multiculturalism in the New Japan: Crossing the Boundaries Within
Edited by Nelson Graburn, John Ertl, and R. Kenji Tierney

For a full volume listing, please see the series page on our website:
https://www.berghahnbooks.com/series/asian-anthropologies

VISIONS OF MARRIAGE

Politics and Family on Kinmen, 1920–2020

Hsiao-Chiao Chiu

First published in 2023 by
Berghahn Books
www.berghahnbooks.com

© 2023, 2026 Hsiao-Chiao Chiu
First paperback edition published in 2026

All rights reserved. Except for the quotation of short passages
for the purposes of criticism and review, no part of this book
may be reproduced in any form or by any means, electronic or
mechanical, including photocopying, recording, or any information
storage and retrieval system now known or to be invented,
without written permission of the publisher.

Library of Congress Cataloging-in-Publication Data

Names: Chiu, Hsiao-Chiao, author.
Title: Visions of Marriage: Politics and Family on Kinmen, 1920–2020 / Hsiao-Chiao Chiu.
Description: New York: Berghahn Books, 2023. | Series: Asian Anthropologies; volume 15 |
   Includes bibliographical references and index.
Identifiers: LCCN 2023007840 (print) | LCCN 2023007841 (ebook) |
   ISBN 9781800738881 (hardback) | ISBN 9781800738904 (open access ebook)
Subjects: LCSH: Marriage—Taiwan—History. | Families—Taiwan.
Classification: LCC HQ686 .C45 2023 (print) | LCC HQ686 (ebook) |
   DDC 306.810951249—dc23/eng/20230323
LC record available at https://lccn.loc.gov/2023007840
LC ebook record available at https://lccn.loc.gov/2023007841

British Library Cataloguing in Publication Data

A catalogue record for this book is available from the British Library

EU GPSR Authorized Representative

LOGOS EUROPE, 9 rue Nicolas Poussin, 17000, LA ROCHELLE, France
Email: Contact@logoseurope.eu

ISBN 978-1-80073-888-1 hardback
ISBN 978-1-83695-119-3 paperback
ISBN 978-1-80073-889-8 epub
ISBN 978-1-80073-890-4 web pdf

https://doi.org/10.3167/9781800738881

The research and writing of this book were funded by a European Research Council (ERC) Advanced Grant under the European Union's Horizon 2020 Research and Innovation Programme, grant agreement No. 695285 AGATM ERC-2015-AdG, held at the University of Edinburgh, which is gratefully acknowledged here.

This work is published subject to a Creative Commons Attribution Non-commercial No Derivatives 4.0 License. The terms of the license can be found at http://creativecommons.org/licenses/by-nc-nd/4.0/. For uses beyond those covered in the license contact Berghahn Books.

Contents

List of Illustrations	vi
Acknowledgements	viii
Introduction	1
Chapter 1. The Migrant Economy and Marriage in the Republican Era	24
Chapter 2. Militarization and Marriage in the Cold War Context	45
Chapter 3. Changing Intergenerational Transmission amid Political and Economic Liberalization	67
Chapter 4. Trials of Marrying	87
Chapter 5. Cross-Border Marriage on the Borderland	107
Chapter 6. The Work of Marriage: An In-Married Woman's Perspective	128
Conclusion	147
References	160
Index	177

Illustrations

Figures

0.1. Minnan-style houses in a village in Kinmen, 2010. © Hsiao-Chiao Chiu. — 5

1.1. An unused *yanglou* in the town of Jincheng, Kinmen, 2010. © Hsiao-Chiao Chiu. — 25

1.2. A memorial arch of chastity in the town of Jincheng, Kinmen, 2018. © Hsiao-Chiao Chiu. — 29

2.1. A disused building of a former military brothel in Anqian, Kinmen, 2018. © Hsiao-Chiao Chiu. — 49

3.1. The bride and groom entering an ancestral hall to greet and worship the groom's remote ancestors in 2017. © Hsiao-Chiao Chiu. — 79

4.1. Steady rise in age at first marriage for both sexes. Source: Department of Household Registration, Ministry of the Interior, Taiwan (https://www.ris.gov.tw/app/portal/674). — 88

4.2. Declining marriage rates in Kinmen and throughout Taiwan. Source: Department of Household Registration, Ministry of the Interior, Taiwan (https://www.ris.gov.tw/app/portal/674). — 89

5.1. The significant proportion of female marriage migrants from China in Kinmen and its recent decline. Source: The Department of Household Registration, Ministry of the Interior, Taiwan (https://www.ris.gov.tw/app/portal/674). — 108

5.2. The changing dynamics of cross-border marriage in Taiwan in the last two decades. Source: Department of Household Registration,

Ministry of the Interior, Taiwan (https://www.ris.gov.tw/app/portal/674). 109

Map

0.1. Kinmen's position between China and Taiwan. © Hsiao-Chiao Chiu. 3

Acknowledgements

I am deeply grateful to the many people in Kinmen for the incredible kindness and hospitality they have shown me during my different periods of residence there. I am especially indebted to my host family who have provided me with unfailing support and unbounded patience, and from whom I learned critical lessons that inform this book.

The research and writing of this book were funded by a European Research Council (ERC) Advanced Grant under the European Union's Horizon 2020 Research and Innovation programme, grant agreement no. 695285 AGATM ERC-2015-AdG, held at the University of Edinburgh, which I gratefully acknowledge here.

The Global Anthropology of Transforming Marriage (AGATM) research team has been supportive and inspiring since the beginning of our collaboration in 2017. I thank my colleagues Siobhan Magee, Eirini Papadaki and Koreen Reece for stimulating my thinking with their constructive comments on my drafts and their own insightful writings. I am extremely grateful to the Principal Investigator of AGATM, Janet Carsten, for having been a constant source of advice, perspective, encouragement and support. She has also given me the benefit of detailed and astute comments on the earlier versions of the manuscript.

I thank the members of the advisory committee of the AGATM project – Ammara Maqsood, Sidharthan Maunaguru, John McInnes, Susan McKinnon, Perveez Mody and David Sabean – for their generous support and comments on our work at different stages. I would especially like to thank Resto Cruz, Ammara Maqsood, Julia Pauli and Charles Stafford for their insightful comments on earlier versions of some chapters in this book. I am grateful to the two readers for Berghahn Books, who gave the manuscript a highly sympathetic reading, and provided many helpful comments.

Finally, I've dedicated this book to my family in Taiwan. Without their confidence in me and unstinting support, I would have not embarked on this journey of becoming an anthropologist and writing this book.

Introduction

Marriage often serves as an index of the wider social changes that were part of the grand force of modernity that swept across much of the globe in the twentieth century. People on the Chinese mainland initially experienced this sweeping force when their government was defeated by the Western powers, including the British and French empires, on their own land in the nineteenth century. The Chinese empire's incapacity to compete with Western forces eventually led to its collapse and the establishment of the Republic of China (ROC) in 1912. Since then, marriage has been highlighted by reformers as a key site of engineering the building of a modern Chinese nation-state. The Chinese Civil War following the Second World War resulted in two Chinese regimes in 1949 – the People's Republic of China (PRC) on the Chinese mainland and the ROC on Taiwan. The two regimes continued to promote modernization in their respective territories, in both of which, despite various contradictions, marriage played a significant role. Rather than focusing on political events, this book explores ordinary people's experiences of marriage on Kinmen – an archipelago under Taiwan's governance and bordering China's southeast coast. I investigate marital experiences across multiple generations over the last century, unpacking the entanglements between marital change and multiple forms of modernity linked to changing global and regional geopolitics.

'Visions of marriage' – the title of this book – reflects my treatment of marriage as a site of creating desired futures from the perspectives of an individual, a family, or a political regime. I also consider marriage as a site of making relatedness between spouses, between an individual and his/her family, or between groups. These future-making and relational aspects of marriage are highlighted and illustrated through ethnographic stories across different political temporal-

---

Endnotes for this chapter begin on page 21.

ities, which reveal the constitutive power of kinship and marriage in regimes of modernity (McKinnon and Cannell 2013). While in subsequent chapters I outline how reformers and political regimes envisioned new futures for their nation through marital reform in different political contexts, my discussion centres on Kinmen islanders' experiences. I explicate how ordinary people envisioned a good life and futures through marriage and kinship practices, and how these visions and practices have changed over time in conjunction with shifting political economies over the last century. Through marital stories across multiple generations in Kinmen, I point out a shift of emphasis in kinship practices from the goal of preserving the patriline in earlier times to the goal of pursuing cross-generational emotional intimacy and material security in the face of increasing uncertainties. This shift, involving challenges to the generational and gender hierarchies of traditional patriarchy (Santos and Harrell 2017), suggests that, rather than zones of conservatism, kinship and marriage are always constitutive of changes and new futures.

Kinmen refers to a group of islands lying about 2 kilometres from China's southeast coast, and about 300 kilometres from Taipei, the capital of Taiwan (see Map 0.1). The available records suggest that Kinmen was officially incorporated into the Chinese administrative system in the late tenth century (Kao 2014; Lin 1993 [1882]), whereas the island of Taiwan was officially placed under Qing's governance in 1683 (Tai 2007). Kinmen and the islands of Taiwan and Penghu diverged politically when the Chinese government ceded the latter islands to Japan in 1895 following its defeat in the First Sino-Japanese War. After the Japanese surrender in 1945 and its resettlement on Taiwan in 1949, the ROC government – led by the Kuomintang (KMT, or the Nationalist Party) – controlled Taiwan, Penghu, Kinmen, Matsu and some smaller islets. But the unresolved civil war between the KMT and the Chinese Communist Party (CCP) again resulted in a different destiny for Kinmen from Taiwan. Due to its geographical proximity to China, Kinmen was shaped by the KMT, backed by the US, as an anti-communist frontline against China in accordance with Cold War geopolitics, and a system of military rule was set up on the island (Szonyi 2008).[1] This military rule, which ended only in 1992, excluded Kinmen from the movements promoting democratization that emerged on the Taiwanese mainland in the 1980s. However, Kinmen's external contacts and people's movements were never entirely blocked during these wars and the period of military rule. The flows of people into and out of Kinmen, due to wars, livelihoods, education and other factors, left imprints on the marital landscape in Kinmen but also linked Kinmen to the Chinese mainland, Taiwan and foreign countries far away. Because of its imbrication in these wider geopolitics, Kinmen is a strategic site for studying the multiplicity of modernity and the vitality of kinship. The stories in this book, across an extended timeline from the early twentieth century to the present, provide a dynamic picture of transforming family and society in Kinmen that is closely linked to but not concordant

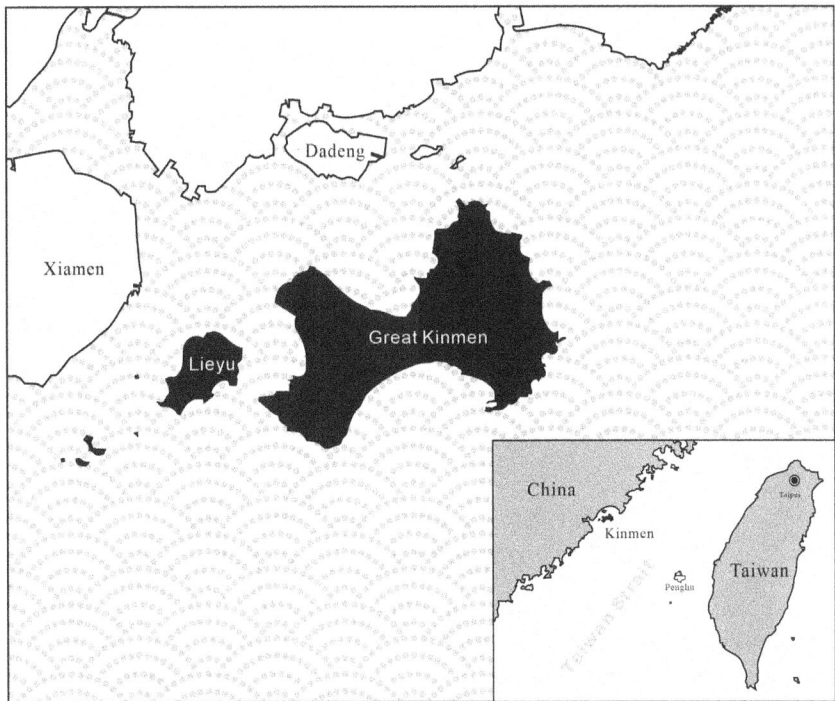

Map 0.1. Kinmen's position between China and Taiwan. © Hsiao-Chiao Chiu.

with the situation on Taiwan. The concept of 'compressed modernity', proposed by sociologist Kyung-Sup Chang (2010), pertinently describes the condensed processes of modernization in various aspects in East Asian societies which resulted in the coexistence of diverse cultural components (including both colonial and postcolonial elements) and multiple social temporalities (e.g. traditional, modern and postmodern temporalities). I argue that such compressed modernity also has multiple representations within the same country as Kinmen islanders experienced different forms of modernity from those on Taiwan in the past century. Marriage provides a productive avenue to explore the intersection and interaction between temporalities under different conditions of modernity in Kinmen and Taiwan, revealing kinship's significance in mediating and generating changes for subsequent generations. Moreover, Kinmen's historical and kinship connections with China, as well as involvement in post-Cold War waves of globalization and expansive neoliberalism, offer suggestive insights for a comparative analysis of family change across Taiwan and China and around the world.

The ethnographic material in this book is arranged chronologically, beginning with the Republican era (1912–1949), followed by the period of military rule (1949–1992), and post-militarization (1992–present), to highlight how marriage has been a knot in which changes in personal lives and politics converged. Rather than projecting a unilinear, progressive understanding of family change, this chronological arrangement brings to light the contestation and negotiation between divergent visions of marriage pursued by individuals, families and successive political regimes. The marital stories of different generations and these stories' cross-generational connections also reveal how wider kin and social ties are still valued and maintained, challenging the assumption by theorists of modernity about the nuclearization of the family and increasing possessive individualism (see also Donner and Santos 2016; Lambek 2011; McKinnon and Cannell 2013). Probing marital change in this specific place over time thus illuminates the interplay between changes in personal lives and the society's transformation into the conditions of modernity as well as the significance of kinship in these transforming processes.

The Setting: Kinmen and Its Experiences of Multiple Forms of Modernity

This section zooms in on Kinmen, introducing the formation of its landscape of Chinese settlements and how the different forms of modernity arising from wars and regime transitions in the past two centuries shaped its current conditions and differences from Taiwan. The following description centres on the two main constituent islands of Kinmen, Great Kinmen (around 134 square kilometres) and Lieyu (around 16 square kilometres, also known as Little Kinmen). Calculation of the resident population on Kinmen has been difficult because of the constant flows of native islanders and outsiders (including soldiers) along with changing politico-economic conditions over the last century, as I describe below.

From the late tenth century, Kinmen received migrants mostly from the southern part of Fujian Province ('Minnan' in Mandarin) on the Chinese mainland. They spoke Hokkien, a dialect used in Minnan, and many of them settled in Kinmen and built houses in an architectural style also observed in Minnan (see Figure 0.1). Their offspring gradually expanded their residential and productive areas, and differentiated between each other according to their surnames (through patrilineal lines). Despite being remote tiny islands, Kinmen produced numerous Confucian scholars and ranked officials mostly between the mid-sixteenth and late nineteenth century. These scholar-officials contributed greatly to the formation of what David Faure (2007: 2) calls the scholarly model of lineage, namely, a lineage with its own written genealogy (*zupu*) and ancestral hall in an official style known as *jiamiao* (see Figure 3.1 in Chapter 3). A commonly-funded estate was set up to finance the maintenance of the ancestral hall and grand rituals worshipping remote ancestors that involved a complex set of etiquette introduced by the scholar-officials from the imperial court to Kinmen. These single-surname set-

Figure 0.1. Minnan-style houses in a village in Kinmen, 2010. © Hsiao-Chiao Chiu.

tlements, or territorialized patrilineages in anthropological terms, were also found in Fujian and Guangdong (Freedman 1958, 1966) and Taiwan, which received many migrants from the foregoing two provinces (Cohen 1976; Pasternak 1972). Nowadays, the boundaries between these single-surname settlements in Kinmen are not only marked bureaucratically (the lines of settlements and administrative villages are basically congruent) but also symbolically by the preservation of ancestral halls and rituals (Chiu 2017). The persistence of these rituals suggests the continued significance of kinship in spite of the expansive marketization today promoting a shift of emphasis from a universe of wider kin ties to the self.

Prior to 1949, Kinmen islanders were mostly engaged in farming and fishing, commuting frequently to the Chinese mainland for trade and purchase of various items from daily necessities to materials for house construction. Despite the achievements in producing numerous scholars, making a living on Kinmen was extremely difficult because of the lack of fertile land to produce enough food. The genealogical records (*zupu*) of local patrilineages indicate the constant outflow of young men eastward to the islands of Penghu and Taiwan, or westward to the Chinese mainland. In the nineteenth century, the growing Western powers which challenged the Chinese empire and colonized tropical lands of Southeast Asia provided Kinmen islanders with another channel of earning a living through migrant labour. The Opium War (or Anglo-Chinese War) in 1842 resulted in China opening five treaty ports, including Xiamen, and the 1860 Beijing Treaty legalized the emigration of Chinese labourers that the Western colonizers coveted. Via the nearby port of Xiamen, young men of Kinmen followed the trend of selling their labour abroad (especially to Singapore, Malaysia and Indonesia in Southeast

Asia) and sending remittances back home. This transnational labour migration and remittance economy was common across the provinces of Fujian and Guangdong – all known as *qiaoxiang* (the homeland of overseas Chinese).

It was through this migrant economy that Kinmen experienced modernity for the first time. As documented in many studies, the initial processes of modernization in *qiaoxiang* across south China were largely attributed to the Chinese migrants who achieved economic success abroad (Ding 2004; Godley 1981). In Kinmen, these successful migrants returned home, investing in the general improvement of local society including in education, public security and public hygiene (Chiang 2011). Many influential Chinese merchants in Southeast Asia supported Sun Yat-sen's 1911 Revolution which led to the collapse of the Qing dynasty and the establishment of the ROC in 1912. Young men receiving a Western education in Xiamen or in the foreign countries where their fathers worked advocated new ideas of marriage by choice and gender equality in Kinmen, echoing the discourses of the New Culture Movement emerging on the Chinese mainland in the late 1910s. Chapter 1 draws on historical material and stories of local women marrying migrants in order to discuss marital change in relation to this wave of modernization.[2]

A few months after Japan's full-scale invasion of China in 1937, Kinmen fell in October to the Japanese army's control. The islanders' transnational mobility was to some extent restricted by the Japanese occupation, and then interrupted by the separation of Taiwan (including Kinmen) controlled by the KMT and China controlled by the CCP in 1949. The post-1949 Taiwan-China conflict, as part of Cold War bipolar politics, led to the second wave of modernization in Kinmen, in which military and geopolitical concerns were prioritized. As compellingly demonstrated in historian Michael Szonyi's (2008) monograph, *Cold War Island*, the lives of Kinmen civilians were significantly altered or disrupted by military strife between the KMT and the CCP in the Cold War era. Houses were destroyed by CCP shelling; civilians were required to conduct militia training and missions, and were ordered to replace the main subsistence food of sweet potatoes on their farms with sorghum, which was used to make alcohol that generated profits to sustain the army. Nevertheless, this militarized modernity had some positive effects which might have been unexpected by the authorities. The remarkable number of soldiers deployed on Kinmen (about 100,000 at their height in the 1950s and 1960s) encouraged the sprouting of various small businesses catering to the needs of the troops. Local women of different ages were the entrepreneurs or main labour force in these flourishing businesses. Based on life stories of local women and men, Chapter 2 unpacks how kin ties and conditions of militarization co-produced new patterns of marriage.

From 1949 to the 1980s, the economic development in Kinmen was shaped and constrained by military concerns. By contrast, the Taiwanese mainland had undergone several waves of industrial development: from cheap, labour-intensive manufactures in the 1960s to an expansion of heavy industry and infrastructure in the 1970s, and then to advanced electronics from the early 1980s onwards (Cheng 2001; Tsai 1999). Like rural areas on Taiwan, Kinmen has been a source of male and female labour, from low-skilled workers to professionals, contributing to Taiwan's economic miracle (Brandtstädter 2009; Kung 1983). On the political side, the KMT regime had confronted growing crises of legitimacy from within and from outside since the 1970s. In 1971, the ROC was replaced by the PRC in the United Nations General Assembly and Security Council; then, in 1979, the US officially recognized the PRC and severed diplomatic relations with the ROC. These diplomatic failures stimulated young intellectuals, including Taiwanese natives and the children of mainland Chinese, to initiate a series of social movements advocating democratization (Hsiau 2005). These events contributed to the lifting of martial law on Taiwan in 1987 (Gold 1986), whereas in Kinmen, due to military concerns, martial law was only lifted in 1992. Taiwan transitioned from the KMT's one-party rule to multi-party democracy, and the Democratic Progressive Party (DPP), established in 1986, won the first presidential election in 2000. Social movements focusing on various public issues (women's rights, LGBT rights, labour rights, etc.) became more active on Taiwan (Chang 2009; Fan 2019; Schubert 2016), but until recently have had only a limited presence on Kinmen (see this book's Conclusion for further discussion).

Though Cold War geopolitics resulted in different routes of modernization for Kinmen and Taiwan, the flows of Kinmen islanders to and from Taiwan to some extent bridged these differences. Chapter 3 explores how parents increased their investment in both their sons' and daughters' advanced studies in Taiwan with a view to guaranteeing their upward mobility and future material security. The younger generation witnessed a transition to the third wave of modernization featuring democratization, expansive neoliberalism, and increasing mobility (including affordable domestic flights and global travel) from the 1990s onwards. Chapters 3 and 4 describe how young people with sojourning experiences in Taiwan articulated their ideas about marriage and planned their weddings in relation to these new politico-economic circumstances.

Following the end of military rule in 1992, central and local governments proposed tourism as a solution to local economic decline following the mass withdrawal of troops from Kinmen. But the effects of these initiatives were limited, and not readily helpful to individual households. Some market towns close to larger military bases that had been established and prospered during the period of military rule became like ghost towns in the 1990s (Szonyi 2008: 206–12). Notably, following demilitarization, the county government of Kinmen began to provide generous benefits and social welfare to its citizens, with financial support from the profitable sorghum distillery founded by the military government in 1952 (Chiu

2017). This encouraged many native Kinmenese living on Taiwan to transfer their household registration back to Kinmen, which resulted in a growing gap between those registered in Kinmen and those actually resident there. The number of people actually living on Kinmen was estimated to be 50,601 in 2017, whereas the number of people with household registration in Kinmen was 136,771 (Liang 2018).[3]

In this book I do not highlight the notion of class to describe my informants in Kinmen. Researchers often use degree of education and type of occupation to categorize people into middle class or working class. For example, Pei-Chia Lan (2018) uses a Bachelor's degree as an index for the measurement of class status in her study of parenting in, largely, urban and nuclear Taiwanese families. However, in Kinmen where joint households remain common and family members vary in degree of education from illiteracy to a Bachelor's degree and above, it is difficult to categorize a family as being middle class or working class. Besides, I knew a couple of local younger politicians, without higher education, who gained upward mobility through participating in electoral politics based on daily networking with their related islanders. The aforementioned generous benefits and social welfare provided by local government also help to reduce the gap in living standards between households. One of these benefits is the monetary compensation to local residents who experienced the period of military rule, which to some extent guarantees the material comfort of many elderly residents.[4] As such, the older generation who accumulated wealth by living very frugally throughout their lives could finance the large expenses of their children's housing and weddings (see Chapter 3). This laid the foundation for the younger generation, with or without higher education, to pursue a middle-class lifestyle in Kinmen as is in urban Taiwan (see Chapters 3 to 6).

Following the waning of military tension between Kinmen and China in the early 1990s, Kinmen islanders began to restore their contact with people in China. In 2001, the governments of Taiwan and China agreed to the establishment of *Xiao San Tong* (lit. mini three links, meaning direct postal, transportation and trade links between Kinmen and China). Local people usually use the term *Xiao San Tong* to refer to the regular ferry service between Great Kinmen and Xiamen (a one-way journey takes about thirty minutes), which has brought a remarkable number of tourists from China.[5] Two tax-free shopping malls and diverse kinds of shops targeting Chinese tourists have been established in Kinmen in recent years.[6] Rapidly growing communications between people in Kinmen and China, as well as the convenient *Xiao San Tong*, had contributed to the surge of cross-border marriage between Kinmenese men and Chinese women between the early 2000s and mid-2010s, as discussed in Chapter 5.

For the Chinese women marrying in Kinmen whom I interviewed, Kinmen was very rural in their eyes when they arrived in the early 2000s. The growing enrolment of students from Taiwan in a local public university and the expanding tourism industry in the last decade have stimulated the local economy to some extent, but most new businesses were established around the market town and administrative centre of Jincheng. A governmental project of preserving traditional Minnan buildings and unused military constructions partly for tourism also contributes to the rural or 'underdeveloped' landscape of Kinmen as a whole. But for in-married Chinese women, their impression of Kinmen as 'rural' also connotes the patriarchal ordering of local family lives, for example, the popularity of patrilocal joint households and the density of familial rituals that are seldom seen in most parts of China and urban Taiwan today. Chapters 5 and 6 discuss how this patriarchal ordering has affected local people's marital experiences, especially from the perspectives of women facing more pressures than their husbands in patrilocal joint households.

Ethnographic Research in and beyond Kinmen

The ethnography in this book is drawn from nearly three years that I spent on Kinmen, including two long-term periods of fieldwork and several short-term visits between 2013 and 2020. Due to its status as a militarized frontline, before 1992, Kinmen was inaccessible to most Taiwanese civilians and was perceived as a place where only soldiers went – and with reluctance. As a native Taiwanese with no kin connections in Kinmen, I was so curious that I first visited the island in 2010. I was amazed by its landscape with numerous traditional Minnan settlements and the density of military fortifications dotting around the islands. But what puzzled me most was, in those seemingly rural and tranquil villages, the kinds of lives local residents had lived through wars and military rule, and were living after demilitarization. In the autumn of 2013, I visited Kinmen again to carry out anthropological fieldwork for my doctoral research aiming to solve these puzzles.

Before my departure, I was told by several people who had friends from Kinmen that it would be difficult to find a place to stay in a village because the available properties were rare and outsiders were usually unwelcome. Rather than the main town of Jincheng where rental housing was easier to find, I managed to rent a Minnan-style house in a larger patrilineal village through several indirect connections. I was not the first researcher from Taiwan in this village but I was the first who intended to stay in the village for more than a year. I could sense the initial suspicion of my landlord at our first meeting. But my landlord's elderly mother and several female neighbours, who were also present, interpreted my single, female and student status as being *tan-sûn* (in Hokkien, meaning simple, without complicated background) and welcomed me.

In a sense, I was fortunate to be able to live in that village for fifteen months because its patrilineal group was comparatively strong by local standards. It had a relatively large population and robust ritual traditions, and several descendants were incumbent political representatives. Moreover, the existence of a voluntary group in the village provided me with a great opportunity to get involved in local social lives. This kind of voluntary group composed of ordinary citizens has flourished in the towns and villages across Kinmen since the late 1990s, encouraged by the Taiwanese government's nationwide policies promoting community building (Lu 2014). Though, in the case of Kinmen, the voluntary groups enabled villagers to go beyond their more exclusive circles associated with ancestral rituals,[7] they have become an efficient way to organize voluntary labour for social events inside and outside the village and to enhance the reputation of the patrilineage (Chiu 2018a).

My participation in the village's voluntary group, mainly composed of middle-aged and elderly women, enabled me to build relationships of trust with many villagers and to enter their households and listen to their family stories. Working with volunteering villagers, I frequently engaged in preparations and proceedings for various traditional events, such as ancestral ceremonies, funerals and celebrations for a new marriage or the birth of a baby boy. Through participant observation, I learned how rituals and customs have been significant media through which kinship and social values (mutual help, reciprocity and hospitality) and interpersonal ties within and beyond the patrilineage have reinforced each other. My fieldwork was not restricted to the above village. Instead, through the villagers' wider social networks building on kinship, marriage, rituals and volunteering activities, I travelled and gathered data across the islands of Great Kinmen and Lieyu, and even in China and Malaysia where my informants had kin connections. These multi-sited experiences were an essential part of Kinmen's biography regarding the complex interaction between kinship, human mobility and political transitions. These research experiences inspired me to explore what role kinship had played in the islanders' everyday lives through the disruption and changes caused by wars, militarization, and then demilitarization, which eventually became the main theme of my doctoral dissertation.

This book is mainly built on my second project in Kinmen, as part of an ERC-funded research programme, 'A Global Anthropology of Transforming Marriage' (AGATM).[8] AGATM aims to re-examine marriage theoretically and ethnographically against the backdrop of profound changes to this institution across the globe. The knowledge gained from my first fieldwork left me with a question: What changes to marriage had come about amidst this resilience of patrilineal values and communities? With a PhD and in my mid-thirties when carrying out my second fieldwork in 2017–2018, I was still categorized by local people as marriageable and encountered suggestions for possible marital candidates. This personal experience signals a significant change in local marriage patterns: the great improvement in women's higher education and the rising trend of delaying marriage among local women and men (see Chapter 4). I therefore tried to understand these changing patterns over time by collecting life histories from local people across multiple generations, including informants of different generations from the same family. I paid attention to how my older and younger informants spontaneously, or in answer to my questions, related their personal experiences and ideas about marriage to the locally dominant views of gender, moral personhood and a good life embodied in persistent traditional rituals and customs, and to wider social changes.

The ethnography of this marriage project builds on an anthropological tradition of longitudinal research in a specific place to make sense of comparable developments and interactions between that place and the broader geographic areas over time. My fieldwork involved a combination of several methods to gather data, including semi-structured interview, participant observation and collecting various publications related to my research, such as local newspapers, the volumes of local people's life stories, and governmental reports. I resorted to my existing local networks to recruit research participants, and found participants myself through volunteering in or attending local public events that had different types of audiences. I also visited China several times to interview people who were relatives of my informants in Kinmen about cross-border marriage. The persons whom I interviewed or had conversation with therefore range across different ages, occupations, social positions and places of origin. I carried out forty-five semi-structured interviews in Kinmen with local people regarding their life stories or views on marriage-related topics based on their personal or work-related experiences. More ethnographic material was accumulated during my longitudinal research spanning eight years, through close interactions and conversations with my informants on various occasions such as dining in their homes, volunteering with them, and attendance at weddings. Notably, most of the marital stories in this book are drawn from women's perspectives because, as a female researcher, I had easier access to women and their intimate lives in present-day Kinmen where the social monitoring of proper male-female boundaries remains palpable. More importantly, this female lens discloses the less visible part of family change in a male-focused society and underlines the importance of gender in making sense of the dialectics of change and continuity.

I discuss my research methods further in subsequent chapters which concern either a specific political period or particular groups of people, and involve data gathered through varying approaches. My framing of this book in chronological order and singling out certain aspects of marriage, gender and intergenerational relations in each chapter was inspired not only by theoretical concerns but also by my long-term and close interactions with local people and families across multiple generations. Most existing studies of Kinmen focus on a specific period, especially the Cold War era. This book, presenting marital stories across multiple generations in Kinmen, links the multiple temporalities of local histories to those of global histories, revealing the mutually transforming processes of kinship and politics.

Family Change and Modernization

Theoretically, this book aims to contribute to the reconsideration of marriage in anthropology and in social scientific studies of family change through unpacking kinship's transformative capacities in regimes of modernity. Ethnographic studies of China prior to 1949 almost unanimously identified the family as the entry point for studying Chinese society and culture (Kulp 1925; Lang 1946). The 'traditional Chinese family' was conceived as an economic unit as well as a carrier and embodiment of Confucian philosophy that envisioned a patriarchal family-based social order.[9] Ideologically, father-son filiation and continuation of the patriline were emphasized, which affected actual arrangements of marriage and transmission of family property. The generational and gender hierarchies intrinsic to the patriarchal structure endowed parents with almost absolute authority over children's lives and marriages, which were highly gendered (Croll 1984). Only male heirs could continue the family line (and uxorilocal marriage and adoption were alternative solutions to the breakdown of the agnatic line) and inherit family property. In contrast, women were destined to marry out and be counted as members of their husband's family providing that they produced heirs for their husbands (Wolf 1972). The 'traditional Chinese family' which suppressed individual autonomy and structured gender inequality was therefore severely critiqued by intellectuals in the early twentieth century amidst the threat, but also inspiration, of Western modernity.

Postwar anthropological studies of Chinese kinship to some extent reinforced the impression of the Chinese family as being oppressive. British anthropologist Maurice Freedman (1958, 1966) drew on Africanist theory of unilineal descent groups to examine patrilineal settlements in south China, proposing patrilineal descent as the key politico-jural principle in organizing Chinese social and family lives. This structural-functionalist approach led to a dominant model viewing the Chinese family as 'an organization characterized by a common budget, shared property, and a household economy that relies on a strict pooling of income' (Yan 2003: 3). Within this corporate family, it was assumed that individuals would suppress their own interests and act in the family's common interests. Accordingly, marriage was considered a pivotal social institution largely in terms of its political and economic significance in the reproduction of the family and society, echoing the mid-twentieth century anthropological scholarship of kinship (see, for example, Evans-Pritchard 1951; Fortes 1949; Lévi-Strauss 1949; Radcliffe-Brown and Ford 1950).

This 'lineage paradigm' (Watson 1982) or 'corporate model' (Yan 2003) had a profound impact on anthropological studies in Taiwan and Hong Kong in the 1960s and 1970s (when China was inaccessible) (Santos 2006). Earlier ethnographies of Taiwan provide nuanced accounts of the interaction between peasant households and industrialization, illuminating how the family made adjustments by rearranging its familial resources and labour (Cohen 1976; Gallin 1967; Gallin 1984). However, these works, based on the corporate model, marginalized the existence of personal desires and emotions (Lee 2004a, 2004b; Yan 2003). On the other hand, the sociology of family, mostly quantitative, has been focused more on how individuals became independent from the family owing to modernization of the economy, education and the growing advocacy of gender equality (e.g. Chen and Chen 2014; Thornton and Lin 1994). In this scholarship, the case of Taiwan has been used to reassess theories of modernization originating from Euro-American experiences given that Confucian-cum-patriarchal values remain effective in enforcing hierarchical relations and gendered expectations (e.g. Lee and Sun 1995; Raymo et al. 2015; Yu 2009).

While the above two bodies of literature vary in theories and methods, they both present Chinese kinship and family as zones of conservatism demanding individual compliance with traditional norms and gendered roles. They implicitly reaffirm a dichotomy posited by theorists of modernity treating kinship as a 'private domain' segregated from the progressive, public spheres of politics and economy effecting changes.[10] Recent anthropological discussion has challenged this 'domaining' framing in the theories of modernity and highlighted the constitutive power of kinship and marriage in generating changes (Carsten et al. 2021; McKinnon 2013; McKinnon and Cannell 2013). On the other hand, I take forward insights from earlier research based on the corporate model, which implied kinship's transformative capacities for the purpose of reproducing the extended family. My doctoral research also showed that while the ritual continuities in Kinmen reflected the conservative aim of preserving the patriline, the continuities actually required people's creativity and innovation to make adjustments in relation to changing conditions (Chiu 2017). To foreground the transformative capacities of kinship, I take theoretical inspiration from the rethinking of the individual-family relations in anthropological studies of Chinese kinship and from new kinship studies.

Individual-Family Dialectics and New Kinship Studies

As discussed above, in light of the corporate model, post-1949 changes in marriage in Taiwan, especially the rise of marriage by choice, were studied as an outcome of the restructuring of household economy and generational hierarchy alongside industrialization. While personal emotions, desires and aspirations for the future might be silenced, neglected or suppressed by individual men and women, and by their parents and wider communities, they were also marginalized by researchers' theoretical preoccupations. Yunxiang Yan's *Private Life Under Socialism* (2003), going beyond this corporate model, is a breakthrough in anthropological studies of Chinese kinship and marriage in foregrounding emotionality, desires and personal freedom that have a vital presence in the private lives of people in post-reform China.

Based on his personal experiences and research in a village in north China between the 1970s and early 2000s, Yan (2003, 2009) theorizes the rise of the individual or individualization following China's transition from collectivization to decollectivization. He shows how young villagers actively pursued personal privacy, desires and a marriage based on romantic love, along with marketization and growing commodity consumption, which since the 1980s had shaped the imaginings and aspirations of rural youth for modern lifestyles in the cities. This quest for modern lifestyles – which were nonetheless hardly attainable in rural areas – has driven many young villagers' ruthless demand for money and property from their parents and created perceived crises of filial piety and elderly support. Yan pertinently captures the role of the socialist state in bringing about this clash of interests and values between generations. The Maoist revolutions replaced traditional values with socialist morality by tearing down the Confucian heritage and the material foundation on which the patriarchal order had been grounded. But this socialist morality collapsed after decollectivization as Chinese citizens, especially in rural areas, were forced to make their own way rather than depending on the state for work, housing and pensions. With neither traditional values nor socialist morality, Yan observed a moral and ideological vacuum widely perceived among the younger population in both rural and urban China. He therefore distinguishes the individualization trend in China from that which Ulrich Beck and Elisabeth Beck-Gernsheim (2001) found in Euro-American societies because of the intervention of the Chinese government and the absence of an internal democracy and welfare state to date.

Though Yan convincingly links individualization to China's compressed process of marketization mediated by the state, there are concerns about his overstating the extent to which individuals have become detached from the family and other social bonds (Donner and Santos 2016; Santos and Harrell 2017). For example, Yan's (2003) rich ethnography of changing intergenerational relations features somewhat less description of the ways and processes in which parents raised their children, and their consequences for parent-child ties. But many studies in post-reform China suggest that parent-child ties are complicated by parental investment in children's long-term well-being (especially through education) in relation to the state's policies (e.g. the One-Child policy) (Evans 2008; Fong 2004; Johnston 2013; Kipnis 2011). These works explicitly or implicitly echo new kinship studies, emerging from the 1980s onwards, which shifted the focus from the question of whether kinship is determined by biological or social factors, to the processual and performative aspects of kinship. The new kinship studies turned attention to how kin ties are established and nurtured over time, and their consequences (Carsten 1995, 2000, 2004; Stafford 2000a, 2000b).

Several recent studies of marriage in China, theoretically in line with new kinship studies, unpack how young people negotiate their marital choice with people, rules and expectations from the broader social networks of which they are part (Donner and Santos 2016; Santos 2021). For example, Obendiek (2016) shows that young people in northwest China rely on their familial and wider social ties to achieve higher education and well-paid employment despite the disadvantages caused by their rural *hukou* (household registration). Despite their espousal of companionate marriage, marital choices are not simply based on affection but influenced by other concerns, such as the potential spouse's *hukou* and the intervention of those who have supported their upward mobility. In metropolitan Shanghai, on the other hand, Zhang and Sun (2014) observe that many parents frequent a 'matchmaking corner' in a park where they look for a suitable partner for their single son or daughter. Though some young women assert their refusal to compromise in their marital choices, they avoid openly rebuffing their parents' matchmaking efforts. Strong intergenerational ties have been enhanced by the One-Child policy and have led to parents' concentration on their only child's well-being, as well as their own, in their old age. In his recent works, Yan (2016, 2021) also notes the increasing expressions of intergenerational intimacy and even the rise of neo-familism in China in ordinary families' response to the problems resulting from compressed marketization and reduced social support provided by the state.

Yan (2003, 2009) made an important theoretical contribution in his shift of focus from the family to the individual in the anthropology of Chinese kinship, which has reshaped the ways that marriage is analysed. Researchers now place less emphasis on how marriage represents and reproduces Chinese patriarchy than on how marriage serves as a vital site in which different imaginings of a good life and future contest with each other. However, as recent ethnographies have shown, we should be wary of overstating the individual's desires and power to disengage from familial and social bonds. My research in Kinmen builds on Yan's move to attend to the individual's subjective experiences and emotions to explore marital change, but also considers these changes in dialogue with new kinship studies. Moreover, my Kinmen ethnography offers a point of comparison with the above studies on China regarding the consequences of the intersections of kinship, the state and policies of reproduction in culturally similar but politically opposite regimes of governance. This comparative perspective also helps to highlight what role kin ties play in preparing people across different social settings for increasingly competitive and precarious living conditions.

Making Relatedness and Fostering Changes in Everyday Lives

Since the late twentieth century, sociologists and demographers using large-scale surveys or demographic statistics as sources of data have consolidated their authority in the study of family change in Taiwan.[11] Chinese kinship and family have been less prominent topics of enquiry for anthropologists of Taiwan.[12] Though growing research on the new global phenomenon of cross-border marriage illuminates the links between sex and commodification, citizenship, and the sovereignty question of Taiwan (e.g. Chao 2004a, 2004b; Friedman 2015; Lu 2008), the theoretical reconsideration of Chinese kinship and marriage via this new phenomenon has been more limited. Notably, with the rising LGBT rights movement in Taiwan, studies of LGBT kinship practices across the fields of anthropology, sociology and gender studies have stimulated rethinking of Chinese kinship (e.g. Brainer 2019; Hu 2017; Lin 2014; Tseng 2018).

These works cite or echo new kinship studies, paying attention to what LGBT people do in their everyday lives to sustain ties with their natal families, or with children who may not be biologically connected to them in their queer families. What they 'do' to keep or make kin ties usually falls within the mainstream cultural framework, that is, the heterosexual, patriarchal structure and gendered roles, but also involves innovation or transgression. For example, Brainer (2017a) describes how a transgender (female to male) research participant took on men's roles in rituals, such as the role of a son during the funeral of his maternal uncle, to construct his maleness but also to create the chance for his kin to recognize his transgression of the conventional gendered boundary. Tseng's (2018) case study shows how lesbian parents in different kinds of non-normative families negotiate with norms grounded on heterosexual marriage and family in order to protect their children and prove their families to be as 'normal' as other normative families. But Tseng also notes that LGBT people's efforts to conform to mainstream norms and gendered roles may make them feel more pressured and anxious while reinforcing dominant norms and values.

The transgression, innovation and anxiety about conforming to dominant norms entangled in LGBT kinship practices reveals the ambivalence of kinship (Peletz 2001). It also echoes the growing anthropological discussion of how transgressions or changes may arise from the unremarkable everyday acts of kinship, which may involve both positive and negative effects leading to kin ties being thickened or thinned out over time (Carsten 2013, 2019; Das 2007; Lambek 2011). Chinese kinship has been well documented for its generational and gender hierarchies that are reinforced through unequal transmission of care, attention and materials to sons and daughters (Croll 1984; Santos and Harrell 2017; Wolf 1972). As this book shows, though these inequalities remain palpable in Kinmen today, the growing parental investment in daughters' education and material security has diversified their life options beyond the traditional gendered destiny (see Chapters 3 and 4). Moreover, I argue that kinship's transformative capacities also lie in the innovation, transgression or unequal treatment made in the processes of parenting that may lead children away from the life paths expected by their parents and reconfigure hierarchical relations between generations.

Most of the protagonists we encounter in this book are heterosexual, and the majority of their marriages and families may be categorized as being 'normative' in relation to the aforementioned queer families. But, like their queer counterparts, my younger informants express the pressure and anxieties originating from parents and wider social networks who demand their conformity to patriarchal social norms that are at odds with their own desires. As we will see, my work and the above LGBT studies have two ethnographic insights in common. First, we have found that our informants try to secure autonomy in their lives and marital decisions while also preserving familial and social ties that are important to them in practical and emotional terms. Second, by including perspectives from people of different generations of the same family in our investigations, we have all detected room for transgressing or subverting norms within the sphere of family (Hu 2018). These life stories across different generations provide subtle material illuminating the accumulation of changes in quotidian lives within the family that potentially contributes to wider social changes, for example, through civil organizations and movements as discussed in this book's Conclusion.

The Intersection of the Personal and the Political

Taking an anthropological approach to kinship in my exploration of transforming marriage and modernity in Kinmen, Taiwan and China, I highlight not only the continued vitality of kinship but also cultural heterogeneity in the age of globalization. This is to critically challenge the global application of grand theories of modernity and intimate lives grounded on Euro-American experiences (Beck and Beck-Gernsheim 2001; Giddens 1992, 1998). Similar attempts have been seen in the bourgeoning scholarship in Asian studies across the fields of social sciences (e.g. Davis and Friedman 2014; Donner and Santos 2016; Ochiai and Hosoya 2014; Yan 2021). Several Asian societies, including Japan, South Korea, Taiwan and urban China, have witnessed increasing trends of later marriage and childbearing, fewer barriers to divorce, and growing commercialized pursuit of (sexual) intimacy, similar to those which occurred earlier in the US and were described by Cherlin (1978, 2004) as the 'deinstitutionalization' of marriage. The volume edited by Davis and Friedman (2014), for example, brought together scholars from the fields of sociology, anthropology and law, highlighting the value of comparison by exploring the political, legal and cultural factors behind these phenomena in different Chinese societies. This book shares a similar aim of comparison but through a different approach in linking Kinmen's specific experiences to wider political and social changes across the world and engaging with relevant anthropological theories (see Santos 2021 for a similar approach). In light of the horizon of new kinship studies, I single out generation, gender and temporality as effective lenses to probe the intersection of the personal and the political.

Generation and gender have been highlighted as two prominent axes of hierarchy and inequality constituting Chinese patriarchy in a collection of anthropological studies edited by Santos and Harrell (2017). This collection has shown how these two axes have been maintained and yet reconfigured by the intersection and interaction between familial norms and state policies in contemporary China, which has resulted in what they called 'transforming patriarchy'. Building on this collection and on insights from new kinship studies, I pay attention to the dynamics among the same generation, and between generations, to explore how acts of kinship contributed to protecting or transgressing patriarchal norms, in relation to actors' more conservative or transformative visions of the future. Through marital stories across multiple generations, I point out a shift of emphasis in kinship practices from a more conservative aim of preserving the patriline to a more open-ended aim of pursuing cross-generational emotional and material well-being today.

Gender, or, more specifically, a female lens, is used to foreground the roles of women in a male-centred society in reinforcing, loosening or subverting gendered norms and inequalities during the processes of raising their children. But examples of fathers' less patriarchal roles in participating in children's life trajectories are also provided to illustrate the gradual reconfiguration of gender and power. Temporality becomes significant in these understandings of generation and gender. In earlier writing from the linked projects of which this book forms part, we focused on the temporalities inherent to the imaginative work that marriage involves (Carsten et al. 2021). This may be concerned with how a person contemplates past familial marriages, or those of children or grandchildren in the future – all of these require imagining relationships beyond the here and now. This imaginative work of marriage affords opportunities for, and encompasses, ethical judgements about, and changes to, ways of performing gender and making relatedness. For example, my ethnography shows how parents who transgressed gender stereotypes (seen in the increased power of mothers to decide family matters) broadened and stimulated the imaginings of their children about non-normative gender images and futures. Children thus became more confident in choosing a life path at odds with their parents' expectations and supported wider changes in society. Moreover, strong parent-child ties encouraged parents to tolerate or protect children who might be non-conformist in their sexuality or social expectations against locally strict patriarchal values (see this book's Conclusion for discussion of emerging LGBT campaigns in Kinmen).

Exploring how marital change across multiple generations is linked to Kinmen's particular experiences of modernity over the past century thus provides a unique comparative perspective on family change in Taiwan and China. It reveals the heterogeneity produced by complex intersections of kinship, politics and different conditions of modernity. It also combines with anthropologists' efforts to reconsider how to study culture and kinship in an ever-changing world where people in different places are linked to each other in varied and complicated ways. By using generation, gender and temporality as analytical lenses, I demonstrate how conservative as well as transgressive qualities presented in the marital stories in Kinmen across the past century embody the increasing reconfiguration of gender and generational hierarchies within and beyond the family. Rather than zones of conservatism, kinship and marriage are sites of animating changes in relation to their agents' visions of desired futures that are challengeable and changeable.

Mapping the Book

This book is composed of six chapters presenting the ethnography chronologically in relation to three political periods that Kinmen experienced between 1920 and 2020. Each chapter is focused on either a specific political period or specific groups of people to provide a suggestive angle on the connections between marital change and shifting political economy. Overall, these different angles together offer a kind of multi-point perspective used in Chinese painting, revealing the coexistence and intersection of multiple temporalities. This helps to foreground how the future-making aspect of marriage becomes less associated with the goal of preserving the patriline than with the goal of ensuring both conjugal bonds and wider kin ties today, and how non-marriage, LGBT intimacy and other relational possibilities are increasingly incorporated into individual and social imaginings of new futures.

Chapter 1 explores marriage in Kinmen in a period when different temporalities of men's transnational mass-migration and China's transition into a republic converged and brought about the first wave of modernity. The 'traditional Chinese family' was 'managed' in this context in the sense that many migrants married women chosen by their parents in Kinmen and their wives were left behind to take care of the household. With examples of young educated men's struggle for marital reform and 'left-behind' women's everyday striving, I discuss how kinship practices and the migrant economy co-produced new arrangements of marriage and maintaining a patrilocal household.

Chapter 2 describes the palpable changes to local marriage patterns conditioned by Cold War geopolitics and militarization in Kinmen. Through stories from veterans originally from China and from Kinmen civilians, I discuss how individuals and families sought to realize desired visions of marriage and the future through transgressing the existing order of sex-gender, generational hierarchy and what constituted a family. The rising power of women in this context is underlined as these women, embodying both the conservative and creative qualities of kinship, had a profound influence in shaping their children's visions of marriage and the future.

Chapter 3 focuses on changing intergenerational transmission amidst significant changes in Taiwan's diplomatic relations and domestic politics since the 1970s which led to democratization and the end of military rule in Kinmen in 1992. Education, housing and weddings are highlighted as three key sites where parents changed their ways of transferring much of their accumulated wealth to both sons and daughters in order to better prepare their children for increasingly uncertain futures. These three sites of intergenerational transmission also witnessed the gradual reconfiguration of gender and generational hierarchies; especially in weddings, there are growing visible expressions of emotions and intimacy between generations through a combination of old rituals and global commodity forms. While the expectation of preserving the patriline remains strong and is expressed through performing old rituals, there is a shift of emphasis in parenting strategies to a desire to enhance intergenerational intimacy and ensure children's material security despite children's life choices being at times at odds with parental expectations.

Following discussions of changing intergenerational transmission in the preceding chapter, Chapter 4 centres on young single people above the age of thirty and their experiences of remaining unmarried in Kinmen. Presenting three young people's life stories, I describe their experiences of deferring marriage not as simply an expression of personal autonomy and freedom but as 'trials' they have to go through on a daily basis. In dealing with three kinds of trials surrounding marriage, they ponder, hesitate and seek to eventually reach their desired visions of life and the future. Moreover, these young single people, rather than embodying possessive individualism, live with their parents and even a married sibling's family and express feelings of obligation and emotional attachment to their families.

Chapter 5 turns to another kind of marital choice emerging in the late 1990s, in which local men decided, very often with their parents' intervention, to marry women from China. I explore how Kinmen's borderland status rendered these cross-border marriages to some extent dissimilar from those found in Taiwan and other Asian countries and, from Chinese women's perspectives, affected their marital decision and navigation of ways of pursuing their desires. Here kinship's conservative tendency became evident in terms of setting local men on a normative life course and pressuring Chinese women to conform to traditional gendered roles. However, Chinese women strove to make the life habitable and even adjust to their desires through transgressing the patriarchal ordering and reshaping relations with their marital families. This suggests a kind of transformation that these women sought to initiate within the intimate sphere of kinship.

Focusing on a young married woman's experiences, Chapter 6 examines the actual marital lives in a patrilocal joint household. While centring on this woman's perspective, I adopt a relational analysis showing how the views and behaviours of her husband, in-laws and villagers encouraged or pressured this woman to make changes to herself in order to sustain her marriage. By situating this woman's marriage within a wider web of kin, I discuss different kinds of relatedness-making in relation to both the conservative and transformative qualities of kinship. This woman's marital story, as well as those discussed in Chapters 3 to 5, demonstrates that younger islanders today tend to search for a balance between pursuing personal desires and sustaining wider kin ties as part of their creation of a good life and desired future.

The Conclusion runs through the key arguments of this book, linking the marital stories across multiple generations in Kinmen to the changing global and domestic political economies over the past century. I end by discussing the emerging LGBT rights campaigns in Kinmen in relation to kinship's transformative capacities, which brings to the fore how wider societal changes in sex-gender, family and marriage can be generated from the relatedness-building and future-making activities of kinship.

Notes

1. Matsu, an archipelago in the East China sea and to the north of Kinmen, also served as the KMT's anti-communist frontline in the Cold War era (see Lin 2021).
2. Note that, from 1895 to 1945, the islands of Taiwan and Penghu were governed by the Japanese, who promoted modernization in various regards, such as infrastructure, production, education, public health, and so on, to maximize their own interests. A growing body of literature has unpacked the tensions between the people of Taiwan and the Japanese colonizers heightened by the former's exposure to ideas about democracy, ethnic self-determination, class struggle, gender equality, and so on, under the concurrent processes of colonialization and enlightenment (e.g. Chang 2014; Li and Lee 2015; Liao and Wang 2006; Wakabayashi and Wu 2000). Despite the difference in their initial approach to modernity between Kinmen and Taiwan, intellectuals in both places echoed the discourses of the New Culture Movement, seeking to reform their society through new practices of gender and marriage (see Chapter 1; see Hong 2017 and Yang 1993 on Taiwan).
3. As many local people told me, the registered population figures include many native Taiwanese people who covet the benefits provided by local government though they have no local kin connections and do not live in Kinmen.
4. The benefits to which people registered in Kinmen may be entitled can be separated into three types: (1) ordinary social welfare, which can be found in other parts of Taiwan, but the level offered in Kinmen is relatively generous, including free public transportation, free medical care, free tuition fees and lunch for pre-university students, and a variety of grants for the elderly and disadvantaged groups; (2) the privilege of buying

sorghum liquor at wholesale price for three traditional festivals and applying for a liquor retailing licence (licence-holders can profit by renting their licences to other bigger distributors); (3) monetary compensation to Kinmen residents for their physical suffering and sacrifice of their civil rights under military rule (Chiu 2017).
5. According to a report issued by the local government of Kinmen in 2019, the number of Chinese tourists visiting Kinmen surged from 68,523 in 2014 to 253,724 in 2015, which was followed by a continuing increase, and the number reached 631,360 in 2018 (see the website of Tourism Department, Kinmen County Government, retrieved 15 March 2023 from https://kmtd.kinmen.gov.tw/Content_List.aspx?n=B159B98318F6F0E6). There was no explanation in the report for this impressive surge, but a news item on *Taiwan News* suggested that this tourist boom was related to the keen promotion of Kinmen as an ideal site for Chinese holiday-makers by county Magistrate Chen Fu-hai at the time. On the other hand, the Taiwanese mainland witnessed a significant decline in Chinese tourists after Tsai Ing-wen (representing the Democratic Progressive Party, DPP) took presidential office in 2016, which was believed to be related to the Beijing government dissatisfaction over Tsai's refusal to accept the 1992 Consensus, under which China defines Taiwan and the mainland as part of one China (see *Taiwan News*, 14 September 2018, retrieved 15 March 2023 from https://www.taiwannews.com.tw/en/news/3530174). This contrast was suggestive of an overall inclination of Kinmen islanders for amicable relationships with China while also being cautious of the DPP's claim about Taiwan's status, which my local informants often commented on publicly.
6. However, due to the Covid-19 pandemic, the ferry service between Kinmen and China has been suspended since February 2020. The day of full reopening is not yet clear at the time of writing this book. As far as I observed, several shops were closed because of the loss of their customers (see also a news item on the website of *CNN*, 3 March 2021, retrieved 15 March 2023 from https://edition.cnn.com/travel/article/kinmen-travel-taiwan-china/index.html).
7. Within the patrilineal village, as the patrilineal group is genealogically separated into several branches constituting smaller units for conducting ancestral rituals, villagers tend to be socially closer to those in the same ritual unit (see Chapter 6 for more on women's communities congruent with these ritual units).
8. AGATM includes five sub-projects carried out in selected sites in Europe, North America, Asia and Africa. With a comparative perspective building on ethnographies from five places across the world, AGATM aims to create a new theoretical vision of the importance of marriage as an agent of transformation in human sociality. See the collective volume by Carsten et al. (2021) resulting from this collaborative research.
9. Francis Hsu's *Under the Ancestors' Shadow* (1948) provides a detailed exploration of how this patriarchal vision of social order was laid out inside the family and shaped its members' personalities through day-to-day internalization of ideas including an emphasis on the father-son relation as the axis of family life, estrangement between the sexes, and authority based on generational and gender hierarchies.
10. Note that a significant body of literature in sociology has shown how the governments in Asia, such as Japan, South Korea, Taiwan and Singapore, proposed policies related to marriage and the family that have created or reinforced familialistic or patriarchal expectations of gendered roles (e.g. Chiu and Yeoh 2021; Lan 2008; Ochiai 2011; Ochiai and Hosoya 2014). Here my discussion focuses on how kinship has been treated as a zone of conservatism in the scholarship of family change in Asia. In subsequent chapters, I relate my findings to the literature on the state policies appropriating or reinforcing conservative or patriarchal familial values.

11. Two on-going projects of the *Taiwan Social Change Survey* (since 1985) and the *Panel Study of Family Dynamics* (since 1999) have accumulated an astonishing amount of data for longitudinal analysis and cross-country comparison (Yi and Chang 2012; Yu and Huang 2018). However, this scholarship has two representative problems. First, some groups of people living in remote areas (offshore islands, mountains, etc.) are often excluded from so-called nationwide surveys. Second, the data is generated and interpreted according to certain theoretical assumptions while the question of how phenomena which seem superficially similar may be engendered by heterogeneous historical or cultural contexts is side-stepped. For example, as I discuss in Chapter 2, the remarkable number of soldiers assigned to safeguard Kinmen between the 1950s and 1980s had a significant impact on the local marriage market: many local women married soldiers and moved to Taiwan. I have not, however, found any reliable official statistics or survey data about these marriages and migration to Taiwan.
12. This is probably related to the diversification of research interests among anthropologists of Taiwan and their division into two research areas, focusing respectively on Austronesian-speaking peoples – the indigenous inhabitants on the Taiwanese mainland – and Han Chinese who constitute the majority of the population.

1

THE MIGRANT ECONOMY AND MARRIAGE IN THE REPUBLICAN ERA

Apart from the military legacies of the Taiwan-China conflict from the Cold War era, nowadays the landscapes of Kinmen impress visitors from outside through various built edifices from imperial times and numerous grand *yanglou* (Western-style houses) mostly built in the 1920s and 1930s (see Figure 1.1). The heritage of the imperial epoch, such as the ancestral halls (*jiamiao* or *zongci*) of local patrilineages and memorial arches in honour of chaste widows (*zhenjie paifang*), epitomizes the imperial vision of a patriarchal family-based social order. The *yanglou* built by local men who achieved tremendous success abroad, especially in Singapore, Malaysia and Indonesia, signify Kinmen's first encounter with modernity in conjunction with China's political transition from a hereditary monarchy to a republic. This chapter explores how this wave of modernity brought about by the migrant economy stimulated the contention between conservative and progressive visions of the future that people wanted to achieve through marriage. With historical and ethnographic material representing different actors' perspectives, I discuss how kinship practices and men's migration co-produced new arrangements of marriage and managing a patrilocal household, and how women, rather than being mere victims of patriarchy, asserted and protected their ways of life.

The coexistence of the above two kinds of architecture constructed in different times is not merely a superimposition of different temporal layers or past residues enfolded in the unilineal progress of time. Rather, I suggest, this coexistence inspires us to consider heterogeneous spatial-temporal experiences that came together, clashed or merged with each other, and reconfigured patterns of marriage in the age of men's mass emigration. In tandem with the recent surge of interest in time and temporality in migration studies (Baas and Yeoh 2019; Barber and Lem 2018), historian Shelly Chan (2018) shifts attention to fragmented and multiple

---

Endnotes for this chapter begin on page 43.

Figure 1.1. An unused *yanglou* in the town of Jincheng, Kinmen, 2010. © Hsiao-Chiao Chiu.

temporalities that have been sidestepped in previous historical studies of Chinese diaspora focusing primarily on spatiality. In her exploration of Chinese history through the lens of the diaspora from the late nineteenth to the mid-twentieth century, Chan uses 'diaspora time' and 'diaspora moments' to conceptually distinguish different temporalities (2018: 12–13). 'Diaspora time' depicts the diverse, ongoing ways in which migration influenced the lifeworlds of individuals, families and communities. A 'diaspora moment' occurred when diaspora time converged with other temporalities and produced broader repercussions, especially responses from powerful leaders or political authorities, such as influential Chinese merchants in Southeast Asia who supported Sun Yat-sen's 1911 Revolution and Nationalist China's anti-Japanese war effort. In this chapter, I borrow Chan's concept of diaspora time to refer to the period in which the migrant economy reshaped the local world of Kinmen. But instead of momentous encounters, my focus is on the conjunctures of different spatial-temporal experiences of ordinary people in Kinmen and their fellow islanders abroad that provoked anxieties, contestations and re-imagination of marriage and social futures.

The diaspora time of Kinmen started in the late nineteenth century and ended in 1949 when the Chinese Civil War resulted in the obstruction of the islanders' transnational mobility. The local world in this diaspora time was composed of larger and smaller territorialized patrilineal communities. As mentioned in this book's Introduction, these patrilineal communities had produced numerous Confucian scholar-officials who promoted the popularization of state ideology in their natal communities in late imperial times. This state ideology, tracing back to the resurgence of Confucian teachings generally known as Neo-Confucianism in the Sung dynasty (tenth to thirteenth centuries), included ritual etiquette and moral norms defining a person's proper conduct and interaction with others, such as a woman's chastity. In the first section of this chapter, drawing on historical material and historians' studies, I explain the popularization of an imperial vision of a patriarchal family-based social order featuring the protection of female virtue in Kinmen. This helps to illuminate how this imperial vision still dominated spatial-temporal experiences of many Kinmen islanders following the modernization brought about by the remittance economy and exerted great pressure on many women with regard to their fidelity to their absent husbands.

Most of the material discussed in this chapter focuses on the latter stage of Kinmen's diaspora time between 1920 and 1949 – a period which witnessed the emergence of progressive visions of marriage following China's transition into a republic in 1912. Though the exact number of migrants across the world during this diaspora time is difficult to verify, the local gazetteer published in 1968 supposed the number to be remarkable given the sharp decrease in Kinmen's population from 79,357 in 1915 to 49,650 in 1929 (Kinmen xian wenxian weiyuanhui 1968: 97). These migrants mostly relied on their kin connections to decide their destinations and occupations. For example, in Singapore which received a large number of men from Kinmen, new migrants followed their relatives to participate in piloting different kinds of boats (e.g. sampan, twakow, motor sampan) and porterage along the Singapore river (Chiang 2010). With the savings they accumulated, some migrants collaborated to establish their own businesses. Anthropologists have scrutinized the significance of kinship in informing and organizing such transnational migration (Oxfeld 1993; Watson 1975), and more recently transnational corporation (Rofel and Yanagisako 2019; Yanagisako 2002, 2013). This chapter will not go into the relation between kinship and transnationalism but will examine male migrants' marriages in light of the constitutive power of kinship and marriage underlined in this scholarship (Yanagisako 2013), and in relation to emerging political discourses surrounding marriage in the Republican era.

Following the establishment of the ROC in 1912, criticism of Confucian traditions that emerged in the late Qing era became more vigorous among young urban intellectuals and, through newspapers and magazines, grew into nationwide campaigns known as the New Culture Movement in the late 1910s.[1] The Western conjugal family ideal (*xiao jiating*, lit. small family), which promoted marriage by choice and the economic and emotional independence of the individual from the family, was advocated to replace the traditional family. The reformers believed that the conjugal family, which encouraged productivity, independence and civic virtue, was the key to the strength of Western countries. Women's roles were underlined by the New Culture advocates in reconfiguring the familial and societal order. By moving women out of the inner sphere and educating them, male reformers hoped that these new women would make satisfactory companions for their modern husbands and raise their children with modern knowledge for the sake of a stronger China and its bright future (Glosser 2003). According to the local gazetteer edited in the early Republican era, some changes that the New Culture Movement called for occurred in Kinmen. For example, bound feet lost their allure as a type of beautification for local women, and girls living in the towns started going to school instead of concealing themselves at home (Liu 1958 [1921]: 150–51). But, as we will see, women's access to education and autonomy in the choice of mate remained limited.

Set against the above context, the second section discusses what roles kinship and marriage had played in linking male migrants abroad to their families staying behind. Featuring the material drawn from publications produced by a local lineage, the third section discusses how young men receiving a Western education echoed the discourses of the New Culture Movement and turned their ideal visions of marriage into writings and into actual practices. But I also examine a dichotomous framing in these men's discourses which overlooked the transformative capacities of kinship in creating new generations and futures. The fourth section turns to the stories of migrant wives, who were left behind to take care of their marital families in Kinmen, in this diaspora time. Building on the life stories of several 'left-behind' women that were collected by Hsiang-Chin Liu (2006) and on my own ethnographic material, I discuss how these women preserved their fidelity despite the long-term absence of their husbands. Rather than fitting these women to the imperial model of female virtue, I draw on Veena Das's (2012, 2018a, 2018b) thesis about 'ordinary ethics' to suggest an alternative understanding of these women's moral striving. The material discussed in this chapter altogether reveals the growing contention between conservative and progressive visions of marriage, where we can detect the transformative capacities of kinship in contributing to a move of societal change through investing in male offspring's upward mobility.

The Imperial Vision of Social Order and Female Virtue

This section summarizes the historical formation of the idea of female virtue, including strict observance of sex segregation and chaste widowhood, in imperial China to explicate why many women in Kinmen in the Republican era complied with the conservative arrangements of marriage and gendered roles that I discuss later. Historians of China have scrutinized the interconnections between marriage, women's sexuality and the maintenance of a patriarchal family-based social order in imperial times (Ebrey 1993; Mann 1991, 2011). To maintain this social order, the imperial governments promoted and rewarded the virtue of female chastity on the one hand and punished the offenders of this virtue on the other. Even though widow chastity had long been praised by the imperial court and was legally sanctioned in the Yuan dynasty (thirteenth and fourteenth centuries), it was in Ming and Qing times that chaste widowhood escalated into a cult and gained systematic legal support, state sponsorship and widespread social prominence (Birge 1995; Mann 2011). The Ming and Qing governments disseminated the value of chastity in towns and villages through strengthening the institution of imperial testimonials (*jingbiao*) honouring moral exemplars across the empire. The women who had the court honour of *jingbiao* conferred upton them were privileged to be commemorated in government-financed memorial shrines and arches.

This protection of women's chastity implied the confinement of sexual activity to marriage. As such, men unable to get married were perceived as threats to the social order and patriarchal stability. Sommer (2000, 2002) argues that, especially during the High Qing era (late seventeenth to mid-nineteenth centuries), the state's attempt to regulate sexuality has to be understood against a social background in which men outnumbered women and a remarkable number of men of lower socioeconomic strata remained unmarried. By reviewing Qing-dynasty legal case records, Sommer (2002) shows that jurists depicted the men accused of illicit sexual intercourse, including both consensual and coercive acts outside marriage, as aggressive violators of the boundaries of the sexes and of the household because a woman's social identity was defined by her relationship with her husband or father. In other words, the politico-jural concern over women's sexuality was not only to defend the state's conception of women's moral and sexual integrity but to preserve the stability of the patrilineal families and the social order in general.

The strict separation of the sexes which worked to sustain the vision of a patriarchal order was not only reinforced by the state but also supported by ordinary families. To guarantee a woman's virtue, a family carefully prevented her having any contact with the outside world and she was taught to do womanly work (namely, to work with her hands inside the home, as a spinner, weaver or embroiderer) (Bray 1997). A sex-gender system revolving around cloistered women was elaborated and espoused by people of divergent social statuses in the nineteenth century. As Mann puts it, 'whether scholars, cultivators, artisans, or merchants, the ability of a family to cloister women, train them for womanly work, and place them in a respectable marriage was a crucial marker of status' (2011: 7).

In Kinmen, there are three memorial arches of chastity (*zhenjie paifang*) granted by the Qing emperor in the nineteenth century (see Figure 1.2). The local gentry and literati joined in the state's moral campaigns by documenting these chaste women in the genres of local gazetteers, written genealogies, biography and poetry. In these records, the women honoured were placed in the categories

Figure 1.2. A memorial arch of chastity in the town of Jincheng, Kinmen, 2018. © Hsiao-Chiao Chiu.

of the 'faithful' (*jie* or *jiexiao*) and 'martyred' (*lie*). A 'faithful woman' meant a widow who never remarried and fulfilled her filial obligation towards her husband's family; a 'martyred woman' meant a widow who took her own life to follow her husband in death. Many martyred women were still young, between their late teens and early twenties, when they committed suicide.

Notably, many of these faithful and martyred women were from the families of commoners rather than elite families. The local gazetteer noted that local women strictly adhered to the separation of the sexes in their everyday lives: girls avoided going out after they reached the age of ten and spent their time at home doing spinning and weaving (Lin 1993 [1882]: 395). This quotidian observance of the sexual boundary seemed to lay the ground for numerous women to choose chaste widowhood or suicide following their husbands' death as the ultimate realization of their female virtue. Many widows also made a difficult living through womanly work at home and they were thus kept away from sexual intrusion. Some women, who had not borne children before their husbands died, not only preserved their chastity but also attempted to continue their husband's family line by adopting a little girl and arranging an uxorilocal marriage for her in the future.

Given that the historical documents that I found were all written by educated men who might emphasize the efficacy of Confucian teachings, one may wonder to what extent local women took the virtue of chastity seriously. The cases of 'faithful maidens' – meaning a young woman expressing her loyalty to her deceased betrothed by living out her life as a widow (*zhennü*) or committing suicide (*lienü*) – in Kinmen and throughout China suggest women's general identification with this virtue.[2] Historian Weijing Lu (2008: 14) argued that what motivated these young women's decisions, regardless of their families' class and their degree of education, was the intertwining of orthodox Confucian values and ideas of *yi* (honour-bound duty) and *qing* (romantic love, feeling) which were widely celebrated in literature and popular theatre. These feelings of *yi* and *qing* were also related to the common practice of child betrothal: betrothed at a very young age, a girl had grown used to viewing herself and being treated as a member of her fiancé's family long before the wedding (Lu 2008: 144–56). Drawing on such faithful maidens' own writings, principally poetry, and biographies of faithful maidens composed by men who knew their subjects personally, Lu argues that these young women, rather than passive followers or victims of Confucian ideology, were passionate actors whose lives were complicated by duty, love, aspiration and fatalism (2008: 15–17). They might use various ways to gain permission from their late fiancés' parents to join their families, and establish authority in these difficult situations.[3] Lu's original discussion on these faithful maidens directs our attention to women's own feelings, volition and choice of life behind their devotion to the protection of their absent husbands' families, as I discuss in the latter part of this chapter.

Marriage in the Context of Mass Men Working Abroad

When asked about the choice of mate before 1949, my elderly informants in Kinmen answered intuitively that almost all marriages at that time were decided by parents, in the form of arranged marriage or little daughter-in-law (*tongyangxi*, meaning a girl being adopted at birth or in childhood to be the wife of her adoptive parents' son in the future when both children grew up). For example, a female informant told me that her parents' marriage (in the 1930s) was exclusively decided by her grandfather, who was a renowned artisan from a prestigious family. When her grandfather visited a village for work, he heard about a pretty young woman in that village who was skilled at weaving and worked hard to provide for the family because of her father's early death. The grandfather viewed this woman as an ideal bride for his eldest son. Without informing his son beforehand, he sent a matchmaker to the woman's family to ask her mother's permission for the marriage. This kind of scenario was common among local marriages at the time despite the absence of the groom who was working abroad. However, rather than merely a replication of marital tradition, I suggest that such parental arrangement for their migrant son's marriage was part of kinship's constitutive power and closely related to the anxieties about preserving the patriline engendered by transnational migration.

For the men who planned to work abroad or had been abroad for a while, their marriages were of great concern to their parents. As my senior interlocutors put it, most migrants had not thought about establishing permanent residence overseas before their departure; neither had their parents. Probably in order to link their sons to the home, many parents found brides for their sons before they left. Lin Ma-Teng, an expertise in local history in his mid-seventies, told me that his grandmother found a *tongyangxi* for his uncle, who was just thirteen years old at that time and preparing to work in Singapore. By doing so, the grandmother also acquired an adopted daughter to accompany her and help with household chores. When this uncle turned eighteen years old in the 1930s, the grandmother urged him to hurry back by writing several letters, in which she overcame her illiteracy by using drawings to indicate a wedding. But returning was not easy for a low-paid labourer, so this man had to borrow money from his fellow countrymen for the journey back home. This instance illustrates a sense of uncertainty caused by the disjuncture between different spatial-temporal experiences of migrant sons and the parents they had left behind at a time when transnational communications were difficult. The negative imaginings of their son's permanent absence triggered the parents' creative use of the existing form of *tongyangxi* and overcome the difficulty of communication.

Similar forms of parental intervention in a migrant son's marriage were also found across *qiaoxiang* (the homeland of overseas Chinese) in Fujian and Guangdong, which were characterized by many well-organized patrilineal communities like those found in Kinmen. Based on his extensive survey in Fujian and Guangdong in 1934–1935, sociologist Da Chen (2011 [1939]: 133–38) notes that the extended family, with three or more generations living together, remained common. Values of ancestral reverence, continuation of the patriline, and cooperation between lineage brothers were also upheld. Migrants' parents contributed to the preservation of the patrilineal family by making every effort to ensure their sons' marriages with native women. Even in a very poor family, parents saved a portion of their son's modest remittances for the expenses of his marriage to a bride they found for him (Chen 2011 [1939]: 150–51). It was not only the conservative vision of marriage with the aim of preserving the patriline but also the anxieties and uncertainties caused by young men's absence that had driven parents to try their best to anchor their son's attention and future to the natal home.

Local men working abroad not only triggered their parents' anxieties, but also generated a stimulus to the local marriage market regarding the association of migration and wealth. Many relevant stories can be found in a bulletin called *Xianying* (it also has an English name *Shining*, used hereafter) established by the Xue lineage in Kinmen in 1928, with funding mainly from the lineage's overseas members.[4] Given its function to exchange news between overseas sojourners and their families in the homeland, news about a returnee's matchmaking, announcements of an engagement or a marriage, and the holding of a wedding accounted for a remarkable proportion of *Shining*'s total publications. There were numerous news reports in *Shining* showing the popularity of young migrants as marital candidates in the local marriage market. One news item describes how a young migrant's return to find a bride attracted numerous matchmakers' proposals and, finally, thirty-two women of different characteristics were introduced to him (*Xianying* 2006: 1760). Some of these news reports mentioned the occupation of the migrant under discussion, sometimes with information about his economic competence, which arguably aroused the imagination of those staying behind about the wealth that a migrant could earn abroad.

Marrying migrants seemed to have become a social fashion across *qiaoxiang* in south China (Chen 2011 [1939]; Hom 2010; Oxfeld 2005). It was not only the bride's parents but also the bride herself who agreed to the marriage not because of an in-depth knowledge of the groom but for his migrant status. In one woman's recollection of accepting marriage to a migrant working in Singapore chosen by her parents in the early 1940s, she said that 'I was like a blind person not knowing him being lame or paraplegic, and pleased to marry a migrant' because 'all people here at that time thought that it was good to marry a migrant' (Liu 2006: 118). However, this fashion of marrying migrants resulted in numerous unfortunate marital stories because not all of the migrants were able to realize their goal of making a fortune abroad and returning home. There is a proverb circulated in Kinmen '*liuwang, sanzai, yihuitou*' meaning that out of ten men going abroad, six died, three stayed overseas, and only one returned home, which suggests the cruel reality that many migrants and their families eventually confronted. I will revisit this topic in the fourth section on migrant wives' marital experiences.

Educated Men's New Visions of Marriage and National Futures

The publication *Shining* is a representation of Kinmen's exposure to Western knowledge and modernity. Its appearance in 1928 was suggestive of the fruitful results of many migrants' years of hard work and eventual success abroad. These successful migrants returned home to build their grand *yanglou*, renovate their lineages' ancestral halls, and carry out the modernization of local society including aspects of education, public security and public hygiene (Chiang 2011). *Shining* and other newsletters funded by these migrants indexed the aspiration of a group of young men who had received Western education for their homeland to transform into a strong modern state compatible with Western powers.[5] Based on the material from *Shining*, I discuss below these educated men's attempts to challenge the Confucian-cum-patriarchal traditions through articulating new visions of marriage and national futures.

Shining, which started as the newsletter of a village-owned primary school also funded by overseas members of the Xue lineage, included school news and written works by students. *Shining* revealed that girls could attend school (and they usually performed very well in their studies) and how they could become conscious of the constraints and inequalities imposed on them. For example, a female student of a higher grade (who seemed to be in her mid-teens) expressed her frustration in a short article because her wish to further her studies was objected to by her parents, who were 'old-fashioned people living in the nineteenth century'. As she foresaw no possibility of advancing her education, which was deemed by her to be the only way for a woman to attain independence, she despaired: 'It might have been better if I had never learned to read' (*Xianying* 2006: 126–27).[6]

Though the editors of *Shining* and most contributors were men, they advocated ideas of gender equality, women's emancipation, and marriage based on free choice and love through writing in various genres. The first chief editor of *Shining*, Shi-Wu, who was also the school's principal, observed rural parents' biased views about their daughters' education. In an essay, he claimed that the migrants' remittances were gradually ruining the society of Kinmen, particularly in moral terms: 'In the eyes of men, women were like toys. [The aim] of a migrant's family marrying in a woman was to gain one more prostitute [for men]' (*Xianying* 2006: 1626). He also bemoaned the fact that the New Culture Movement only had a limited effect on Kinmen because, according to his observations, parents sent their daughters to school to elevate their daughters' value in the marriage market with a view to requesting a greater sum of bridewealth from wealthy migrants in marriage negotiations (*Xianying* 2006: 1627). The articles by the female student and Shi-Wu instantiate shared views among Chinese reformers at the time in which women's education was treated as an index of a society's progression into modern civilization, and the 'traditional family' appreciating education's symbolic value of facilitating a woman's hypergamy was criticized as being reactionary and materialistic.

Several essays authored by men in *Shining* painted pictures of new futures by contrasting traditional marital practices with their new visions of marriage. For example, Jing-Xin, a highly-educated man residing in Southeast Asia, wrote an essay to argue against the old marital customs including parental authority over children's marriages (*Xianying* 2006: 2041–45). He criticized people's obsession with the formalism of traditional marital ritual in Kinmen, advocating the couple's genuine love (*ai*) for each other as the core of a marriage. Despite these educated men's critiques of the patriarchal repertoire on paper, their visions of a new society and national futures could hardly overturn the conservative practices focusing on preserving the patriline observed by their fellow islanders. In his reply to Jing-Xin's inquiry about his thoughts regarding marital reform, Shi-Wu expressed his sense of shame over his eventual submission:

I could do nothing but go with the flow. I don't want to pour out my despair. I admit I am a person with no ambition, and can only stand aside and send my blessing to you. Alas! Jing-Xin, I was not qualified to be counted as the vanguard of our times. I am willing to bear the sneers of those people who uphold a revolutionary spirit. Nevertheless, there is still a tiny bit of hope. In next season, for my livelihood, I may go somewhere else ... I am truly desperate to leave this dead-end of [life in the] Minnan as soon as I can. (*Xianying* 2006: 2046)

Shi-Wu wrote this reply to Jing-Xin when he was approaching graduation from Xiamen University. From other news items in *Shining*, we know that Shi-Wu married a school teacher in Kinmen, whom he had befriended during a long intellectual exchange, and he did leave for Singapore after marrying (*Xianying* 2006: 1847, 2121–22). Shi-Wu 's marriage took the form of *tongju*, which was also adopted by his fellow villagers as shown in several news items in *Shining*. By comparing these news items, *tongju* seemed to mean a marriage based on the couple's own decision and without involving traditional, elaborate marital rituals – apparently different from its contemporary connotation of a couple's cohabitation whether or not they plan to get married. Shi-Wu appeared to put the new ideas and practices that he promoted into practice by marrying a woman of his own choice and formalizing his marriage in a much simpler way. Nevertheless, his frustration at what he considered conservative and even depraved in his homeland ultimately drove him away.

The Missing Aspect of Kinship's Transformative Capacities

The articles from *Shining* mentioned above reveal the problems resulting from the interaction between remittance economy and traditional marital practices on the one hand, and the new visions of marriage closely linked to new futures of China that young intellectuals possessed on the other. Their arguments, as well as similar articulations by young reformers across the societies of China and Taiwan at the time, all repeatedly constructed and emphasized a dichotomy between patriarchal traditions and modern civilization. It seemed that this dichotomous framing justified their harsh critique of the 'backwardness' and inequalities of the 'traditional family', to be replaced by progressive and civilized family valuing personal autonomy and gender equality. The rhetoric formation of marriage as a political issue concerning a nation's futures by these young intellectuals appeared to marginalize the place of kinship, which was conceived as being reactionary because of its aim of preserving the patriline. But, with an anthropological perspective of kinship, we may move beyond this dichotomous framing to reconsider what role kinship practices had played in enabling these men to receive a Western education and advocate the modernization of their society.

In her discussion of how Italian family firms survive in today's very competitive global market by turning themselves into transnational corporations, Yanagisako (2019: 232) highlights another meaning of 'generation' – that is, 'creation' – beyond the habitual association of generation with intergenerational transmission. Rather than employing a model of biological reproduction in studying these firms' persistence, she argues that these firms should be considered as kinship enterprises involving constant reassessment and reformulation of their goals and strategies. This transformative process involved the incorporation of modern management techniques and organizational forms into their firms, through sending children to pursue degrees in business and finance, information technology, marketing and economics, in order to forge a modern family capitalism, which might lead to the generation of new firms following the demise of old ones. These transformative capacities of kinship were actually intrinsic to the 'traditional Chinese family', which, in Kinmen, had produced several scholar-officials from agrarian families in late imperial times. For families of different conditions, the goal of reproducing the family might not be about making sons follow their fathers' careers but mostly about cultivating sons, especially talented ones, to gain a higher social status so as to *guang zong yao zu* (to glorify their ancestors). Marriage served as a key institution of reproducing a patrilineal group not only by procreation of male descendants but also by enhancing social status through building alliance with affines of compatible status.

Similar kinship logic was implied in several news items about marriage throughout the publications of *Shining*. For example, a news item describes how a young male migrant of a merchant family based abroad, through an introduction, married the daughter of a Chinese businessman also based abroad. The author noted that as these two families were both well-established merchant families with wider social networks, their wedding must be magnificent (*Xianying* 2006: 3545). This kind of 'arranged marriage' between two well-off migrant families, rather than conservative, could be supportive to their homeland's enterprises of modernization. For instance, a migrant getting married after the end of Japanese occupation of Kinmen (1937–1945) donated a sum of money from the monetary gifts that he received from his family's networks to celebrate his marriage to the publisher of *Shining*, with the wish that the money be used to purchase reading materials for children (*Xianying* 2006: 3220). The publisher of *Shining*, which had resumed in 1946 and was suffering a great financial deficit, then openly called for donations in order to continue the publication. Afterwards, there were several news items about newlyweds' donation of their monetary gifts to support the publisher and their operation of a school in their natal village. In reward, the publisher published thank-you notes in *Shining*, usually with a photo of the newlyweds dressed in Western wedding attire.

The above-described instances suggest that the transformative capacities of kinship and marriage are an intrinsic part of the seemingly conservative aim of reproducing the patrilineal family. Acts of kinship intersected with new politico-economic circumstances to ensure the upward mobility of new generations and the preservation of the patriline, which was not necessarily opposed to the creation of a modern Chinese society. However, this is not to deny that gender inequalities and oppressive elements existed. For less resourceful migrant families, the reproduction of the patrilineal family might involve a great deal of sacrifice that women were pressured to endure.

Left-Behind Wives Leading Patrilocal Households

'We just owed each other' (*sio-khiàm-tsè*, in Hokkien), Grandma Su, as I called her, said when answering my question about her late husband, who went to Singapore a few months after the birth of their only son and died there at a young age in the early 1940s. Due to her father's work in Shanghai, Su and her three elder brothers were born there. Returning to Kinmen in the early 1920s, Su's father resettled his family in a patrilineal village other than his natal village, and they became one of the few families with different surnames (i.e. of different patrilineal lines) in that village. Su's parents gave birth to their youngest son in this new residence; both Su and her younger brother followed their parents' arrangements to marry persons belonging to the lineage dominating their residential village. Despite growing up in the same village, Su said that she barely knew anything about her future husband beforehand because at that time women rarely went outside and interacted with men.

Su gave birth to her son about one year after marriage, and then her husband suddenly decided to go to Singapore before their son's first birthday. At the age of twenty, without time to absorb her husband's abrupt decision to leave home, Su started to take on the burden of leading the household (her parents-in-law seem to have passed away before her marriage). By describing her relationship with her late husband as *sio-khiàm-tsè*, Su declined to recall anything further about her marriage. But from her son Woody, whom I befriended in 2013, I learned that Su's husband went to Singapore to earn money and he may have been killed by the Japanese army occupying Singapore during the Second World War. Woody's paternal uncle, the elder brother of his father, had worked in Singapore for a long time (and eventually established permanent residence there). He was a member of the Kuomintang (KMT) and involved in the anti-Japanese activities that the KMT organized among overseas Chinese in the 1930s and 1940s.[7] This uncle told Woody that his father might have been implicated in an anti-Japanese mission and killed by the Japanese when Woody was five years old. As such, Su's memory of her husband was understandably tenuous but also traumatic; after her statement above, she shook her head and was unwilling to say more. During the five years of her husband's absence, Su lived as a grass widow heading a patrilocal household. After her husband's tragic death, Su continued her life as a widow, feeding herself and her son by helping in agricultural work on a relative's farm.

Absent Husbands and Tough Wives

The patrilocal household that was sustained by a young married-in woman, as was the case of Grandma Su's, became common across *qiaoxiang* during the diaspora time. Many women of Su's generation were left behind by their migrant husbands who rarely or never returned home. These migrants' marriages to local women involving their parents' expectations and intervention constituted pressure on them as they were supposed to bear the twofold responsibilities of feeding their marital families and caring for their old parents. Besides such familial burdens, they faced expectations from the wider communities in their occasional visits to their homeland. As mentioned earlier, despite local imaginings of upward mobility and the fortune that male migrants were expected to earn overseas, there were few successful cases. Lin Ma-Teng, whom we saw earlier, said that many migrants were afraid to make a return visit due to the great expenditure that the journey involved and, more crucially, the moral pressure to prepare gifts for their families and wider social networks back home. This gift-giving not only mattered to migrants' social reputation, but also served as a token of gratitude for the small sum of money, food and necessities that they had been given on their first departure. To manifest their proper manhood in the homeland, low-paid migrants had to live very frugally in harsh conditions abroad, which undermined their manhood materially and psychologically.

Male migrants lived apart from their wives and children but the form of the patriarchal household was maintained in terms of the gendered division of labour. Men were breadwinners working abroad and sending remittances back, whereas their wives stayed at home and took care of domestic chores (Hsu 2000; Mazumdar 2003; Mckeown 2001; Shen 2012). Nevertheless, due to the conditions that male migrants encountered abroad, including disease, misfortune, second marriage and death, many men could not meet their responsibilities of providing for their families. Instead, their wives who were left behind became the backbone of their marital families economically and symbolically. Like Grandma Su, many women saw their husbands depart for Southeast Asia soon after they married or after the birth of a first child; then, suddenly, they no longer received any news or remittances from their husbands who were dead or had established another family overseas. To feed themselves, their children and probably their co-resident parents-in-law, these women started to make money through their skilled female labour at home (e.g. making textile goods of various kinds) or, like Su, by learning to do heavy agricultural work which they had never done before marriage.

Some scholars argue that migrants' wives did not emigrate with their husbands because they played important roles in managing the family estate, including remittance-funded investment, and even generating income by labouring in productive activities of various kinds (Mazumdar 2003; Szonyi 2005). Concepts of the corporate property-holding unit or *jia* (household) economy put forward by anthropologists (e.g. Cohen 1976; Watson 1975) have been used to analyse the divided family as a strategy of maximizing a family's common economic interest. While this argument seems logical, as Szonyi (2005) admits, it is limited because many migrants from poor families actually earned little abroad and hence hardly improved their family's economic conditions, nor acquired any property. This argument also implies a teleological view of migrants and their families as instrumental and acting out of economic interest, without considering non-instrumental motives and human sentiments. The story of Madam Suhong described below exemplifies a more complicated picture of the divided family maintained by a migrant's wife.

Migrants from Kinmen were often engaged in low-paid work in Southeast Asia, but some managed to come back to ask their families to go abroad together, like Madam Suhong's husband (Liu 2006: 113–15). Suhong's husband left his pregnant wife to go to Malaysia in order to take over the role of earning money for the extended family that his elder brother had held for years. However, he failed to keep his promise to return home after three years, and he married a second wife overseas who looked after him when he was ill. When Suhong's daughter was seven years old, her husband finally came back and asked her to go with him to Malaysia. Suhong rejected the proposition because she could not leave her elderly parents-in-law behind and she worried about the burden for her husband to feed the large family including two wives and their children. Suhong never saw her husband again. Nevertheless, with a sewing machine that her husband sent home and by collaborating with female relatives in her marital family, she made a living by making and repairing clothes. In this story, narrated by Suhong herself, the divided family was not a strategy of maximizing the familial common economic interest but a difficult decision made by Suhong, based on her multiple concerns and care for others, and respected by her husband who could only offer limited economic compensation for his absence.

The decision of Madam Suhong to stay in her marriage and stay with her parents-in-law in Kinmen, as many women in similar situations did at that time, symbolically preserved the patrilineal family. They fulfilled the filial obligations, on behalf of their absent husbands, to their parents and ancestors by caring for their parents-in-law and bringing up their children, especially sons, with aspirations of their children's continuation of their patrilines in the future. They contributed to the formal and moral intactness of the patrilineal family by excluding the option of remarriage and guarding their fidelity in their everyday exposure to various ways of monitoring their sexuality, such as gossip and the reporting of behaviour to husbands abroad, by members of close-knit communities (Hsu 2000: 107). The story of Madam Zhou in Liu's (2006: 107–108) collection shows that she preserved her fidelity even though her husband married a second wife in Singapore. When Zhou took her adopted daughter to Taiwan to escape the Chinese Communist artillery attack on Kinmen in the late 1950s, her parents-in-law, who stayed behind, were very worried about whether she would run away with someone else. Some villagers' suspicious comments about the freedom that Zhou might enjoy in Taiwan intensified her mother-in-law's anxiety, so she sent numerous letters to hasten Zhou's return. In retrospect, Zhou said that if she had ever considered remarriage, she would have done it earlier but not after more than ten years of her husband's absence, and she would have not brought in a girl as an adopted daughter to her marital family.

Exemplars of Faithful Women and Ordinary Ethics

During my conversation with a retired school teacher about the stories of women marrying migrants before 1949 in his village, he drew an analogy between these women and the faithful widows (*jiefu*) honoured by the imperial court. These women, whom he knows personally, like those described above, became the breadwinners of their marital families due to their husbands' death, misfortunes or second marriages abroad. They preserved fidelity and fulfilled filial obligations on behalf of their absent husbands. My interlocutor commented that these women, who lived out their lives as chaste (grass) widows, deserved the award of *zhenjie paifang* (memorial arches in honour of chaste widows) granted by the President of Taiwan, had the honouring system still been in practice today.

As we have seen, the imperial vision of a patriarchal family-based social order, in which the model of faithful women was embedded, remained influential in the Republican era despite the forces of reform and modernity. This vision still significantly informed and shaped many parents' gendered upbringing of their children, the ways in which marriages were established, and the gendered division of labour in the household. One could argue that these migrants' wives' endurance of hardship and solitude – the construction of the female self in accordance with the dominant cultural paradigm – was structured by gender inequalities in various aspects. This is true but by drawing on Das's (2012, 2018a, 2018b) discussion of ordinary ethics, I reconsider these women not as mere observers or victims of patriarchal norms but as moral subjects endeavouring to make everyday life habitable. Instead of understanding these women's behaviour through the exemplar of faithful women as the above retired teacher suggested, I look at how these women sustained their lifeworlds and formed their moral subjectivities, not by escaping from the ordinary but rather by descending into it (Das 2012: 134).

In Das's discussion of ordinary ethics, rather than viewing ethics as composed of human judgements made in relation to their ordinary practices, she proposes thinking about the ethical as being 'much more diffused into one's life lived as a whole' (2018a: 547). Here 'the ordinary' or 'the everyday' is more than routines, habits and traditional maps of social action, which have often been equated with the everyday in anthropology. Building on her readings of works of Freud, Cavell, Austin and Wittgenstein, Das proposes seeing 'the everyday as haunted by the possibilities of scepticism, a scene of trance and illusion, and of the uncanny' (2018b: 57). In this sense, the maintenance of the everyday itself constitutes an achievement, which involves innovations, improvisations and moral strivings 'to give birth to the eventual everyday from within the actual everyday' (Das 2012: 134). Given that I did not collect most of the stories presented in this chapter directly from women marrying migrants before 1949, I lack the ethnographic nuances to build on information and insights derived from my interactions with these women over an extensive period. Despite this limitation, in light of Lu's (2008) attention to faithful maidens' personal feelings as discussed previously and Das's thesis of ordinary ethics, I highlight these women's sentiments of resentment, disappointment, empathy and dignity as well as their everyday striving to make life habitable.

The aforementioned remarks of Grandma Su about her relationship with her late husband as owing each other indexes the rejection of associating her chaste widowhood with her affectionate ties with her husband, as well as her feelings of resentment but also acceptance of what had happened. Madam Wang, a respondent in Liu's (2006) collection of oral histories, made a similar statement: 'My husband rarely contacted me after he went abroad (and had a second marriage there), so I barely had *zhen qingyi* (genuine affection) for him' (2006: 112). She stayed in this marriage because she did not feel it was right to leave her mother-in-law, who had become a widow at a young age, and she was concerned about the possible damage that a divorce would do to her natal family's reputation. Like Madam Suhong and many of her female coevals, Wang attributed one of her reasons for staying in her marital home to her care and empathy for her widowed mother-in-law, rather than to an articulation of a daughter-in-law's filial piety to her parents-in-law as demanded by the patriarchy. What made this life full of hardship generated by poverty, a husband's irresponsibility, and a mother-in-law's sometimes bad treatment bearable to Wang was, as she herself said, that 'I was wholeheartedly devoted to bringing up my only son' (Liu 2006: 112).

Though Grandma Su did not explicitly articulate her son's importance to her, the strength of their ties was illustrated in her son Woody's words to me. Woody told me several times that, if not for his concern about his widowed mother, he would have pursued a military career: it is conventionally deemed that such a career should be avoided by a man because the potential sacrifice of his life threatens his filial duty to his parents and ancestors (see Stafford 1995). I propose to read Grandma Su and Madam Wang's lives as enduring periods in which the upset caused by their husbands' disappearance was enfolded in their everyday striving to sustain their families and rear their children, through which they constituted their moral subjectivities. This understanding avoids an over-hasty reduction of their lives to a mere realization of the patriarchal model of female virtue.

The Confucian teachings of female virtue appeared to remain effective in shaping the social expectations of women's lifelong fidelity to their husbands despite the latters' irresponsibility and second marriages abroad. Women, whose subjectivities were shaped in their quotidian experiences of social and self-surveillance of their sexuality, inevitably viewed the preservation of fidelity as crucial to their ethical existence in the world. In the early 1950s when the KMT troops from China occupied part of Kinmen civilians' houses (see next chapter), the father-in-law of Madam Zhou, whom we saw earlier, stayed all day in the main room of the traditional house, which faced the courtyard, to monitor the soldiers' movements. Zhou herself also avoided coming out of her bedroom (Liu 2006: 108). Women's everyday prudence in safeguarding their proper distance from men was not just their response to social expectations about their fidelity but, more importantly, mattered to their self-recognition of their moral integrity and dignity. When replying to a question about remarriage, Liu's respondent, Madam Li, claimed that 'no matter how hard the life was, I never considered marrying another man' because '[I] had not done anything wrong, how could it be to marry two [men]' (Liu 2006: 125–26).

Madam Zhou's and Li's assertion of their moral and sexual integrity implied their self-distinction from other widows who remarried soldiers coming from China in 1949. In retrospect, my elderly informants commented that these women had no choice but to remarry because of extreme poverty. But this kind of empathy was not readily applied to those women back then. Auntie Lu, as I called her, told me that her late husband could not forgive his mother, a widow with no support who remarried a soldier to Taiwan in the early 1950s. Lu's husband was in his early teens at the time, and refused to go with his mother to Taiwan. He even refused to meet his mother after he established his own family. Lu had served as a mediator between her husband and mother-in-law. She sent her eldest son to spend some time in Taiwan with her mother-in-law, who indulged this grandson with love and financial help with his education. These episodes, recounted from a third-party's perspective by Auntie Lu, reveal the difficult feelings that her mother-in-law and husband experienced over decades. With no easy and perfect solution to the mental trauma that she caused to her son, Lu's mother-in-law tried to make her life habitable by mending her relationship with her son by various attempts and mediation from her daughter-in-law.

The above-mentioned stories of women who preserved their fidelity and women who remarried altogether reveal their great efforts undertaken to keep their lives going in ways that were bearable and felt ethically right to them. Their stories were nicely captured by Das's words that 'our sense of life as a whole as ethical involves us in finding ways of containing these disappointments and not allowing them to be converted into a curse on the world' (2018a: 541).

Conclusion

This chapter has focused on marriage in Kinmen in a period featuring the intersections of temporalities of mass male emigration and transition of political regimes, during which marital reform was proposed as a crucial approach to modernizing China. Traditional arranged marriage, which remained dominant during this period, was not merely the result of the powerful influence of Confucian traditions or ordinary people's resistance to change. Instead, I argue that it was the constitutive power of kinship involving actors' practices to create a future in line with local people's expectations of preserving the patriline. Marriage played an important role in realizing this conservative aim by linking the male migrants to their natal homes or building alliance with affines of compatible status.

Despite the prevalent conservative arrangements of marriage during the diaspora time, the core work of kinship in creating the next generations involved constant interaction with new politico-economic circumstances in order to ensure the upward mobility of male offspring and to glorify the ancestors by their achievements. This opened up opportunities to animate changes in society from the intimate sphere of kinship. The migrant economy built on kinship networks nourished a group of young men who had experiences of sojourning abroad and received Western education and ideas. The differences between these educated men and their kin left behind in their spatial-temporal experiences led to the rising contention between conservative and progressive visions of marriage. Echoing the New Culture Movement, they articulated new visions of marriage and national futures and tried to put these new visions into practice. Though many of these young men's struggles against patriarchal conservatism ended in failure and feelings of frustration, their endeavours to break with tradition, such as in the adoption of new forms of formalizing a marriage (e.g. *tongju*), signalled the possibility of carving out alternative paths. Rather than reinforcing the dichotomous framing between traditional and modern marriage that these male intellectuals devised, I have drawn attention to the transformative capacities of kinship in co-producing these changes and progression towards modernity.

This chapter has also discussed the negative effects resulting from the conservative aim of reproducing the patrilineal family which was suffused with gender inequalities and oppressive elements, particularly the ideas revolving around women's chastity. Though the forces of reform initiated by intellectuals in Beijing reached Kinmen and had some impact in the Republican era, the patriarchal order still dominated many islanders' everyday lives, especially the social surveillance of women's sexuality. The obstruction to women's access to education and gainful employment outside the home confined their spatial-temporal experiences to a clear separation of the sexes, a division of inner and outer spheres, and generational hierarchy. As we have seen, many left-behind wives constantly self-regulated their sexuality and rejected remarriage, even though their husbands were dead or had second marriages abroad. Instead of viewing these women as duplicating the imperial model of chaste widowhood, I argue for an understanding of their everyday striving to make life habitable through Das's thesis of ordinary ethics. Their everyday lives, presented outwardly as their adherence to the patriarchal repertoire, were suffused with their ethical responses in their empathy towards their parents-in-law who were also left behind, their devotion to rearing their children, and their complicated feelings towards their husbands who were barely present in their marital lives.

The stories of left-behind women's everyday ethical striving and young men's struggles against patriarchal dominance in Kinmen illuminate the complicated pictures of Chinese intimate lives in the first half of the twentieth century. Moving beyond the earlier framing of the Chinese family as a property-holding entity acting on the family's common economic interest in anthropology (e.g. Cohen 1976; Freedman 1958, 1966; Watson 1982), this chapter has shown the personal emotions, desires and ethical judgements surrounding the contention between conservative and progressive visions of marriage. While the conservative aim of preserving the patriline involved gender inequalities and oppressive elements, kinship or the 'traditional Chinese family' was not entirely reactionary against change, as young reformers tended to emphasize. The practices of kinship actually joined in the creation of new social futures through adopting both old and new resources to prepare the next generations for the changing world, despite a focus on male offspring in this initial stage of the Chinese society's march towards modernity. In subsequent chapters, we will see how this constitutive power of kinship enabled families to sustain kin ties while creating diverse options of life paths for the new generations along with Kinmen's encounter with new waves of modernity.

Notes

1. It is generally agreed that Chen Duxiu's famous essay 'Call to Youth' (*Jinggao Qingnian*), published in the September 1915 issue of *Xin Qingnian* (New Youth), marked the beginning of the New Culture Movement. This movement reached its zenith on 4 May 1919 when university and high-school students in Beijing initiated a protest against the Treaty of Versailles which was criticized as a secret agreement between Britain and Japan to allow the latter to take over the territories in Shandong previously controlled by Germany. The May Fourth Movement has thus become a well-known

appellation of the New Culture Movement (see Chow 1960; Glosser 2003; Schwarcz 1986).
2. The phenomenon of faithful maiden surfaced in the thirteenth century and reached its zenith from the mid-Ming and throughout the Qing dynasty. The Qing court honoured nearly 5,000 faithful maidens who remained celibate and 1,000 who had committed suicide between 1644 and 1850 (Lu 2008: 4–5).
3. Faithful maidens who were permitted to join their late fiancés' families (so that they were prevented from committing suicide) usually faced immense challenges because their presence entailed an economic and emotional toll for the families. But they gained certain authority in individual circumstances. Some educated women served pedagogical roles for their younger female relatives by teaching Confucian classics or writing poems. Some became the primary breadwinners for the families by working in the vegetable garden or making shoes, food or other products to sell in the market, instead of womanly work at home (Lu 2008: 173–75).
4. The publication of *Shining* was suspended during the Japanese occupation of Kinmen (1937–1945) and ceased permanently in 1949. There were in total 21 issues: 15 issues in 1928–1937 and 6 issues in 1946–1949. In this book I use the collective volumes of *Shining* which includes all issues reprinted by National Kinmen Institute of Technology (upgraded and renamed as National Quemoy University in 2010) and Jushan Xue's Association in 2006.
5. There were other migrant-funded newsletters established by other villages or organizations in Kinmen in the 1920s and 1930s, but only the copies of *Shining* are well preserved to the present day (Chiang 2016).
6. All the articles in *Shining* were written in Chinese, and all the quotes from *Shining* in this chapter are my own translations.
7. Regarding overseas Chinese's involvement in Nationalist China's anti-Japanese war effort, see Kuhn (2008); Wang (1991).

2

Militarization and Marriage in the Cold War Context

In 1949, after losing the war to the Chinese Communist Party (CCP) on the Chinese mainland, the Kuomintang (KMT) retreated to Taiwan, together with the government of the Republic of China (ROC). At this time, the KMT still controlled several islands along the mainland's southeast coast, including Kinmen. Later in October of the same year, the KMT's army defeated CCP troops in a ground battle in Kinmen – a significant victory that allowed the KMT to secure control of Kinmen and Taiwan. Kinmen immediately entered a state of '*ad hoc* militarization', as historian Michael Szonyi (2008: 26) terms it, followed by the establishment of military rule, *Zhandi Zhengwu* (War Zone Administration), in 1956. This system endured until 1992 when martial law on Kinmen was lifted, five years after martial law ended on the Taiwanese mainland.

Szonyi's monograph on Kinmen, *Cold War Island* (2008), compellingly depicts local civilian experiences of wars and military rule from a broader perspective of the global Cold War, revealing the mutual constitution of local, regional and global histories. His work contributes to emerging scholarship in Cold War historiography that shifts the focus from the superpowers of the US and the Soviet Union to 'peripheral' countries, and from the study of high politics and diplomacy to the study of the social and cultural dimensions of the Cold War (Kwon 2010; Masuda 2015; Zheng et al. 2010). The framework of bipolar politics that Szonyi highlights illuminates how Kinmen was constructed as 'a beacon of freedom' and a metaphor of 'the commitment of the US-led Cold War alliance to resist Communism' (2008: 4). It also provides comparative understandings of how both the ROC and the People's Republic of China (PRC) sought to define themselves in opposition to the other, though often in practice they mirrored each other.[1] This chapter builds on this broad historical and comparative horizon to explore what happened to marriage when Kinmen civilians had to live with massive numbers of

---

Endnotes for this chapter begin on page 65.

troops for an indeterminate period in the 'hot war' between the ROC and the PRC in the Cold War context.[2] But based on an anthropological approach to kinship, my discussion complements Szonyi's work through foregrounding how kinship practices sustained local families and animated marital change in these extraordinary circumstances.

The framework of bipolar politics that Szonyi uses to explicate KMT governance on Kinmen in the Cold War era, which was intended to oppose the CCP in China, is also evident in the two regimes' policies concerning Confucian traditions. In contrast to the CCP's radical measures of destroying Confucian and patrilineal heritages, the KMT sought to build a modern nation-state grounded on these heritages. Such opposing attitudes towards Confucian legacies between the two sides can be traced back to the period prior to 1945, and the KMT continued its pre-war policies relating to gender and the family in the Cold War era.[3] Unlike socialist policy in China, where women were asked to work equally with their male counterparts with the support of state-sponsored childcare (Stockman et al. 1995: 191; Zuo 2016: 35–36), the KMT expected women to be mothers focusing on rearing their children. In Kinmen, while young women were ordered to undertake militia training and service, they were spared this after marrying so as not to interfere with the important duties of childbearing and childrearing for the national interest. Given the KMT's emphasis on women's domesticity and its Chinese Cultural Renaissance Movement launched in 1967, in competition with the Cultural Revolution (1966–1976) in China, the Confucian vision of a patriarchal family-based social order was retained, unchallenged, across Taiwan.

The KMT's attitudes towards Confucian traditions allowed Kinmen civilians to keep their ancestral heritage and rituals manifesting patrilineal values. However, the KMT's military measures – shaped by its goal to retake the Chinese mainland – engendered problems and stimuli which unsettled this patriarchal order. The large number of troops retreating from China to Kinmen after 1949 aroused local anxiety over women's sexuality because civilians were forced to share their houses with soldiers. Unfortunately, there were cases of soldiers raping local women and, in response to this, in 1951 the first military brothel was established in Kinmen. Notably, sex workers in the military brothels were employed from Taiwan, rather than recruited locally (Chen 2006). Szonyi highlights the linkage between military prostitution and marriages between soldiers and civilian women because 'they comprised the two major *legitimate* modes of sexual relations between soldiers and civilians' (2008: 159; my italics). I emphasize the adjective 'legitimate' because some marriages between soldiers and civilian women were 'illegitimate' according to a special law regulating soldiers' marriages in the 1950s. The first section that follows examines how the KMT's aim of recovering the Chinese mainland engendered unequal access to marriage and family life among the servicemen from China, and tensions between soldiers and

Kinmen civilians. Stories of veterans are provided to illustrate how they pursued their intimate desires through unconventional ways of establishing a marriage or intimate relationships.

The second section scrutinizes relations between militarization and marital change among Kinmen civilians between the 1950s and early 1980s. During this period, local residents suffered loss of life, physical and mental injury, and considerable damage to family property due to continued shelling from the PRC. The agricultural modernization promoted by the military government could not overcome the basic ecological constraints of the island. But, as mentioned in this book's Introduction, the remarkable number of soldiers deployed on Kinmen created economic incentives for ordinary residents. They set up various small businesses catering to the needs of the troops, locally called *a-ping-ko sing-lí* in Hokkien (lit. business with soldiers, hereafter '*a-ping-ko* business'). Local women of various ages were the entrepreneurs or main labour force in these novel businesses. Together with the military government's measures to restructure the local economy (e.g. through the sorghum distillery), local average living standards gradually improved, and women's and men's heterosexual experiences and marital options diversified.

Szonyi also examines how the dominant presence of mass troops impacted on the local marriage market (2008: 158–66), and how the geopoliticization of Kinmen was gendered through women's potential roles as entrepreneurs, prostitutes (referring to women from Taiwan), wives and mothers, and soldiers (see Chapter 10 of his book). My discussion differs in my sources of data and my theoretical approach. While Szonyi mostly relied on local men's generalized remarks about the past and other indirect material to describe marital change under militarization, my analysis is built on the biographical stories of local women and men that I collected myself. I take an approach inspired by new kinship studies to explore how kinship practices constituted reproductive and transformative power to sustain local extended families but also to animate changes to the patriarchy-prescribed gendered destinies in the circumstances of militarization. Through the intimate stories of soldiers and civilians in the Cold War context, this chapter demonstrates how marital change in this period embodied the intricate entanglement between the personal and the political, in which individual intimate desires were contested and negotiated in relation to national and familial futures.

State Control of Soldiers' Sexuality and Marriage

With the declassification of certain government archives in recent years, we now can trace the KMT's logic and measures to control soldiers' sexuality and marriage, especially those soldiers coming from the Chinese mainland after 1945 (hereafter 'mainland soldiers'). It is estimated that the number of mainland soldiers who moved to Taiwan between 1945 and 1953 amounted to approximately 600,000 in total (Lin 2009: 333–36). Though native Taiwanese men were conscripted into the army after 1949, mainland soldiers were professional servicemen and constituted the main force in various military attacks on China in the 1950s and 1960s (Cheng 2018). The KMT's policies regarding military brothels and soldiers' marriages specifically targeted these mainland soldiers whose military morale was essential to the KMT's anti-communist struggle. In what follows, I initially draw on studies based on archival sources to summarize how the KMT's measures to regulate soldiers' intimate lives were closely linked to its war preparation. I then move on to the life stories of mainland soldiers, demonstrating how they built intimate relationships despite the constraints to their normal pathways to marriage and family life. I did not interview any retired mainland soldiers in person and therefore my discussion relies on ethnographic studies and a collection of the life histories of these veterans made by Han-Yu (2012), a Kinmen-based female writer.

Regulating Soldiers' Sexuality

Military brothels first appeared on Kinmen, at sites on the Taiwanese mainland, and on Penghu, between 1949 and 1953, before the legal regulation of military brothels was formally enacted in 1954 (see Figure 2.1 for a photograph of a military brothel in Kinmen). According to military archives and former officials' recollections, military brothels were set up to ease soldiers' (especially mainland soldiers) feelings of loneliness and sexual need, and prevent further cases of raping civilian women (Chen 2006: 11–14; Yao 2019: 19–24). The archives suggest that some high-ranking officials were concerned about the damage to military morale as a whole caused by soldiers' mental instability and by sexual needs that might result in their deserting the army, suicide, masturbation and crimes of rape. On the other hand, the establishment of military brothels was linked to the legal restrictions on many soldiers' marriages, and thus their normal access to sexual life.

The first version of a law governing soldiers' marriages was promulgated in 1952, followed by various modifications, before its repeal in 2005. The 1952 version was the most restrictive, and mainland soldiers who constituted the central part of the army at the time were naturally its targets. This law forbade active ranking officers and certain servicemen under the age of twenty-eight, or those involved in battles or an emergent mission, to marry. All the enlisted soldiers who were not ranked – most of whom were mainland soldiers – were forbidden to marry during their terms of service. As the KMT expected mainland soldiers to stay on active service till the age of forty or even fifty because of the on-going war with the CCP in order to retake the Chinese mainland, this meant that many mainland soldiers could not marry before retirement. However, numerous cases

Figure 2.1. A disused building of a former military brothel in Anqian, Kinmen, 2018. © Hsiao-Chiao Chiu.

of transgression by ranking and non-ranking servicemen by 1958 resulted in the liberalization of the law the following year.

Reviewing the relevant archives on the military's internal debates about cases of infraction of the restrictions, Fan (2006) summarizes the authorities' concerns about military morale, military finance, and the goal of recovering the Chinese mainland. As mainland soldiers were encouraged to devote themselves to the struggle for the return to the homeland, having a family in Taiwan was deemed harmful to the revolution and to military morale in general. The authorities were also concerned about the additional financial burden generated by looking after soldiers' dependents, which was essential to sustain military morale, and with the possibility of soldiers marrying spies sent by the CCP. But when transgressions occurred, military superiors in charge tended to tolerate them because they were afraid that punishment might trigger soldiers' depression or resentment and harm military morale. They also tried to explain transgressions in terms of soldiers' homesickness and sexual needs, easily provoked by the sub-tropical weather of Taiwan.

The archives reveal that military leaders believed that many soldiers' troubles were related to the denial or suppression of their normal access to sexual and family life. But they determined to prioritize military concerns while reducing these difficulties to soldiers' sexual needs aroused by homesickness, loneliness and the hot weather. Military brothels were proposed as the solution, and justified by the long history of military prostitution tracing back to ancient China and the existence of similar systems around the world, especially the Japanese system of military prostitution during the Second World War (Chen 2006: 12; Yao 2019: 23–24). The military leadership emphasized the function of military brothels to raise military morale and to prevent servicemen from forcing unwanted sex on female civilians. These justifications reflected the KMT's attempts to establish its legitimacy in Taiwan while preserving its goal of recovering the Chinese mainland. Especially on the anti-communist frontline of Kinmen, it was deemed crucial to maintain friendly and peaceful relationships between the army and civilians in the joint effort of fighting the communist enemy a few miles away.

Chen Changching, a local writer who was a member of staff in a military brothel on Kinmen in the 1960s and 1970s, argues that military brothels worked to prevent trouble over intimate matters between the troops and civilians (2006: 143). However, though civilians might have believed that military prostitution was a necessary precaution against soldiers' rape of civilian women, this did not mean a full curb on sexual violence. Jia-Lin, my informant who was born in the mid-1960s when military brothels had existed for years, recalled:

> Why was there 831 [a colloquial term for the military brothel initially used by soldiers and then commonly used by civilians (Chen 2006: 131–32)]? There were a lot of soldiers staying in or around civilian houses. We dried our laundry in the courtyard and women's underwear was very often stolen. Very often! Then, 831 appeared… When I was in my third or fourth grade at primary school, an incident happened. A girl who was about two years my junior was raped by a soldier in a bomb shelter. I was just a child at that time and we were all horrified. Several men in our village took sticks and tried to find that soldier. They seemed to catch the soldier, but that girl's family left the village and moved to Taiwan afterwards… This incident was not the only one. There were many children who were taken to the shelters and raped. That's why 831 appeared.

Jia-Lin's recollection suggests that military prostitution could not fully avert the miseries of rape. Civilian worries about the threat to women's security and the social order caused by the soldiers remained unrelieved. Though the military leaders recognized the complexities of soldiers' mental and sexual problems, they were inclined to treat these problems as merely men's 'biologically rooted sexual needs', which Sor (2000: 61) pinpoints as the same logic as the Japanese excuse for military prostitution, in order not to question the military mobilization itself. Military leaders could not attribute the origin of these problems to the state of war and the emergency, to which they themselves contributed. Under the KMT's banner of fighting for the recapture of the homeland, the ways in which soldiers' and civilians' personal concerns and traumas were dealt with were highly militarized.

Mainland Soldiers' Intimate Lives

As mentioned above, there were numerous transgressions of the 1952 law restricting soldiers' marriages. When the military attempted to figure out the approximate number of illegitimate marriages by servicemen of different types and ranks, they used the criteria of working conditions and income to make the calculation. It turned out that soldiers with inferior working conditions and the lowest incomes were estimated to constitute the lowest percentage of illegitimate marriages (Fan 2006). This calculation made sense because, although the law was liberalized to allow non-ranking soldiers to marry in 1959, marriage remained a luxurious dream for many low-ranking soldiers. Several ethnographic studies have shown that a large number of non-ranking mainland soldiers experienced lifelong bachelorhood, unstable intimate relationships, or a significant age gap with their wives from China whom they married after visits to China became possible in the late 1980s (Chao 2004a, 2008; Hu 1999; Li 1998; Wu 2001).

In the 1950s and 1960s, mainland soldiers' own perceptions and experiences of their masculinity may have differed from state and civilian ideas about them. Mainland soldiers were expected by the state to be patriotic warriors, but were probably viewed as dangerous outsiders by civilians. However, especially for low-ranking soldiers, personal experiences suggest that their masculinity was fragile when judged by traditional social-moral standards. The following text from a military document in 1962 highlights how mainland soldiers experienced matters differently from their Taiwanese counterparts, and reveals these soldiers' visions of a desired future to have been in line with the traditional patrilineal values:

> The *volunteer* soldiers who followed the army from the [Chinese] mainland to Taiwan have been far away from home and serving in the army for a long time. They were not allowed to resign without a sensible reason, nor to get married. This actually deprived them of the rights they were entitled to. On the contrary, the Taiwanese soldiers can enjoy warmth from their families and can leave the army after completing their fixed terms of service. It is understandable that this sharp contrast might generate emotional bitterness [among the mainland soldiers]. Rumours circulated [within the army] and complaints aroused. When a military superior encouraged soldiers by saying: 'You all have a bright future ahead', the old soldiers responded: 'There is no future if we are not going to have male heirs'. (Fan 2006: 13; my translation and italics)

I emphasize the adjective 'volunteer' used to describe the soldiers from China as a whole in the above text because it is highly problematic. Nowadays we can see from the oral histories of many mainland veterans that, rather than joining the army voluntarily, they were seized by the KMT's army on its retreat to Taiwan in 1949 (Chao 2004a; Han-Yu 2012). Chao (2004a) argues that these 'snatched' soldiers at the bottom of the military hierarchy were forced into conditions of sexual and emotional deprivation, first by the armed forces coercing them into exile and into long-term military service, and then by the legal proscription of their marriages. Though the law was relaxed in 1959, marriage and building a family were still unaffordable dreams to many rootless and impoverished soldiers, even after they retired. Many mainland veterans, as a result, developed various kinds of intimate and affective relationships with women, which deviated from dominant moral lines (Chao 2004a; Wu 2001). For instance, Mr Jiang, a mainland veteran in Chao's (2004a) study, called four women with whom he had previously had close relationships *laopo* (wife), though these women were already married to other mainland veterans who also knew Jiang. These women usually came to stay with Jiang at weekends, doing domestic chores such as laundry, shopping, cooking and dining together that were normal for a married couple. No matter how his behaviour might have been judged according to mainstream norms, Jiang himself emphasized that he always focused on one relationship at a time and did not try to damage these women's marriages. Instead, one way that he showed his genuine love for these women was to have studio photos taken of themselves in wedding attire (Chao 2004a: 17–18).

Kinmen was a key military site where many mainland veterans stayed for short-term or long-term periods during their terms of service. Han-Yu's (2012) published collection of the life histories of twenty-two mainland veterans provides rich information about these men's military experiences and intimate relationships with local women. Most veterans married local women in the 1960s and 1970s when they were more than thirty-five years old – much older than men's average age of marrying at the time – and this points to the constraints posed by the law restricting soldiers' marriages and by their socioeconomic status. The ways in which these veterans met their wives varied. For example, one veteran met his wife during a militia training exercise for local young women; another man married his colleague in the local bus agency where he worked after leaving the army. The marriage of a veteran named Zhao Guo-An was rather special: he accepted a woman's request to marry her deaf and dumb younger sister who was junior to him by eleven years. He also agreed on an uxorilocal marriage, with his wife's surname added to his full name, so that his widowed mother-in-law could receive government subsidies for soldiers' dependents (Han-Yu 2012: 220–21).

The story of Ke Bing-Yan in Han-Yu's collection illustrates an unconventional way of building a family. Ke decided to join the KMT army after being 'snatched' in Guangdong in 1949 because he had been upset by his girlfriend's earlier participation in the CCP. From the age of twenty-one, Ke served in the army for thirty-seven years and constantly shifted between the bases on Kinmen, Matsu and Taiwan. He was once in love with a woman on Kinmen but he did not dare to ask for her hand because he had no money. Some years later, he and another woman together adopted a girl whose mother was a Kinmen native (Ke's relationships with these two women were not explained). This adopted girl was taken by her adoptive mother to Taiwan for some years. After Ke retired and settled down on Kinmen, he brought his adopted daughter back to live with him. As a single parent, he devoted himself to raising his daughter, who at the time of the interview had a good career and in 2010 married a man in Taiwan. During the interview, Ke told Han-Yu that his only wish was to become a grandfather (Han-Yu 2012: 48–61).

These stories about mainland soldiers' intimate lives show that, despite the KMT's protection of a patriarchal family-based social order, its goal of retaking the Chinese mainland led to the denial of, or various obstacles to many soldiers' normal pathways to marriage. Rather than attaining socially recognized manhood through marriage and childbirth, the KMT emphasized the status of soldiers as patriotic and tough warriors, ready to sacrifice their lives for the greater Chinese nation-state. But, from the archives and soldiers' personal stories, we see how the traditional values of marriage and continuing the family line became particularly desirable for many mainland soldiers who were rootless and lonely in Taiwan. Some soldiers got married despite this being a transgression of the law, and their superiors understood their situations and tended to dismiss their transgressions. Marriage seemed to be both a means and an end that soldiers pursued in order to rebuild their manhood and personal lives, which had been damaged and exploited by the dreadful conditions of war. Even in cases where they remained officially unmarried, mainland soldiers in the lower social strata tried to perform the roles of husband or father through unconventional ways of building intimate relationships with others.

Changing Marital Patterns in Militarized Kinmen

We now shift to the other side of stories about Kinmen civilian intimate experiences. As we have seen in Chapter 1, the emphasis on sex segregation and women's fidelity remained strong on Kinmen in the early twentieth century despite some modernization brought about by the remittance economy. The increasing number of soldiers in Kinmen after 1946 heightened islanders' worries about women's security and young widows' efforts to protect their sexual virtue. Many women whose husbands were dead or abroad tried to sustain their families by making textiles or through agricultural work, but life was too difficult for some women without other support. Remarriage to a soldier became a solution for these lone women but they could suffer moral blame from their communities as well as mental trauma through their lifetime.

Though there was barely any paid employment for women in the early 1950s, local women of different ages started to earn money by washing and repairing military uniforms at home, and making snacks to sell on the street. Many women became entrepreneurs of *a-ping-ko* business, which grew and diversified rapidly across the island. More and more shops, such as snack bars, souvenir shops and pool halls, appeared and employed young women in their late teens to early twenties whose youthful faces and bodies could attract more soldier-clients (Chou 2009: 66–75). As their work involved intensive contact with soldiers, the number of young women who married soldiers originally from China or from Taiwan increased.[4]

Lin Ma-Teng, an expert on local history mentioned in the previous chapter, made the link between militarization, a changing local economy and marriage during my interview with him in 2018. He stated that local residents were under constant pressure to feed the family, especially throughout the 1950s when the CCP launched two intensive artillery attacks on Kinmen. For a young woman, marrying a soldier might therefore have been better than marrying a local farmer. He listed three types of local women's marriages to soldiers: (1) a married woman who had received no news from her husband abroad or had been widowed might prefer to marry an army chef because at least daily meals were guaranteed; (2) a young, fashionable woman would be easily attracted by a young soldier driving a military car, even if he was on duty; (3) a prudent woman could wisely choose a ranking officer who might become a general in the future.

Rather than representing all cases at the time, Lin's categorization points to the emergence of alternative imaginaries of intimate relationships, marital lives and futures among local women evoked by the comings and goings of soldiers with various characteristics. It also points to local women's growing autonomy in deciding their own life and marriage thanks to their newfound economic power largely building on *a-ping-ko* business. But this does not mean that conventional ideas about sex-segregation and parental authority over children's marriages had no part in these women's individual circumstances. Based on my collection of life stories of women born in the 1950s and 1960s, I describe below how local women's heterosexual experiences and marital options diversified along with expanding opportunities to study, to work outside the home, and to meet men from different backgrounds. I discuss their economic power and autonomy in relation to their familial bonds. Lastly, I turn to local men's marital experiences, unpacking how militarization generated different effects for local men and women.

Diversification of Women's Heterosexual Experiences and Marriage

From imperial times to the early 1950s, investment in daughters' education had been viewed by most parents as a waste of money and pointless in Kinmen. As the KMT gradually settled its governance in Taiwan and Kinmen, policies of improving levels of education were promoted. In the 1960s, mandatory education was extended from six to nine years and some programmes guaranteed a certain number of Kinmen students' university admission and funding for their studies in Taiwan (Li 2009). With the gradual improvement of local living standards, families that were relatively affluent sent their daughters to the only senior high school where female and male students from different neighbourhoods could meet. Some of my young informants said that their parents met each other at the senior high school and got married a few years after graduation. On the other hand, I heard numerous stories about women who went to Taiwan to work after graduating from junior high school, and married men they met in the factories or at gatherings of friends in Taiwan. Though women's increasing mobility in the outside world, beyond the reach of the watching eyes they constantly sensed in Kinmen, was entwined with sending their remittances back home, they gained opportunities to develop romantic relationships and marry the men of their choice. But there were also cases in which women were more reserved about their interaction with men, as illustrated in the story of Yu-Fen.

Yu-Fen, a retired teacher at a local school, was born into a prestigious family in the early 1950s. When recalling her life history to me, Yu-Fen emphasized repeatedly that she was very careful about her proper behaviour and distance from men because of her family teaching. One of the several examples she provided was that she never talked to a male classmate who lived close to her home during her years at primary school. Though her father, like many of his coevals at the time, deemed further education after senior high school unhelpful for a girl, she gained the emotional and financial support from her mother and eldest brother to carry on her studies in Taiwan. Yu-Fen said that her mother told her, 'You should continue your education as far as you can. Don't be illiterate like me'. This story instantiates the transformative capacities of kinship as kin ties, like the mother-daughter ties and the ties between siblings in this case, could support the transgression of dominant patriarchal rules of prioritizing sons' education and upward mobility.

Without any hesitation, Yu-Fen headed home directly after completing her undergraduate studies because her parents wanted her back and her eldest brother informed her of a suitable teaching job. Her return brought about a meeting with her future husband, a man from Taiwan who was also a teacher in a local school. Her husband seemed to fall in love with her at their first encounter, and tried to create chances to meet her. Yu-Fen, who might have been shy of recalling the details about their courtship during an interview, quickly concluded by saying smilingly: 'My husband was the first man I knew. He was *si-pi-lai-lian* (impudent and brazen-faced); since we met, he has always been *si-pi-lai-lian* and waiting for me'. Finally, after seven years, Yu-Fen agreed to marry this man. Her father, who had always wanted her to marry a local man, agreed because this son-in-law stayed in Kinmen after the marriage.

Yu-Fen's story suggests that her prudence about sex-segregation was cultivated by her upbringing in a high-status family. But cautious attitudes towards sexual boundaries were actually common among local households. Besides cases of rape, unhappy stories about young women deceived by soldiers who hid their married status or abandoned the women who followed them to Taiwan came to light from time to time. Locally tight social networks also intensified the circulation of these stories as gossip beyond these women's natal communities. Their personal reputations and marital prospects were thus seriously damaged. As such, many parents believed that it was better to follow the customary approach to marry their daughters to local grooms whose backgrounds could be known in detail in advance. Many women who were economically competent accepted their parents' arrangement out of filial piety but also out of a reluctance to marry far away from home. For the families relying on *a-ping-ko* business, as illustrated in the two stories below, some focused their relationships with soldiers on business only, while others were more open to closer relationships with soldiers, including marriage.

Mei-Hua, born in the mid-1950s, was the second daughter of six children in her family. Her elder sister sacrificed her own education to look after her ill mother and earn money by washing military uniforms. Their father then invested in a pool table to expand their *a-ping-ko* business and his eldest daughter was the primary manager. This business enabled Mei-Hua and her younger siblings to continue their education. Mei-Hua originally planned to further her studies in Taiwan after junior high school, but she missed the school registration because of a ferry delay from Kinmen to Taiwan. After she finally arrived in Taiwan, she decided to stay and work in a factory in Taipei and send remittances back home – which was common for female teenagers across rural areas in Taiwan (Kung 1983; Yin 1981). Two or three years later, she was called back to take over the *a-ping-ko* business because her elder sister was getting married. She ran the business excellently, but her parents started to worry about her marriage prospects when she was approaching the age of thirty. Despite this, her parents warned her repeatedly to keep a proper distance from soldier-clients; Mei-Hua did not fancy a romance with a soldier either.

When Mei-Hua attended a regular militia training session for unmarried women, she met a girl junior to her who offered to introduce her uncle to Mei-

Hua. This girl's uncle visited her home some days later but Mei-Hua was absent. Her mother asked this man jokingly to help her harvesting sorghum; he agreed and appeared next day. When they were working on the farm, Mei-Hua's father came to inform them that another man had just visited and had expressed his wish to marry Mei-Hua. Her mother then told the young man she was with on the farm, 'You go to select an auspicious date and then visit our home for the formal proposal of marriage'. Mei-Hua was surprised by this sudden decision without her consent or her meeting the man beforehand, but she accepted this marriage because her mother said, 'As I gave birth to you, I could decide your marriage'.

The following story about Wan-Zhen shows a family's rather friendly relationships with soldiers. Before Wan-Zhen's birth in the early 1960s, her family's economic situation had been improved by the income her mother and two elder sisters earned through washing and repairing military uniforms, and selling hot food to soldiers. These two elder sisters then married soldiers who were frequent clients of their family business. I met and had a conversation with one of these two men in Kinmen in 2018 when Wan-Zhen invited me to join their family lunch. This man, a Taiwanese native and former professional serviceman, told me that when he was stationed in Wan-Zhen's village, he visited their food stall often and became acquainted with his future mother-in-law before his future wife. He said, 'my mother-in-law was extremely nice and always took care of me as if she was a living Bodhisattva'. Wan-Zhen's female relative sitting next to us added, 'Their mother was very kind to all the soldiers, and always asked them "*youmeiyou e dao*" (lit. "Are you hungry?", a common expression for care about others)'.

Wan-Zhen started to help the family business, from her time at primary school until her graduation from senior high school. She spent most nights during her childhood and teenage years ironing uniforms while reading her textbooks. Wan-Zhen originally wanted to further her studies in Taiwan after junior high school because going to Taiwan had always been her dream. But for unforeseen reasons, she continued her studies in the local senior high school. Her second attempt to go to Taiwan after graduation was objected to by her family, especially her elder sisters who felt unjustly treated because they had sacrificed their education to earn money for the family. Wan-Zhen therefore took an examination for administrative posts in military-associated institutions in Kinmen. She passed the exam and got a job in a military agency, where she met her Taiwanese husband who was undertaking his mandatory military service in Kinmen in the early 1980s. Wan-Zhen told me that her parents accepted their three daughters' decisions to marry soldiers from outside, but expressed some concern about their eldest daughter's marriage to a mainland soldier who was senior to her by more than ten years. But, as their parents had known about their daughters' courtships with these soldiers beforehand and had carefully observed these men in their frequent interactions, they were relieved to go along with their daughters' choices.

Kinship and Women's Increasing Power and Autonomy

The ways in which the marriages of the three women described above were decided varied according to the differences in their family conditions. We can see the gradual reconfiguration of generational and gender hierarchies as women gained more power in deciding their own marriages owing to their economic competence and contributions to their natal families. Mei-Hua explained that she agreed to marry an unknown man from a poor family because she trusted her mother who judged her husband to be honest and diligent. Similarly, some women told me that their trust in their fathers' choice of mate for them lay in their feelings of being cared for by their fathers who allowed their daughters to go to school despite their poverty. This suggests that an arranged marriage was not simply a marker of parental authority but involved emotional bonds and trust between generations.

The arrangements of these women's marital residence also varied according to their husbands' situations given that patrilocal residence was an almost unchallenged norm at that time (and remains powerful today). Yu-Fen and Wan-Zhen stayed in Kinmen, living close to or in their natal home, because their husbands had local jobs and their families also accepted this residential decision. By contrast, Mei-Hua, who married a Kinmen native, had no choice but to take patrilocal joint residence. Mei-Hua and many of my elderly female informants who married local men in Kinmen appeared to live their lives in compliance with the patriarchal norms and local moral standards. They took care of all the household chores, including looking after parents-in-law and preparing food offerings for the frequent rituals of worshipping gods and ancestors. They contributed to the maintenance of their marital families' social networks in their unpaid labour, helping with the preparations for other people's weddings, funerals and other tasks. They felt great and continuous pressure to give birth to a son in order to continue their husbands' agnatic lines (see also Chiu 2017).

Compared to Mei-Hua, marriage seemed to create alternative futures for Yu-Fen and Wan-Zhen as they were to some extent relieved of the pressure and burden of living in a patrilocal joint household. However, this kind of future might not have been expected by the women themselves. For example, Wan-Zhen told me that she was frustrated when her dream of going to Taiwan was shattered again because of her husband's difficulty in finding a job in Taiwan and his subsequent success in securing a stable job in Kinmen. To save money from renting a residence and to look after her own parents, Wan-Zhen became the only one of four siblings who stayed behind and she headed an exceptional uxorilocal household. While she was relieved from the duty of caring for her widowed mother-in-law, she bore the burden of attending to all the household chores and ancestor worship (on her brother's behalf) in her natal home. This case encourages us not to think of marriage as necessarily the springboard to a desired future but as being enfolded within a story of creating one's own life and future, which might involve agentive power of both the individual and the family (Carsten 2021). It is through this point that I re-examine these women's stories to explore how gender hierarchy in traditional patriarchal families was gradually reconfigured.

Elsewhere, I have drawn on Alfred Gell's (1988) interpretation of kinship as a fundamental technology of reproduction to explore how kinship practices allowed ordinary families in Kinmen to sustain and gain upward mobility in the period of military rule (Chiu 2018b). Kinship practices involved the cultivation of next generations with certain dispositions and abilities, which not only socialized them into a given social world but also laid the foundation for them to create their own lives. As we have seen, Yu-Fen and Mei-Hua adhered to their family teachings of sex segregation to protect their own and their familial reputations. Mei-Hua and Wan-Zhen learned from their mothers and elder sisters how to turn their skills of doing household chores, such as cooking and repairing clothing, to be a business catering to soldiers' daily needs. These skills and the money they earned supported their younger siblings' (especially brothers') education and their natal families' upward mobility. These women gained self-confidence through these work experiences and quickly drew on these experiences to augment income for their marital families. Mei-Hua was a full-time homemaker after marrying but, to help augment the family income, she suggested making money by selling watermelons, planted by her husband, to soldiers stationed nearby. Wan-Zhen continued her full-time job in the same workplace but used her excellent cooking skills, which she had learned from her mother when helping in the family business, to make snacks for her husband to sell to soldiers when he was not working. These women's economic contribution to their marital families earned them recognition of their authority over family matters from their husbands and children.

These women's stories also invite us to consider how transgressions or changes may arise from the positive or negative effects of the ties and interactions between kin (Carsten 2013, 2019; Das 2007; Lambek 2011). Yu-Fen's, Mei-Hua's and Wan-Zhen's siblings played different roles in constituting their life trajectories. In Yu-Fen's case, her eldest brother's emotional and financial support enabled her to pursue undergraduate studies in Taiwan, in opposition to her father's wishes. Her brother also encouraged her to continue working as a school teacher rather than marrying quickly and becoming a homemaker. As such, Yu-Fen viewed her returning to Kinmen after graduation as reciprocation of her brother's support to her. Both Mei-Hua and Wan-Zhen continued their education beyond junior high school thanks to their elder sisters' sacrifice of their own education to earn money for the family. Though Mei-Hua and Wan-Zhen also worked to support their younger siblings' education, they faced their elder sisters' complaints about being unfairly treated. While Mei-Hua might have given up her further studies in Taiwan voluntarily, Wan-Zhen explicitly articulated her ethical and emotional struggles between her own desire to study in Taiwan and her elder sisters' feelings of bitterness and envy.

The above cases illustrate how familial bonds and personal ethical striving (Das 2007) were intertwined and drove people to make less transgressive decisions or compromises on their routes of creating their own life beyond the patriarchal prescriptions of gendered destiny. But I also heard other stories about women who were confident and determined in pursuing their own desires despite objections from their families. Jia-Lin, whom we met earlier, described the story of her aunt (born in the mid-1950s) as being extraordinary. Her aunt had started to work in *a-ping-ko* business in her early teens and, by her late teens, she was already the owner of a snack bar. Jia-Lin and her aunt have only a ten-year age gap between them, and were very close to each other. They shared a dream of going to Taiwan and of self-transformation into a modern image of womanhood. For example, they witnessed the changes in a female neighbour who became fashionable and lost her local accent after some years of working in Taiwan. They painted colourful pictures about lives in urban Taiwan where they could find various new and interesting things that were absent in Kinmen. But Jia-Lin's aunt actually rejected the opportunity to go to Taiwan by marrying one of several soldiers pursuing her. With savings accumulated from her hard work in Kinmen, Jia-Lin's aunt ultimately made her own way to Taiwan regardless of her parents' strong disapproval. Here we see that, rather than a springboard to a desired future, marriage was enfolded within a woman's self-creation of her desired life and her future.

Local Men's Experiences of Marriage under Militarization

Militarization engendered different experiences of marriage for local women and men. While many women gained opportunities to meet marital partners of different origins through their newfound economic agency, local men were forced to compete with soldiers on the local marriage market. As Szonyi (2008: 161–63) notes, given that the number of men (including local males and soldiers from elsewhere) far exceeded the number of local women, there was a notable rise in bridewealth that local men were requested to pay. The term *san-ba* (lit. three eights) – including NTD 8,000 in cash, 800 *jin* (roughly one pound) of pork, and 8 ounces of gold – was coined to describe the new standard of bridewealth (Chou 2009: 112). Though most of my senior interlocutors said that *san-ba* was exaggerated, they all agreed that it was not easy for a local man without any inherited properties and a stable income to find a bride, especially in the 1950s and 1960s. A report in the local newspaper *Zhengqi Zhonghua Ribao* issued by the military on 13 March 1962 described two local men marrying each other's younger sister so as to avoid paying *san-ba*. The scarcity of local brides also resulted in local men 'marrying down'. An elderly villager told me that his older brother who was a school teacher was unable to find a compatible partner to be his wife in the early 1960s except for an illiterate woman.

But as suggested in my previous discussion of women's divergent marital experiences, many women married local men whom they had met at school, the workplace or through parental arrangement. In Mei-Hua's case, her mother decided on her marriage to a man from a poor family who was the only one of three sons who stayed behind to look after his widowed mother. I also heard several stories of arranged marriages in which, although the groom was impecunious, the bride's parents evaluated him as a good mate in terms of whether he was upright, honest and diligent. Moreover, like their female counterparts, local men's marital options began to diversify along with the growing number of men studying or working in Taiwan. However, the enduring military conflict with China sometimes had unexpected effects on individual men's life plans, as illustrated in Guo-Hong's story.

Guo-Hong, born in the early 1950s, was the fourth of seven sons in his family. While studying on an evening programme at a university in Taipei in the early 1970s, he worked in the daytime for a company where he met his future wife, Chun-Yue, from a rural area in northern Taiwan. In my interview with Chun-Yue, she said that people in those days were shy and reserved, and Guo-Hong initiated the first step by giving her a *zhitiao* (lit. a piece of paper on which he wrote sweet words to Chun-Yue). Gradually, they developed a romantic relationship. Chun-Yue became hesitant about this relationship because her mother said that Kinmen was too far away and too dangerous, but she was eventually moved by Guo-Hong's persistence. Before Guo-Hong's graduation, they visited Chun-Yue's mother together to ask for her permission for their marriage, as Chun-Yue recalled:

> He promised my mother that he would not return to Kinmen, and it was not necessary because some of his brothers remained there. He said he would find a job in Taiwan. My sister-in-law told my mother that my marital life would be easier because I would not live with my parents-in-law. Otherwise, my mother... If my father was still alive, he would have definitely opposed this marriage. My father only agreed my elder sister's marriage to a man living nearby.

Guo-Hong and Chun-Yue got married and lived in Taipei. Guo-Hong graduated the following June, and Chun-Yue gave birth to their first son two months later. However, in September of the same year, Guo-Hong announced suddenly that he had to return to Kinmen because he had found a job there and he was anxious about the possibility of being drafted into the army.

Under the system of military rule in Kinmen, Guo-Hong had become a member of the militia when he was sixteen years old. Given that he was supposed to continue militia training until the age of fifty-five, he was recognized as a 'trained class B militiaman' and was exempted from the compulsory military service which applied in general to male citizens of Taiwan. As native men of Kinmen might leave for Taiwan for a certain period and be absent from regular militia training, they were subject to *linshi zhaoji* (temporary mobilization) as long as they were within the age for militia service. If they were in Taiwan to study, they could apply for deferral of their military service. The problem emerged when Guo-Hong graduated and intended to reside in Taiwan, as he explained:

> If there were enough soldiers, there was no need to draft us. But it was hard to say whether the draft notice would come or not... After graduation, I continued working in Taipei, just as I promised my wife. But, as it happened, the schools in Kinmen were in desperate need of teachers because many teachers (from China) who previously served in the army were going to retire, and very few Taiwanese people were willing to come to Kinmen. Also, I became anxious about the draft because several men of my generation in Kinmen got their draft letters. Anyway, I applied for the teaching post and I got the job. I was told to come back immediately to confirm my acceptance of that job.

Chun-Yue was totally shocked when she suddenly heard this news from her husband, as she recalled:

> He was afraid to tell me what had happened... At that time, I had just given birth to my son and was staying in my natal home so that my mother could look after us. My husband stayed alone in Taipei for work and came to see us every Saturday. But, one day, it was a Wednesday, he came suddenly. I asked whether he had taken leave from work. He shook his head and kept quiet. He was afraid... Next day, he finally told me the truth. I cried and my mother also cried terribly. We continued weeping for one or two weeks... Because we Hakka women followed our husbands no matter what their fortunes were, I had no other choice but to accept what had happened.

Despite her reluctance, Chun-Yue followed her husband to Kinmen in the mid-1970s and lived with her parents-in-law. Because I had known Chun-Yue and Guo-Hong for several years, since 2013, I was able to observe this couple's interaction and heard about the tensions and arguments between them from other villagers. Chun-Yue very often said, 'I came to Kinmen because my husband cheated me', as if Guo-Hong's concealment in their early marital life was a weapon she used to blame her husband whenever something went wrong between them. Guo-Hong admitted his concealment when recalling the story to me, but, from his standpoint back then, it was the best option he had – given that he and his newly established family might have encountered more difficulties if he had been conscripted into the army. His story sheds light on the unanticipated effects of the KMT's military mobilization on the lives of ordinary citizens. This intricate entanglement between the personal and the political was actually expressed in various ways in the lives of Kinmen islanders during the period of military rule.

Conclusion

Compared to the period prior to 1949 when Kinmen islanders travelled abroad and brought back with them Western ideas about gender equality and marriage, the general social atmosphere in Kinmen in the Cold War era was much more conservative. There were no revolutionary voices articulating new social imaginaries which differed from the vision of a patriarchal family-based social order promoted by the state. However, the KMT's protection of this patriarchal order was highly militarized, which generated the paradoxical effects of obstructing many soldiers' access to marriage while also encouraging civilian women's devotion to childrearing in the national interest. As this chapter has demonstrated, this extraordinary situation, structured by the KMT's goal of retaking the Chinese mainland, perhaps made the normative life courses of marriage and childbirth particularly desirable for mainland soldiers who had no roots and connections in Taiwan. Many ranking and non-ranking servicemen transgressed the law to get married, or developed unconventional intimate relationships with others, which allowed them to perform the roles of husband or father.

Despite the concerns of the state and of Kinmen residents about the sexual boundary between soldiers and civilian women, contact was inevitable because of war mobilization and women's earnings derived from catering to soldiers' daily necessities. The stories of women described in this chapter have shown how both the positive and negative effects generated from the intimate sphere of kinship had played a significant part in shaping their life trajectories, which also involved challenges to the gender and generational hierarchies. Kinship, as a technology of reproduction, laid the foundation for women to draw on skills acquired in the family to improve their family income by, for example, cooking, washing and repairing military uniforms. Familial ties and local patriarchal ordering created pressure for young women to sacrifice their own education and earn money for the family. But these women, with their newfound economic agency, were sometimes able to gain power in deciding their own marriage or establish their authority in their marital families. During the Cold War era, for local families with several children, it was often the case that elder siblings, usually sisters, worked hard to allow their younger siblings to pursue higher education. These highly educated siblings, especially men, attained upward mobility and marked the continuous growth of their patrilineal family. But there were feelings of unfairness and envy among elder siblings who had made sacrifices and this sometimes engendered emotional and ethical struggles for younger siblings.

As more and more local girls and boys pursued education in local high schools or went to Taiwan for study and work, their heterosexual experiences were enriched by increasing opportunities to interact with the other sex beyond their familiar neighbourhoods, and their marital options diversified. But, as demonstrated in this chapter, women's newfound economic power did not necessarily lead to the rejection of parental intervention in their life and marriage, or to resistance to the patriarchal ordering of local social and family lives. Besides the KMT's moral inculcation of women's devotion to the domestic domain for the national interest, the local kinship system was effective in reproducing these gendered dispositions. Nevertheless, rather than being merely obedient, women's contribution to the preservation of the patrilineal family and values involved ethical struggles between their own desires and their care for others. Moreover, women's economic capacities and skill in managing the household and social networks earned them respect and power within and beyond their intimate circles (Chiu 2017, 2018b).

The historical and ethnographic material presented in this chapter highlights the lack of attention to the military aspects of Taiwan in the Cold War era in anthropological research. A theoretical preoccupation with the lineage paradigm or the model of corporate family has encouraged researchers to focus on the impacts of modernization on the structure and organization of the Chinese (extended) family (e.g. Cohen 1976; Gallin 1984; Pasternak 1972). This has ignored the ways in which the lives of a significant proportion of the Han Chinese population (including soldiers and civilians) in Taiwan were deeply affected by militarization. It has also placed undue emphasis on the Chinese family as a corporate unit in which individual emotions and desires had no means of expression. This chapter has shown how the life trajectories of mainland soldiers and Kinmen civilians were intricately entangled with the Cold War geopolitics, and how individuals articulated their desires and emotions regarding the constraints or unjust treatment they experienced.

Drawing on examples of the intimate experiences of mainland soldiers and Kinmen civilians in the Cold War era, I have demonstrated how the context of military mobilization engendered unequal access to marriage and alternative imaginings of the future. These individuals were not merely passive recipients of state policies but active agents trying to exercise control over their own lives. For soldiers in the lowest ranks of the military and male civilians without disposable wealth, the normative life course of marriage and childbirth may have been luxurious dreams or required greater efforts to achieve. Militarization created a constant threat of sexual violence for female civilians but also broadened their imaginings of intimate futures. The reproductive as well as transformative capacities of kinship practices equipped local women and men with the resources and opportunities needed to improve the lives of their families but also to pursue their own desires, albeit involving the sacrifice of some of their kin. The intertwining of familial bonds and personal ethical struggles contributed to compromise or compliance with the conservative expectations of gendered roles. But the increasing power of women to provide for the family gradually reconfigured local generational and gender hierarchies, leading to transforming intergenerational relations, which are discussed in the following chapter.

Notes

1. For example, land reform on Kinmen in the 1950s was aimed at drawing attention to the contrast in governance between the ROC and the PRC. An agency called Joint Commission on Rural Reconstruction, funded by the US, published numerous pamphlets with photos showing Kinmen farmers holding giant sweet potatoes as evidence of its achievements. However, these photos resemble those released by the PRC as evidence of the triumphs of the Great Leap Forward (Szonyi 2008: 126–34).
2. Besides the ground battle in late 1949, Kinmen experienced two periods of intensive artillery attacks from the PRC in 1954–1955 and in 1958, known as the First and Second Taiwan Strait Crises, which caused significant casualties and loss of property for many local families. After the 1958 Crisis ended in stalemate, both the ROC and the PRC settled upon a routine of bombarding each other every other day with shells containing propaganda leaflets until 1979.
3. After confirming its governance of China in the late 1920s, the KMT exploited the state-building possibilities of *xiao jiating* (lit. small family, meaning Western conjugal family ideals) discourse proposed by the reformers of the New Culture Movement, but differed in its emphasis and direction. Glosser points out that '[w]hereas New Culture radicals had envisioned a state strengthened by the cumulative effects of individual freedom and productivity, the Nationalists made the state both the primary beneficiary and the central agent of reform' (2003: 81). In an attempt to distinguish its campaigns from those of the CCP (founded in 1921), the KMT proposed new laws and policies focusing on educating women and supporting party-affiliated women's organizations on the one hand, but with limited space for issues of gender equality and building women's consciousness and autonomy on the other (Hsu 2005). The image of women that the KMT sought to construct was illustrated in its New Life Movement launched in 1934, in which women were regarded as crucial actors in the implementation of the KMT's desired changes within families (Croll 1978; Diamond 1975). Neo-Confucian teachings of self-cultivation and maintaining family order were applied to mothers, who were to bear primary responsibility for cultivating their children with proper dispositions and assuring family order for the sake of the state. After the Japanese invasion of the Chinese mainland in 1937, the KMT began mobilizing women for the war effort by asking them to assist in upholding the morale of the nation in its greatest trial through focusing on care of the household and children.
4. The exact number of local women marrying soldiers from outside is unknown because, as Szonyi (2008) notes, the phenomenon was never distinguished as a category in

compiling statistics. Szonyi therefore cites the evaluation of one local man to suggest this phenomenon's significance: '[after 1949] [m]any women were married to soldiers; in total over one thousand. My own estimate would be that it was about one in five of the female population' (2008: 159). But this estimate is still approximate as it does not specify the period taken into account.

3

Changing Intergenerational Transmission amid Political and Economic Liberalization

The first wedding feast I attended on Kinmen was hosted by a family from the village where I stayed in 2013. I had been invited by the groom's aunt without knowing anything about the newlyweds. As at similar events, I was brought up to date while seated with nine elderly village women around a table at the wedding feast. These women told me that the groom was thirty-five years old, who worked in a high-tech company in Taiwan, and the bride was five years senior to him and was pursuing her doctoral degree. A woman next to me mentioned in a lowered voice that the bride was pregnant. Without further comments on the newlyweds, these women all said that the groom's widowed mother could now feel relieved as her only son had finally settled down. One village woman sitting at another table, who had volunteered to be my *meiren* (matchmaker) when we first met, came by and said, 'See, it's not too late to get married. You can marry a man younger than you' (I was in my early thirties at the time).

Despite local women's diversifying intimate experiences after 1949, as described in Chapter 2, this delayed first marriage, and the fact that the bride's education and age were above those of the groom, as well as the pre-marital pregnancy, would probably have been unthinkable decades before. However, my elderly female interlocutors appeared to downplay or dismiss these factors. Instead, they emphasized the value of marriage closely tied to parents' duty of seeing their children settle down and, in the case of a son, the continuity of the family line. I describe this local flexible but also conservative response to marital change as 'creative conservatism', a suggestive term coined by Magee (2021) in her discussion of marriage counselling in the US. In her research in Christian communities in Lynchburg, Virginia, Magee observed that conservative dis-

---

Endnotes for this chapter begin on page 85.

courses about stable family structures and anxieties about divorce go together with creative ways of thinking about what marriage is. For example, despite the widespread religious conceptualization of a married couple as 'a unit', people seeking counselling were advised to work on a happy and successful marriage by pursuing intimacy and togetherness with their spouses while maintaining their respective individualities. 'Creative conservatism' captures how these Christian communities appreciate marriage as something that must change with the times and respond to 'new dangers in the world' through creative approaches (Magee 2021: 73).

In this chapter, I use creative conservatism as a suggestive lens onto the changes taking place in intergenerational transmission and marriage in Kinmen, where the conservative goal of preserving the patriline remains remarkably strong today. I explore creative conservatism as a transformative aspect of kinship in producing new generations of persons in conjunction with shifting global and domestic political economies since the 1970s. As described in this book's Introduction, from 1949 to 1992, Kinmen islanders experienced severe political and economic constraints under the system of military rule. By contrast, the Taiwanese mainland had undergone several waves of industrial development, creating an economic miracle. Politically, changes in the relations between the ROC, the US and the PRC in the 1970s led to vibrant social movements for democratization and eventually the end of martial law on Taiwan in 1987. The groom in the above-described marriage, like many of his coevals, left to study in Taiwan and stayed there in a professional occupation, meeting his future spouse. Though these islanders, residing in Taiwan, were not part of my research, they become present in the stories depicted below which show how their move to and settlement in Taiwan were facilitated by their parents but also stimulated their parents' creative conservatism.

The ethnography presented in this chapter draws on my collection of life stories from Kinmen residents of different generations. The older generation of my informants, who were born between the early 1950s and late 1960s, experienced artillery attacks from the PRC and conditions of extreme material austerity. By contrast, the younger generation, who were born between the late 1970s and early 1990s, has witnessed significant improvement in living standards and has become familiar with urban lifestyles through their stays on Taiwan. The stories that I collected from young islanders who returned to or remained in Kinmen reveal the various ways in which their personalities, careers, life plans and marriages were influenced by their upbringing and their relationships with their parents. The discussion that follows focuses on the themes of education, housing and weddings, which figured prominently in my older and younger informants' accounts of their parent-child relations and (adult children's) marriages. These three aspects of life bring to light the new dynamics of intergenerational transmission and interaction amid the gradual improvement in local living standards and Taiwan's political and economic liberalization.

Theoretically, I build on new kinship studies (Carsten 2000, 2004), especially Charles Stafford's (2000a, 2000b) theorization of the Chinese folk model of *yang* (to care for), to highlight the processual and performative aspects of making parent-child ties. In Stafford's thesis, the concept of *yang* is cyclical and reciprocal as children, particularly sons, are expected to return the *yang* of their parents by providing *fengyang* (respectful care) when they are elderly. The cycle of *yang* is therefore tied to Confucian traditions prescribing generational and gender hierarchies, and to some extent overlaps with the notion of filial piety (Ikels 2004). But *yang* directs attention to everyday intergenerational interaction, revealing conflict but also increasing emphasis on emotional intimacy between generations, which redefines filial piety in contemporary Chinese societies (e.g. Evans 2008; Lin and Yi 2013; Yan 2016, 2021; Yeh and Benford 2004). In other words, the processes of *yang* or parenting do not simply result in a reciprocal return of *yang* or caring for aging parents but may animate new perceptions and practices regarding intergenerational relations. Furthermore, the expansive quality of *yang* enables us to consider how education, housing and weddings serve as important sites in which parents participate in a significant way in the shaping of their children's personhood and futures, and the two generations co-produce intergenerational bonds.

Recent anthropological scholarship has increasingly examined education in relation to kinship and relatedness (Cruz 2019; Fong 2011; Kipnis 2009). Though education is often examined as an investment or strategy of the family for upward social mobility or class reproduction, Resto Cruz (2019) makes a theoretically productive move, suggesting that it be considered as an inheritance that is empirically evident across the world amid the global postwar expansion of schooling. In this analysis, Cruz unpacks how education propelled by kinship has generated ruptures and inequalities, and produced contradictory consequences for persons and their relations in the post-1945 central Philippines. Following this lead, and informed by my ethnography, this chapter examines how education has been increasingly conceived as an inheritance by Kinmen parents in the upbringing of their children along with state policies broadening access to higher education. I pay attention to how gender inequalities in local patriarchal environments were challenged or persisted amid growing investment in daughters' education. I also explore how this conception of education as an inheritance has in practice been considered by parents in relation to their arrangements for children's housing and marriages in their allocation of available resources. Housing is one of the most important items transferred from parents to sons in Chinese settings (Croll 1984) and, in contemporary times, this is often a one-off occurrence upon marriage (Yan 2003). In the past and today, weddings have usually involved great expense on the marital rituals and gifts paid by parents of the groom and the bride, including the bride's parents' monetary gifts to her known as *jiazhuang* (dowry). I argue that parents' material input in children's education, housing and weddings can be conceived as three types of inheritance not only in their material aspects but also in terms of their future-making aspect as this inheritance is expected to be the foundation for children's upward mobility and future material security. The following ethnography illustrates how Kinmen parents allocated their available resources to different kinds of inheritance for sons and daughters, and how this might reinforce or unsettle gender inequalities and result in the thickening or thinning of parent-child ties (Carsten 2013, 2019; Cruz 2019).

This chapter follows the discussion in Chapter 2 showing how new dynamics between gender, family and economy in the Cold War era have given women power, transcending the women's domain of the 'uterine family' (Wolf 1972). The latter emphasizes mother-son emotional bonds in contrast to highly valued father-son filiation in patriarchal settings. Subsequent sections of the chapter demonstrate how mothers have played significant roles in arranging their children's education, housing and weddings, informed by their own visions of a good life, which often involved gender stereotypes and inequality. However, transgressions or innovations of both parents (including fathers who are less patriarchal) and adult children became palpable and have reshaped and enhanced intergenerational ties and intimacy. Weddings manifest this creative co-making of intergenerational bonds through drawing on a cultural repertoire and on contemporary commodity forms amid rapid expansion of the neoliberal economy since the 1990s. Changing forms of intergenerational transmission illuminate kinship's transformative capacities in making new generations of persons with new futures in relation to wider changes in politics and economy. This emerging creative conservatism signals a gradual shift of emphasis in parenting from the aim of preserving the patriline to the aim of ensuring the material and emotional well-being of children of both sexes.

Education, Gender, Livelihood

As described in Chapter 2, access to education in the early stage of military rule was uneven not only between the sexes but also between siblings, as (elder) daughters often sacrificed their education to earn money for the family. Education conceived as an inheritance was, therefore, not just unidirectional from parents to children but also horizontal as it involved contributions from siblings, some of whom, however, found it unfair and grumbled about their sacrifice (Chiu 2018b; see also Cruz 2019, Lee 2004b). On the other hand, several of my elderly female and male participants told me that they had not studied beyond primary or secondary school because they had no interest in studying, though their families' economic constraints were also an important factor. They engaged in farming, *a-ping-ko* businesses, and low-waged and labour-intensive work in the sorghum distillery and other sectors. In light of their own experiences of hardship and their observation of the links between education and stable livelihoods, the generation growing up during the peak period of military tension became more concerned about their children's education.

Governmental policies have also enabled students who have performed well academically and who are from economically less well-off families to pursue higher education. Kinmen students can apply for a programme allowing a certain number of them to skip the national test for university admission. They can also apply for university funding schemes in certain disciplines linked to the future occupations of school teachers and doctors, though they are required to work in Kinmen for some years after graduating (Huang 2019; Li 2009). These schemes are designed to deal with the constant shortage of teachers and physicians in the offshore islands and remote areas in Taiwan. Several studies have shown how the government-funded training system for teachers has contributed to the upward mobility of those from low-income families (e.g. Fwu 1999; Guo 1997; Tsai and Lee 2016). Moreover, in recent years, wage stagnation has frequently been in the headlines with suggestions of a stagnant, alienating and precarious future for young people.[1] While I heard that some funding recipients viewed the obligation to work in a designated place for some years as not in accordance with their life plans, many of my local interlocutors praised these young people for their success in securing respected jobs with steady incomes amidst the gloomy prospects of Taiwan's economy.

Higher education has been closely linked to upward mobility and future material security for children of both sexes in Kinmen. Though most of my young informants whose stories are described in this book did not take up the government programmes, their pursuit of higher education was usually inseparable from their parents' support. Below, my discussion focuses on the relations between gender, household economy and intergenerational transmission through two examples showing how mothers reshaped the gendered outlook of their daughters by investing in their education.

'Women Must Be Economically Self-Reliant Whatever the Circumstances'

Li-Mei (who was born in the early 1950s) made the above remark when describing her reluctance to ask her mother-in-law for money to purchase daily necessities early in her marital life. She felt bad about being financially dependent and supervised by her mother-in-law, who controlled her son's salary, because she had been the main breadwinner in her natal family before marriage. As the eldest child of her parents, with three younger brothers and two sisters, Li-Mei left school when she was in the fourth grade and started her *a-ping-ko* business of laundering soldiers' uniforms. She then worked in other *a-ping-ko* businesses till the age of twenty-three when by her own choice she married a man in her village, whom she had known since childhood. At that time, the salary that her husband earned as a school teacher was stable but relatively low. In her attempts to augment her family income and gain financial autonomy, after giving birth to her second child Li-Mei restarted her *a-ping-ko* activity by opening a snack bar among a variety of shops close to a larger military base. This business continued to operate till the late 1990s, when the policy of demilitarization made it no longer profitable.

Like many *a-ping-ko* businesses established by the islanders in this era, Li-Mei's enterprise involved the maximization of all available family labour and constantly expanded, for example, by building individual shower rooms, in order to attract more soldier-clients. Cherry (born in the mid-1980s), the youngest child of Li-Mei, recalled that her father would be asked by her mother to deliver hot food to the soldiers in his spare time. She also helped by sitting in the entrance to the shower rooms in order to receive the soldiers' payments, and in other ways during her childhood. Though she was very reluctant to help the business, Cherry admitted that these experiences had trained her to be outgoing and sociable, and influenced her decision to pursue a Master's degree in marketing in the UK. Cherry attributed her smooth path to education abroad, followed by a well-paid job in Taipei, to the financial foundation laid by her mother, who accumulated wealth through her successful enterprise and her sound investment in China's budding real estate market in the late 1990s. The wealth that Li-Mei earned also funded the reconstruction of a large house on her husband's inherited family land, the respective down-payments of her two sons' houses upon their marriages, and another daughter's postgraduate study abroad.

When recalling her endeavour to establish a business after marriage and childbirth, Li-Mei emphasized several times the importance for women to 'have their own careers and be economically independent' in order to be self-confident. She also asserted that 'marriage should be based on [a woman's] own choice and affection [for her partner]'. Her remarks revealed what she might think about her daughter's marriage. Cherry told me that after she resigned from her job in Taipei and returned to Kinmen in 2016, rather than pressuring her to get married, her mother gave her advice about managing her money in order to secure her financial security and independence. Li-Mei's reaction was arguably related to her recognition of Cherry's views about her parents' marital relationship. Toward the end of my interview with Li-Mei at their home, where Cherry was also present, Li-Mei's husband came back in a state of slight drunkenness. Cherry immediately expressed discontent at her father's behaviour. She complained to me that although her father was a nice man, she disliked the typical kind of Chinese masculinity embodied by her father who would leave all family affairs to her mother while out enjoying himself with his friends, and who behaved disreputably when drinking. She then spoke in unequivocal terms, 'I would rather stay unmarried than marry a man like my father'. Li-Mei tried to intercede for her husband by saying with a sigh, 'he just likes spending time with his friends'.

Educational Investment in A Stable Livelihood for Children

Mei-Hua (born in the mid-1950s), whom we encountered in the preceding chapter, had similar experiences to Li-Mei as both their natal families' economic situations were significantly improved by their *a-ping-ko* businesses. Mei-Hua was more fortunate in the sense that, as a second daughter, she received nine years of mandatory education owing to her elder sister sacrificing her own education and establishing the business. From her late teens to her late twenties, Mei-Hua also worked hard to fund her younger siblings' higher education in Taiwan. Unlike Li-Mei, Mei-Hua's husband was arbitrarily chosen by her mother, and she had no knowledge of the debt her husband's family owed before marriage. While Mei-Hua was constrained by her duty to care for her ill mother-in-law and children at home, her economic acuity building on her previous work experience helped her to generate several strategies to increase the family income. She not only cleared her husband's debt within a few years, but also financed the construction of their current residence and her four children's education beyond high school.

Despite her marital family's constrained economic circumstances, Mei-Hua told me that she had invested a lot in her children's education. She did not let her children apply for student loans for their undergraduate studies as many students of working-class families did, nor did she ask them to pay money back after they started working. Mei-Hua claimed that her investment in her children's education was aimed at enabling her children to 'have their own bowls [*you yige ziji de wan*]' meaning to have the necessary capacity to earn an independent living. Here, education was conceived as an inheritance that could become the foundation for the children's livelihood (see also Kunreuther 2009) rather than academic achievements. When her youngest son decided to prepare for the highly competitive civil service examination instead of going to university, Mei-Hua gave him her full support. She also dissuaded her first and third daughters, who held Masters' degrees from the two leading universities in Taiwan, from pursuing doctoral degrees. In our conversations, Mei-Hua clearly related her advice to her children to her perceptions about the increasingly precarious job market and future for young people today.

Mei-Hua did not intervene in what subjects her daughters studied at university, but her first daughter's major in finance and third daughter's major in social work were related to observing their mother's financial shrewdness and her devotion to volunteering. Mei-Hua's profound influence on her daughters' career-paths was also shown in her encouragement of these two talented daughters to participate in the examinations to secure stable public employment (and their success). When I first met Mei-Hua in 2013, these two daughters were not yet married and Mei-Hua avoided intervening too much in their private lives. Nevertheless, she upheld an idea that she and her husband would not have fulfilled their parental duty until all of their children had married and established their own families. Rather than spending time and money on doctoral studies, Mei-Hua wanted her daughters to accumulate their savings and prioritize their marriages. These two daughters got married in the following years.

Reshaping a Gendered Outlook and Its Limits

The two mothers described above instantiate an image of women that recurred among many of my older female interlocutors in Kinmen. On the one hand, they embodied the patriarchal ideals of womanhood in their skill in managing domestic chores and looking after children and parents-in-law. On the other, their ability to augment the family revenue reconfigured the power dynamics between themselves and their husbands (see also Brandtstädter 2009; Judd 2009), leading to their children's recognition of them as the actual matriarchs in their families (Stafford 2009). Their power in their marital families was reflected in their leading roles in allocating funds to their children's education, but the reshaping of a gendered outlook might have been restricted by the mothers' conservative visions of a good life and future. Despite these limits, the daughters who received higher education might have sought to break away from the normative life course, including marriage.

The stories of Li-Mei and Mei-Hua both show mothers' substantial roles in shaping their daughters' personhood and life paths. Their investment in their daughters' education to some extent guaranteed the latter's material security amidst the gloomy prospects of Taiwan's economy. While Mei-Hua's daughters appeared to take a normative path of life as expected by their mother, Li-Mei's daughter, Cherry, expressed discontent with this normative destiny. As Cherry told me, her observation of her mother's excessive sacrifice for the family and disapproval of her father's behaviour negatively affected her own interest in marriage.

Being aware of the association between Cherry's current single status and her views about her parents' marriage, Li-Mei left her daughter's marriage aside for the moment while serving as a financial mentor to her economic security. This is not to say that Li-Mei accepted the possibility of her daughter's lifelong singlehood, but her support kept her daughter close and frank in sharing her life with her. As we will see in the next chapter, the emotional ties between generations have led parents to accommodate their children's deferral of marriage, and has sustained children's filial sentiments for their parents. But parental accommodation may be a strategy of patience and waiting for their children's eventual marriage – a sign of creative conservatism, as suggested in my elderly informant's remark at the beginning of this chapter: 'it's not too late to get married'.

Inheritance and Unsettling Gender Inequality

Because Kinmen's teenagers had to go to Taiwan for their undergraduate and further studies, education and housing were increasingly bound together in parents' allocation of financial resources. Several of my younger interlocutors lived in a house their families had purchased in Taiwan when they studied and worked there, rather than in college residences or rented property. A retired school teacher told me that, since the 1980s, more and more local parents, including himself, had bought properties in northern Taiwan, where there were universities with good reputations and more job opportunities. Parents who were civil servants or school teachers also often seized the chance to change their place of work, as allowed by the government system, in order to seek better educational resources for their children while keeping their jobs (Hsu 2009: 49, 70). They targeted districts in Taipei where there were plenty of good schools and where living expenses were affordable. This strategy is still very common among Taiwanese families today as parents seek to prepare their children for a world of competition by settling in educationally prestigious districts in the capital (Lan 2018).

The *yang* provided by parents that bound education and housing together is often read as a parental strategy to ensure children's upward mobility or class reproduction. But this strategy, which also creates physical distance between generations, is double-edged as it potentially enlarges their emotional distance, and prevents parents from knowing about and interfering in their children's lives. Several of my elderly interlocutors said that they knew almost nothing about the intimate lives of their children working in Taiwan and could not understand why they remained unmarried past the age of thirty. Moreover, purchase of property in Taiwan implies parents' preparation for the possibility of living apart from their adult children, especially sons, in the future. For example, Cui-Lian, in her early sixties, has two sons who work in Taiwan and who lived together in a flat purchased by their parents before the elder brother got married. Prior to her first son's wedding in 2016, Cui-Lian and her two sons made the decision that the second son would take ownership of the flat and be responsible for the remaining loan, and the first son would receive financial help from his parents to buy a new residence in Taiwan. Cui-Lian told me that though she – like many local parents – desired to have at least one son live with them in Kinmen, she had expected for a long time that her sons might establish permanent residence elsewhere for employment purposes.

The increased uptake of advanced studies among women suggests a significant shift in women's entitlement to family wealth from almost zero in the early twentieth century to a growing expenditure on their education today. Nevertheless, the prevalent male-focused attitude in Kinmen has placed women in an inferior position, especially in families with more than three children (including sons and daughters). Ya-Fen, a single woman born in the late 1970s, shook her head when asked whether her parents had prepared a dowry for her marriage as several of my older informants did for their daughters. Ya-Fen said that her family was not wealthy enough to fully support six children's education (two daughters and four sons), and her mother, who oversees all the family's affairs, has strong ideas of son-preference. Her father once said that the dowries for his two daughters were nothing more than the money spent on their education. When Ya-Fen's younger sister expressed her desire to attend an intensive preparation course for the university entrance examination, their father persuaded their mother to pay the fees. In the way Ya-Fen described her parents to me, it was her mother who was the actual matriarch in their family and her father had less patriarchal attitudes.

Due to financial constraints, Ya-Fen's parents only paid the tuition fees for their daughters' undergraduate studies in Taiwan, so Ya-Fen and her sister had to work part-time to feed themselves. By contrast, their younger brothers received full funding up to the completion of their undergraduate studies. Ya-Fen said that her brothers might have no idea about the mortgage for a flat in Taipei bought by her mother years ago, when Ya-Fen had just started working. Except for the initial down payment paid by her mother, Ya-Fen paid off the remaining loan. Nevertheless, she did not expect to have a share of the property under her mother's name in the future.

Ya-Fen has long felt the unfairness of demands from her parents to help more in family affairs because she is the eldest daughter. One of the reasons that she returned to Kinmen was her prediction that her parents would ask for her assistance with the preparations for her younger brothers' weddings as she had done for her sister's and one brother's weddings while working in Taiwan. Ya-Fen told me that she constantly reminds herself about being cautious about the balance between her own interests and her parents' requests. She remarked jokingly, 'If I keep doing so much for my family, I may suffer from *youyu zheng* (depression)'. Based on her recognition that she is unlikely to inherit any family property, Ya-Fen has devised some strategies to ensure her own financial security. One method of augmenting her savings was to let out the unused property in Taiwan, and she defended her own rights by dismissing her mother's enquiries about the rent. Anthropologists have noted that inheritance, which usually indexes the relationships between kin, matters to a person not merely in its material aspects but also emotionally, and in the substance of what a person is (Cruz 2019; Knight 2018; Lambek 2011). Inequalities involved in the transmission of wealth, care and attention from parents to children may create ruptures in family relations and may also stimulate innovation challenging hierarchical and unequal relations. Ya-Fen's reaction to her mother favouring her sons illustrates how kinship is not always a site of amity and comfort but may cause harm and alienation to varying degrees (Carsten 2013, 2019; Das 2007; Lambek 2011).

The story of Ya-Fen instantiates the relatively slow overturning of gender inequality in the processes of *yang* that I found across Kinmen. A larger proportion of family wealth was usually spent on sons before their marriages, and houses remain reserved primarily for them. This male bias in transmission of family fortunes is also evident in the popular pattern of patrilocal co-residence in present-day Kinmen. As far as I observed between 2013 and 2020, many local married men live with their parents in the parental home. For aging couples with more than one son, it is common that one married or unmarried son decided or was asked by his parents to stay in the parental home. The conventional pattern of patrilocal co-residence has been maintained by this mingling of a son's economic interest and his filial sentiments of caring for his parents in light of the cycle of *yang*. But there are also cases in which souring relations between parents and adult sons (and their wives) or a young couple's desire for their private space led to the sons' moving out (see Chapters 5 and 6).

Nevertheless, Ya-Fen's case also illustrates rather close father-daughter relations in defiance of the valued father-son filiation in patriarchal settings. Ya-Fen said that though her father loves to spend time outside the home (like Cherry's father described earlier), he is different from most men in Kinmen in that, for example, he actively takes part in household chores. Ya-Fen's younger brothers are also familiar with the sharing of housework, which they had learned from their father since childhood. Ya-Fen and her siblings learned a less patriarchal image of men from their father during the long-term processes of *yang*, which shaped their personhood and emotional bonds with their father. Ya-Fen described her closeness to her father by mentioning that she often communicated her thoughts to her mother indirectly via her father. While I often heard about fathers' patriarchal demand of their children's thorough obedience to their orders or expectations, I also heard several stories from my young female informants which articulated their emotional bonds with their fathers. These intimate father-daughter ties became increasingly palpable and expressive in weddings.

Weddings and Changing Expressions of Parent-Child Ties

As many young people settled on Taiwan or elsewhere for education and work, their parents barely interfered in their choice of spouse. However, instead of being merely informed about and then invited to their children's weddings, parents played active roles in planning, including a series of traditional marital rites followed by a *xiyan* (wedding feast).[2] The *xiyan* mentioned at the beginning of this chapter instantiates this conservative expression of parental authority: the hosts of the feast were not the newlyweds but the groom's parents (in that case, his widowed mother), and most guests were members of the groom's patrilineage and his parents' social networks whom the groom might not have known before. The same holds for the feast hosted by the bride's parents. As several of my young married informants described, while abiding by their parents' arrangements for the traditional marital rites, they devoted their time and money to 'novel rites' to create their own memorable moments of marrying, in particular through bridal photography (see Adrian 2003 for a detailed ethnography in urban Taiwan). This mixing of traditional and modern elements in today's weddings can be seen as a further expression of creative conservatism: on the one hand, a social order building on generational hierarchy and kinship-based networks is maintained through old rituals, and on the other, conjugality and emotional ties between generations are manifested through new modes of celebration.

Parents show flexibility about the weddings of their sons who reside in Taiwan in only asking them to come back for a *xiyan*, while other rites are largely omitted. The weddings for men who belong to larger patrilineages and live in Kinmen are more complicated. A wedding that I attended in 2017 involved the newlyweds' observance of the rites of *yingqu* – in which the groom formed a procession comprising his groomsmen, one *meiren* (marriage ritual facilitator), and a music ensemble to bring the bride from her home to his – touring the groom's village to worship gods and ancestors. This groom, who lived with his parents in his large patrilineal village, performed these rites to fulfil his grandfather's wish. The grandfather was over ninety years old at the time and wanted to see, before the end of his life, at least one of his several grandsons carry out the rite of touring the village for worship (see Figure 3.1). It took nearly two hours for the couple to complete their tour of several sites, including village temples and ancestral halls, to worship gods and ancestors, during which the grandfather appeared at various points and quietly witnessed their conduct. The couple's ritual act symbolized a liminal process in which they renewed their personhood as the groom reconfirmed his membership in his patrilineage and the bride transferred her loyalty from her natal family to her marital family.

As Stafford (2000a) has noted, besides the remaking of personhood as described above, Chinese marital rites also concern two other systems of relatedness, which he termed 'the cycle of *yang* (to care for)' and 'the cycle of *laiwang* (reciprocal movements between people)'. These two systems, I suggest, shed light on why modern governmental attempts at reforming traditional marital rites failed. As discussed in Chapter 1, following the establishment of the ROC in 1912, Chinese intellectuals targeted the patriarchal, costly marital rites as objects ripe for reform, with the aim of building a modern Chinese nation-state and making 'new' Chinese persons. These reform movements were adopted by both the KMT and the CCP, and implemented in the territories they controlled. However,

Figure 3.1. The bride and groom entering an ancestral hall to greet and worship the groom's remote ancestors in 2017. © Hsiao-Chiao Chiu.

in Kinmen and Taiwan as a whole, the traditional practices of bridewealth and hosting a *xiyan* remain popular today because they are concerned with making kin and social ties.

As we have seen, many parents in Kinmen still view their children's marriages as their final duty of *yang*, which includes a great deal of money saved for the wedding. But, beyond this formal and moral duty as a Chinese parent to his/her children, I noticed the changing emphasis on more explicit expressions of their affection for their children in my elderly informants' narratives about their children's weddings. Normally, the groom's parents are responsible for most wedding expenses, including the monetary component of *pinjin* (bridewealth) and other gifts to the bride, the cost for *xibing* (wedding cakes or biscuits) on both the groom's and the bride's sides, and a *xiyan* on the groom's side.[3] I heard of some cases where the groom's parents accepted their affines' request of unreasonable amounts of *pinjin* and gifts, and they kept this secret from the groom to avoid endangering the newlyweds' relationship. In the past, most parents would not host a *xiyan* for their daughter's marriage due to economic constraints and, more crucially, the idea that a daughter would eventually become a member of another family. By contrast, nowadays many parents of a bride not only decline *pinjin* from the groom but also host a large *xiyan* to show their affines that their daughter is loved and they are not marrying her off as if they were selling a commodity.[4]

During the period of miliary rule, the military government tried to reduce the costly *xiyan* by introducing *jituan jiehun* (a group wedding ceremony). But it was still common for civilians to host a large *xiyan* and rely on voluntary labour from female relatives for catering. While the host family might reward the helpers with certain gifts or *hongbao* (red envelopes with money inside), it was the principles of reciprocity and mutual help that mobilized voluntary labour (see Chau 2004 for similar phenomena in post-reform China). Nowadays the *xiyan* is fully commoditized by resorting to the professional catering of restaurants, but some other life course events still rely on female relatives' voluntary labour (Chiu 2017). Thus, the family staging a wedding asks their female relatives to help to distribute *xibing* to all the households in their village.

The islanders' observance of traditional rituals does not exclude innovations which may strengthen the cycle of *laiwang*. With improved living standards, the practice of posting messages of congratulations for an engagement or marriage in the local government-owned *Kinmen Daily News* has become very popular since the 1980s. The appearance of these messages manifests the wider social ties and *mianzi* (face or reputation) of the groom's family which, however, bears an additional moral and financial burden as they usually prepare more expensive boxes of *xibing* in return. Similarly, in light of the principle of reciprocity, it is common today for the family staging a wedding to reject *hongbao*, usually used to cover the costs of the feast, from their related villagers. Reciprocity and mutual help are emphasized as socio-moral values related to the processes of producing social persons, in opposition to the marketable value of commodities (Graeber 2013; Turner 2008). The older generations who revitalize their webs of reciprocity through old and new practices are concerned not only about their own moral personhood but also about the re-embedding of their children in wider social networks, which may help them in times of need. Here we can see the generativity and persistent vitality of kinship under conditions of capitalist modernity where various kinds of labour and exchange can be monetized but fail to generate meaningful relations in the long run.

Most of my young married informants explained their submission to their parents' arrangements for their weddings by articulating their respect and affection for their parents, without directly using the term *xiaoshun* (filial piety). Some said that they were just '*sui tamen de yi*' (doing what their parents asked them to do) to avoid conflicts; some said that they did the rituals '*zhiyao tamen kaixin jiu hao*' (as long as their parents were happy). This submission may also be related to a stereotyped impression of what a Chinese wedding should be that was held by many young people. An experienced *meiren* (marital ritual facilitator) told me that, partly because of the rise of cultural nostalgia, today many young couples try to create a culturally authentic Chinese wedding by adding in several 'traditional' elements they learned about from the internet, but which had not really been practised in Kinmen. Indeed, young couples tend not to question the patriarchal order implied in the traditional marital rites but focus on how to create their special memories of marrying. Whether or not they viewed the traditional rites as necessary elements in making their unique weddings, young couples did not exclude new rites promoted by the bridal industry. This is illustrated in the case of Eve and her husband, both natives of Kinmen, who planned their wedding in 2016.

For Eve's husband and both sets of parents, a memorable wedding had to be ritually complete, including the rite of *yingqu* and large feasts hosted by the two families respectively. But Eve objected to the rite of *yingqu* and preferred a small-scale banquet with only the two families attending. Her mother wondered why she wanted to marry out so 'quietly'. Eve explained to me, as she replied to her mother, that she disliked the part of the rite of *yingqu* that involved bidding farewell to her parents, because 'I am still a daughter of my parents even though I was marrying out'. This claim suggests that women suffer from the rupture of leaving their natal family implied in the ritual and in their marital lives afterwards (Judd 1989, 2009; Wolf 1972), which Eve and many women today firmly refuse to accept.

Significantly, Eve also stated that, 'all of the traditional rites were not what I truly wanted because they were built on family, on the given customs of our society'. But she added immediately that it was just her individual preference, which differed from the original plan of her husband who was present throughout our interview. She further asserted, 'It's not easy to earn money after all', as those rites and feasts were costly. Whether or not Eve's remarks were intended as a critique of patriarchy, she eventually made compromises with her husband and parents on both sides regarding the wedding arrangements. They omitted several rites, including *yingqu*, and only held a betrothal rite at Eve's home, followed by two large feasts respectively hosted by the parents of the bride and the groom, because Eve knew that both parents viewed the feasts as their duty as well as an expression of their love for their children.

While expressing no enthusiasm for traditional rites, Eve declared that 'I wanted to wear a most beautiful wedding gown at that moment'. Her desire was realized through purchasing a package of bridal photography, which usually includes rented gowns (for photography and the wedding), professional photography, and photo albums and cards from a bridal salon. They initially bought a package from a bridal salon in Taipei, but had a bad experience as they were pressured by the photographer and stylist to finish the shoot on time, with the salon thereby failing in its promise to respect customers' preferences (Adrian 2003). Due to this negative experience, Eve asked a professional wedding photographer who had just established his business in Kinmen for a second shoot in several places which were memorable to the couple and at both of their parental homes. When they were at the groom's home, Eve encouraged her husband and his mother to reconstruct a scene from her husband's childhood in which he asked his mother for pocket money but she was too busy to answer him. As Eve recalled, the entire process of photography constituted a shared unique memory of this marriage for them and for their parents on both sides, suffused with emotions and mutual care between generations. The wedding photography was no longer a mere commodity but a medium through which affection and care between generations could be objectified.

While in Eve's case her parents and parents-in-law appeared to enjoy the moments of intergenerational intimacy created by the consumption of photography, several of my elderly informants grumbled about their children spending too much money on wedding commodities that had no benefits beyond temporary personal pleasure. However, kinship practices involving creativity and innovation can surpass the market value of commodities. A young local wedding photographer told me about a client's (the bride's) father, a carpenter who made a *hunli beiban* (a large upright board installed at a wedding feast as the background for photographs of the newlyweds with their guests) as a gift for his daughter. Anthropologists have noted how people lay claim to each other as kin through the objectification of labour as tokens of value (Graeber 2013; Turner 2008). This father appropriated the form of *hunli beiban*, a popular commodity in the wedding industry, and made the item himself, thus objectifying his affection for his daughter and confirming his ties to her. This is very different from the old ritual requiring the daughter to sever her ties with her parents. There were also cases in which the newlyweds sought to hold a do-it-yourself wedding involving the voluntary labour of kin and friends. This kind of wedding might draw on elements from the wedding industry but all the participants recalled the event physically and emotionally as a time of reaffirming their ties and flows of affection for each other.

Echoing Bruckermann's (2019) discussion of a novel ritual celebrating children's birthdays in post-reform China, the co-existence of traditional rites and globalized commodity forms in Kinmen's weddings today could be read as making relatedness between parents and adult children, and among wider social networks. The combination of old and new practices is itself a manifestation of mutual care and affection between generations. As the old rituals are less about the expression of personal emotions, both the old and the young increasingly adopt new forms to express conjugal intimacy as well as intergenerational ties. The desire to express affection between generations can overcome a market logic by appropriating commodity forms to make new objects with no market value. These emerging phenomena illustrate the capacity of kinship practices to animate innovation and change, as well as the continued significance of kinship amidst an expansive neoliberalism that promotes the shift of an individual's attention from a universe of wider kin ties to the self.

Conclusion

Emerging intimate practices, such as late first marriage and pre-marital pregnancy, in the case described at the beginning of this chapter, have often been viewed in mainstream modernization theories as signs of rising individualism amidst a society's transition to capitalist modernity. Little attention has been paid to what role kinship has played in these changing processes. In this chapter, I have used the lens of 'creative conservatism' to explore how kinship practices may animate generational differences in life paths and the pursuit of intimacy in Kinmen. Changing kinship relations, together with a shifting politico-economy since the 1970s, have created new generations of persons with new imaginaries of the future. In line with anthropological challenges to assumptions that kinship becomes restricted to nuclear constructs of family and to possessive individualism (Bruckermann 2019; Cruz 2019; Lambek 2011; McKinnon and Cannell 2013), I have also shown how intergenerational ties and wider social bonds are still valued and maintained.

In this chapter, we have seen that education, housing and weddings have been three key sites of intergenerational transmission and future-making in Kinmen, in which parents participated in a significant way in shaping their children's personhood and futures. These three sites have required parents to carefully allocate their available resources to their children, relying on mixing sources of income from *a-ping-ko* business, farming and other sectors. While an increasing proportion of family wealth has been allocated to daughters, the idea of privileging sons remains dominant in the local patriarchal context. For a family with several children and limited resources, such as that of Ya-Fen, a daughter might not receive a dowry in the form of monetary gifts from her parents upon marriage because the money had already been spent on her education. Persistent male-focused attitudes have also led many parents to allocate much of their accumulated wealth and inherited property to sons, including money spent on their education, housing and weddings.

On the other hand, I have also shown how mothers and fathers deeply influenced their children's trajectories, and nurtured strong mother-daughter or father-daughter ties in defiance of the emphasis on father-son filiation in local patriarchal settings. This contributes to anthropological accounts of how kinship is suffused with ambivalence, and transgressions or changes may arise from everyday unremarkable acts of kinship (Carsten 2013, 2019; Das 2007; Lambek 2011; Peletz 2001). While transmission of care, attention and material property to the next generation is still often unequal by gender in Kinmen, increasing investment in daughters' education has created more diverse life options for them. Young women with higher education gain economic independence and the confidence to defer their marriage or reject parents' excessive demands for their contribution to the family. Parents who transgressed gender stereotypes also showed their children different images of women and men beyond the patriarchal prescriptions, thus strengthening intergenerational bonds and contributing to the possibility of wider, meaningful progress towards gender equality.

Kinship practices not only produce new generations who have more opportunities than those available to their parents but also enhance the ways in which wider kin and other social ties are rendered valuable and desirable – particularly in current times of growing uncertainty. In Kinmen, changes in the nature of parent-child ties are reflected in the mixing of traditional rites and contemporary commodity forms in weddings in an era of expansive marketization. Newlyweds' relational personhood is reaffirmed through old and new practices that revitalize wider kinship and other social bonds. This relational personhood does not exclude personal autonomy as the newlyweds embrace both conjugal intimacy and intergenerational bonds through wedding consumption. Nonetheless, although the desire to materialize the expression of affection between generations may be prompted by the market, kin ties and practices may surpass a market logic through appropriating commodities to strengthen affective ties.

The case of Kinmen offers a comparison with China regarding the consequences of the intersections of kinship, the state and policies of reproduction in culturally similar but politically opposite regimes of governance. As Yunxiang Yan (2003, 2009) has compellingly shown, state-driven transition from collectivization to marketization in China since the 1980s has led to the rise of individualization characterized by egoism. Young people have increasingly emphasized personal desires and conjugal interest by demanding wealth from their parents, especially men's parents, to satisfy their material needs. The older generation in rural areas – who, unlike their urban counterparts, were not protected by the state's welfare system following reform – have faced not only the loss of parental authority but also a crisis of elderly support. In the cities where the One-Child policy (from 1980, and replaced by the Two-Child policy in 2016) was more effective, parental devotion to raising their only child contributed to strong parent-child bonds. Daughters, in particular, emphasized their affective ties with their parents and their filial duty to provide elderly support (Fong 2004; Liu 2008; Xie 2021). They echoed discourses circulated in the state media in which traditional family values, especially filial piety, were emphasized to resolve the problem of elderly care (Zhang 2016; Zhang 2017). By contrast, the Taiwanese government had long treated childcare and elderly care as family duties, and relevant policies of public support have only been proposed in recent years (Chyn 2019).

As fertility rates in China continue to decline because of the earlier One-Child policy, and with increasing competition following marketization, a third generation has now become the locus of family life. There is a rising emphasis on intergenerational solidarity and mutual dependence as young couples have relied on their parents' and/or parents-in-law's support to provide the best care for their children (Bruckermann 2017, 2019; Santos 2021; Yan 2016, 2021). Emotional intimacy between generations has been emphasized and is desired more than ever before. In a recent publication, Yan proposed the term 'neo-familism' to describe these new trends in China where new discourses of the state and ordinary citizens 'invoke familism as the primary strategy to pursue both individual happiness and family prosperity through the collective efforts of a multi-generational domestic group' (2021: 15).

The emergence of creative conservatism in Kinmen and the rise of neo-familism in China, I suggest, demonstrate the constitutive power of kinship in relation to the impact on ordinary lives of different political ideologies and policies. Rather than losing significance, people have drawn on old and new kinship knowledge and resources, in relation to changing politico-economic circumstances, to better prepare the next generations for increasingly uncertain futures. Kinship practices that include various rituals to secure kin relations and other social ties problematize assumptions about the secularization of kinship under capitalist modernity (McKinnon and Cannell 2013; Sangren 2000; Thomas et al. 2017). Kinship labour that can be objectified as tokens of value and care promotes the recognition of kin ties as separate from the capitalist calculation of labour and value (Bruckermann 2019; Graeber 2013; Turner 2008). In the face of similar demographic crises in Taiwan, China and across the world, including declining fertility rates, aging population and rising divorce rates, kinship and familial values have been appropriated and emphasized by neoliberal governments as measures to alleviate crises and ease or shrink governmental responsibilities (see Ochiai and Hosoya 2014). Ordinary families adopt creative approaches to nurture their kin ties within and beyond nuclear or joint families as they seek affection, support and material resources for survival, and attempt to secure the well-being of future generations.

Notes

1. Scholars have noted the trends of economic recession and stagnation of real wages in Taiwan since the late 1990s (Hsu et al. 2015; Huang 2015; Lee and Lin 2017).
2. The traditional marital rites in Kinmen are in principle similar to those in southern Fujian, China and on Taiwan because of the shared regional cultural heritage. But there are many variations and differences in the details; in Kinmen, these variations can be categorized into three geographic areas (Yang and Lin 1997).
3. Take Cui-Lian's case as an example. For her son's wedding in 2016, Cui-Lian had to prepare more than 300 boxes of *xibing* for all the households in their relatively large patrilineal village, and another 200 boxes for social networks outside the village. The *xiyan* consisted of forty-five tables (modest by local standards), and about thirty tables were for co-villagers (a table had ten persons and on average cost 5,000 to 6,000 New Taiwan Dollars, 160–200 USD, in a local restaurant in 2016). Though the prices for

wedding banquets in Kinmen are much lower than the prices in Taipei, where a table for a feast costs three to four times the average price in Kinmen, the total expenses still constitute a great burden.
4. This refusal of *pinjin* implies the bride's parents' definite dissociation from the negative cases sometimes reported in the Taiwanese media in which some parents were criticized for treating their daughters as if they were commodities by requesting an unreasonable amount of *pinjin*. But very often in Kinmen and Taiwan, the groom's parents still prepare a large sum of money in cash or a cheque as *pinjin* to display in front of their affines who have previously stated their refusal to accept *pinjin*. As several senior informants told me, even though their affines reject the *pinjin*, they have to *xingshishang* (lit. nominally; just for performance) prepare the *pinjin* out of courtesy, their own *mianzi* (face or reputation), and the intention to prove their family's financial status.

4

TRIALS OF MARRYING

In the preceding chapter, we have seen examples of marital change in Kinmen following Taiwan's political and economic liberalization. The official statistics indicate that Kinmen is in line with the national trends towards later and less marriage (see Figures 4.1 and 4.2). The shifting demography of declining marriage rates, extremely low fertility rates and a rapidly aging population in present-day Taiwan, and across East Asia, resembles earlier trends occurring in Euro-American societies. But researchers have noted a significant difference between East Asian societies and Euro-American ones: rates of childbirth out of wedlock are much lower in the former than in the latter (Ochiai 2011; Ochiai and Hosoya 2014; Raymo et al. 2015). The Taiwanese government has viewed these demographic changes as threatening the nation's survival, and has begun to propose policies aiming to boost marriage and fertility rates (Chen 2012). For example, in the government White Paper for Population Policy of 2013, one of the reasons given for the declining marriage rates is the decreasing chance of young people meeting potential partners. A policy was put forward to encourage governmental departments and private companies to organize *weihun lianyi huodong* (matchmaking activities for single people) (The Executive Yuan of the Republic of China 2013: 89). This policy continued in 2020 but its effects appear to be limited because of the small number of participants in these matchmaking activities and other factors discouraging marriage.

Recent studies based on large-scale surveys have pointed out that one key factor discouraging Taiwanese citizens, especially women, from marriage is the persistence of patriarchal norms demanding that women take on the main responsibilities of housework, child-rearing and possibly elderly care (Cheng and Yang 2021; Raymo et al. 2015). Intriguingly, while recent survey results show the general trend towards more liberal arrangements of marital lives (e.g. marriage

---

Endnotes for this chapter begin on page 105.

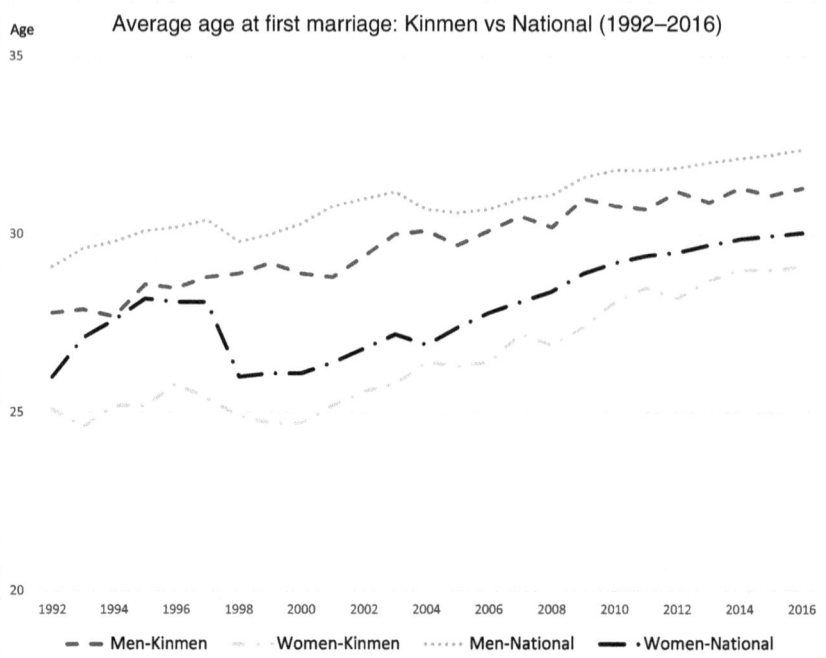

Figure 4.1. Steady rise in age at first marriage for both sexes. Source: Department of Household Registration, Ministry of the Interior, Taiwan (https://www.ris.gov.tw/app/portal/674).

without children), the idea of having at least one son to continue the family line has grown in strength between 1994 and 2011 (men outnumbered women in supporting this idea) (Cheng and Yang 2021). This persistent expectation of preserving the patriline is not surprising in relation to my research experiences in Kinmen, where islanders keep performing various rituals manifesting patrilineal values and maintaining kinship-based social networks. Local parents' enthusiasm for arranging their children's weddings is closely connected to these socio-moral values, but growing expressions of emotional ties with children through new commodity forms are also noteworthy. Nevertheless, marriage is not today the universal experience it used to be for young people above the age of thirty.

During my two periods of fieldwork, I heard many older people articulate their worries about the single status of their adult children or younger relatives who worked in Kinmen, on the Taiwanese mainland or elsewhere. I myself, as a woman of marriageable age from Taiwan, frequently encountered queries about my marital status and my interest in marrying in Kinmen from older people – an experience I seldom had in urban Taiwan. While some elderly female villagers wanted to introduce me to their sons or junior relatives, they expressed concerns about my doctoral degree, which was far beyond the level of education that

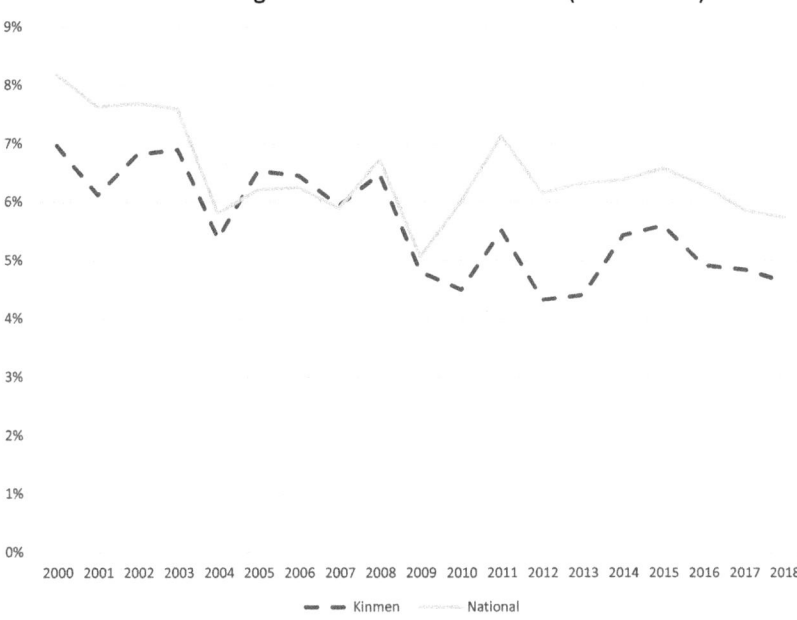

Figure 4.2. Declining marriage rates in Kinmen and throughout Taiwan. Source: Department of Household Registration, Ministry of the Interior, Taiwan (https://www.ris.gov.tw/app/portal/674).

most local men attained (see Inhorn and Smith-Hefner 2020 on highly educated women's constrained marital options across the world). My experiences suggest that finding a marital partner in Kinmen can be very difficult, but staying single is not easy either. These experiences are shared by my local informants who were between their late twenties and early forties and still single when I interviewed them in 2017–2018. Rather than probing what factors discourage people from marrying, as most survey-based research has done, this chapter foregrounds young people's experiences of deferring marriage in the close-knit society of Kinmen. With a focus on the future-making and relational aspects of marriage, my ethnography demonstrates how young single people reflected on their current lives and futures through questions related to marriage and how they interact with their families while staying unmarried.

Informed by my interviews and interactions with young single people, supplemented by data derived from other groups of research participants, I analyse young people's experiences of deferring marriage not simply as an expression of personal autonomy and freedom but as 'trials' they have to go through on a daily basis. I discuss these experiences of 'trials' in three senses: (1) they are constantly subjected to the judgement of others about their social status and marriageability (and they themselves often judge potential marriage partners); (2) they struggle with vexatious people and circumstances pertaining to their private lives; (3) they go through a trial or 'testing process', during which their past experiences, present conditions and imaginings about the future have intertwined with each other and moulded their actions and ideas concerning marriage. In my discussion, I highlight temporality as a productive lens onto the imaginative work that marriage involves (Carsten et al. 2021). In these young people's stories, we can see how whether to marry or not is not simply a decision originating from individual choice or familial obligation but is enfolded in a transforming process during which an individual constantly reshapes his or her ideas of marriage and his or her relations with family. Amidst this process, the imaginative work that marriage involves opens up opportunities for, and encompasses, ethical judgements about ways of making relatedness and pursuing personal desired lives and futures.

My ethnography of young people's experiences of postponing marriage in Kinmen echoes a collection of studies exploring the emerging worldwide trends of later marriage and childbearing through the notion of 'waithood' (Inhorn and Smith-Hefner 2020). In this collection, waithood denotes 'an extended period of young adulthood in which young men and women are waiting to marry and have children, sometimes delaying indefinitely, and sometimes opting out altogether', and this state may be intentional, unintentional or a mix of both (Smith-Hefner and Inhorn 2020: 2).[1] The studies in this collection, mostly based on anthropological fieldwork across different cultural settings, elaborate and expand upon the notion of waithood to better reflect the varying conditions that their informants faced. They point out that waithood is not just a state of passively waiting; instead, it usually involves young people's innovation and action to redraw their life prospects beyond familial and social expectations. This volume therefore presents an expansive view of waithood that involves both agency and constraint. Similarly, my use of 'trials' not only reflects my informants' daily challenges of marrying but also underlies a testing and transforming process in which, rather than 'waiting' to be married, they constantly reshape their visions of their futures with or without marriage.

In what follows I elaborate these three senses of trial, demonstrating how the intersection and interaction between personal trajectories, wider socioeconomic changes and a resilient cultural repertoire make marrying difficult, unattractive or only one possible life option for young people in various social positions. Lastly, I move to everyday scenes of young single people's interaction with their families. Following my argument in the preceding chapter, my ethnography shows how young people try to create their own life while valuing familial ties and obligations. Deferring marriage is not straightforwardly an expression of an individual's autonomy and freedom but a mixed outcome of striving for a desired life against social constraints (see also Lamb 2018 on being single in India). Moreover, I argue, this emerging phenomenon of deferring marriage encompasses changes generated from the intimate sphere of kinship that have encouraged the creation of new visions of marriage and the family beyond conservative patriarchal vision.

Judgements about a Person's Marriageability

Through the Cold War era, the economy of Kinmen was remarkably transformed but also restricted by military concerns. The only new kind of industry developed locally since the 1990s has been tourism and tax-free shopping, targeting in particular tourists from China, together with the expansion of the sorghum distillery and the public facilities of the airport and ferry port. These have provided more job opportunities for local people but have had limited effects on attracting young natives with higher education and professional skills to return home. My first sense of trial depicts, in Kinmen's post-militarized economic circumstances, young people's experiences of being stratified into a hierarchy of social status according to the combination of their level of education, occupation and economic capacity and, following this hierarchy, how their marriageability is judged by potential partners and society more generally.

A large proportion of young people, who have university degrees or further training and live in Kinmen now, work as civil servants or schoolteachers. These two careers are highly valued in local society not only because of the educational investment involved but also because of their stability and comparatively good salaries and welfare in the context of Taiwan's lingering economic recession. Local men and women who have passed the very competitive examinations to become civil servants or teachers are therefore part of a new middle class enjoying high credit in the marriage market. For example, a village woman told me that her nephew's family had given a large amount of bridewealth (*pinjin*) as requested by the bride's grandmother, who considered her granddaughter, a teacher in a local public school, to have a higher social status than the groom, who was employed in a managerial position in a local private company. This case instantiates a constant tension between conservative and progressive visions of marriage in Kinmen since the early twentieth century. While this young couple might view their marriage as a union of two persons of equal standing, the bride's grandmother emphasized their status difference and marriage's function of exchange in the interest of the bride's natal family.

Young people working in the sorghum distillery or at manual jobs, such as labourers in construction and parcel delivery, were judged by locals to be in an inferior position on the local marriage market. When I had an unexpected talk with several elderly men about my research on marriage in 2018, one mentioned how a female schoolteacher in her early forties whom he knew remained single. He said that this woman had not been able to meet a suitable man in Kinmen and, as a teacher, it was not easy for her to accept a man with an inferior career. Another man added, 'It's impossible for a teacher to marry a *gongren* [labourer or workman]'. Based on my understanding that people now compete for jobs in the sorghum distillery for their good salaries and generous company welfare, I asked, 'How about an employee in the distillery? Isn't that a well-paid job?' A third man replied that 'An employee in the distillery is still a *gongren*'.

These men did not comment on the female teacher's single status by using any pejorative terms, such as 'leftover women' (*shengnü*), used by the state media and general public in China to ridicule young women who have higher education and professional careers but remain single beyond their late twenties (Hong Fincher 2014; To 2015).[2] They appeared to find it reasonable that a female teacher would not marry a *gongren* because of the higher social status associated with her career in local standards. This example also shows that a well-paid job in the distillery alone is not enough to elevate a person's social status and marriageability. Marriageability is evaluated by comparing the status of the potential groom and bride, which echoes a Chinese idiom, *mendang hudui* (marriage between spouses of equal standing), though a woman's hypergamy is very often expected objectively and subjectively. This phenomenon is also observed in contemporary China (Gaetaro 2014; Obendiek 2016) and India (Lamb 2018), where marriage is still viewed by many as a highly gendered means of pursuing upward mobility or reproducing status and class. To a certain extent, the popularity of cross-border marriage between the men of Kinmen and women from other less wealthy countries, especially rural China, around the turn of this century, was driven by the lower credit of male *gongren* on the local marriage market (see next chapter).

Intrusions on Personal Privacy

In an era of globalization and an expanding neoliberal economy, young people from Kinmen appear to enjoy higher mobility and broader channels for developing romantic relationships than earlier generations. Several of my male and female acquaintances married Chinese citizens whom they met during a tourist visit or during their study or work in China. It was not their lack of marriageability on the local marriage market but their mobility and autonomy that led them to a cross-border marriage. I also heard some cases of marriage established through online dating. But for people who avoid using virtual platforms for matchmaking, mobility can be very restricted in day-to-day life. My younger interlocutors who are single and work in different sectors all said that 'Kinmen is too small' (*Kinmen taixiaole*) so they barely get to know new people during their everyday life on the island. Living in Kinmen, where there is only a small proportion of younger residents of marriageable age, means limited opportunities to meet a suitable partner face to face. A female friend told me that she was a bit anxious about the possibility that she would never be able to get married when she decided to come back for a long-term stay at the age of nearly thirty, and she emphasized, 'I'm not joking'.

Research participants also remarked that 'Kinmen is too small' when describing how the local kinship-based social networks have disrupted their daily work and private life – the second sense of trial that I refer to. For example, a friend of mine working in local government said that she would judge the situation in order to decide whether she would admit her identity as a Kinmen native or pretend to be a person from Taiwan. This was because when she met local people in her workplace, most of them asked about her identity so as to see whether they had any connections with her, and whether they could gain any benefit by using this connection. The tight-knit social circles also leave little, if any, room for young people to protect their personal privacy, including intimate life, as my informant Wade described below:

Wade: A problem that local young people face in developing a romantic relationship is that Kinmen is too small. I heard a very ridiculous remark, that a boy and a girl who went hiking on Mount Taiwu [the highest mountain in Kinmen] by themselves means that they are going to marry [laughed loudly]. Ridiculous.

Hsiao-Chiao: I heard similar remarks from many of my older interlocutors ...

Wade: But I heard this from a person of my generation.

Hsiao-Chiao: Yeah, gossip [*xianyan xianyu*] ... If your acquaintances spotted us having a meal here, they might gossip about our relationship.

Wade: That's it. The social relationships in Kinmen are too close-knit. One time, I and my ex-girlfriend strolled in the high street in Taiwan; the next day, in my workplace, I found that gossip about my date was circulating among my colleagues. I thought: 'Didn't I have the date in Taiwan? How come you got to know about it?'. Frankly speaking, gossip won't do much harm to a man but this environment is stressful or unfair to women of marriageable age or who long for a romantic relationship. It is impossible for a woman to have a try [*shishikan*] with a man she feels okay with, and then break up with him if things don't go well. She will soon be judged badly in local social circles by doing so.

Wade's words reveal that local tight-knit social circles not only make it hard to safeguard personal privacy but also put pressure on the development of intimate relations. Some gossip, like that of Wade's colleagues who talked about his date, is annoying to the person(s) involved but not harmful as long as it is based on what really happened. However, some gossip, which is simply made up from partial understandings about an event – for example, a man and a woman who are not in a relationship are spotted meeting each other outside – potentially causes problems for those involved, whose integrity may be unfairly judged by others. Wade's comments about a woman's avoidance of *shishikan* arose because it is almost impossible for her to hide her romantic history from locally narrow social circles, and a woman who has several romantic relationships before marriage – even if they were serious – may be judged as reckless and a bad marital partner. I myself was also cautious about this kind of moral judgement, so I avoided meeting any young married men alone during fieldwork. When I had an interview in a coffee shop with a man who was about to be married, I asked him if it was OK for him to meet me alone. He quickly grasped what I meant and said that he had already reported to his fiancée about our meeting and obtained her permission to share their stories with me.

Like my own experiences of encountering older villagers' recommendations of local men to me, my informants face these proposals and pressing questions about when they are going to marry all the time, in their kin communities and workplaces. In the stories of my three informants in the next section, we will see how they tackled this kind of trial.

Deferring Marriage as A Testing Process

In the preceding two sections I have discussed two kinds of trial faced by young people in their everyday lives, which pressure them to get married but also reinforce the stratification of social status that reduces some people's marital prospects. This section focuses on young single people's personal experiences that have placed them in a 'testing process' – my third sense of trial – of figuring out the meaning and place of marriage in their life. The testimonies of my three informants below illuminate that they were not simply justifying why they remained single past the age of thirty – the new threshold for when young Taiwanese people schedule their marriage plans today (Huang 2013). Instead, they were articulating what marriage means to them regarding their personal circumstances, and they do not foreclose the possibility of getting married in the future.

'Marriage Is Just A Possible Outcome of A Relationship'

Wade (born in the early 1980s) gave up his plan of finding a job in Taiwan after completing his tertiary education there because he could not leave his divorced mother alone in Kinmen. He secured a contract-based job suited to his profession in local government, and he has been working there for several years. Though he dislikes many things about his workplace, his desire to change his career has been suppressed by his filial and financial duties. To fulfil his mother's dream of having a house of their own, Wade took out a mortgage which, together with other expenditure, has prevented him from finding different work outside Kinmen. When speaking of the house, Wade asserted, 'I am not like most men in Kinmen. I don't treat buying a house as a definite goal in one's life, nor a marriage'. Rather than excluding marriage from his life, he emphasized that he still wants to have a partner but that 'marriage is just a possible outcome of a relationship'. I responded that many people of his generation have similar thoughts, but Wade countered, 'Not really. Many of my colleagues have made remarks like, "It seems the time to get married", which sounds like "It's lunchtime so let's eat something". This is how marriage is considered in Kinmen'.

Wade's remarks suggest deviation from his male coevals, who appeared to view marriage as a task that a man must complete in his life course, in line with the conventional understanding of marriage as a passage to socially recognized adulthood. Wade has therefore faced pressing questions about his marriage not only from his mother but also from people at his workplace, as shown in our conversation below.

Wade: My mother tried to pressure me to get married, but as several years passed, she realized it's useless because I simply ignored her interrogation. My relatives also always asked about my marriage during the family reunion in the Chinese New Year holidays but I dismissed their questions.

Hsiao-Chiao: How about your colleagues?

Wade: The same, but they tended to ask about my marriage just as they had a gossip – 'You are not young any more. You should get married as early as possible' or 'You are one of the only two people in our office who are still unmarried'. They used these words to hurry me into marriage. Some colleagues said they wanted to introduce someone to me but they were seldom serious. If they did find someone interested in meeting me, what we usually do in Kinmen is have a meal together and see if we both feel alright about exchanging our contact details. Even though we made the exchange, most of the time we didn't try to contact each other because we didn't find a reason to do so. What matters is whether or not we can *liaodelai* [have things to talk about with each other].

Hsiao-Chiao: Haven't you met anyone you feel *liaodelai*?

Wade: There was a woman with whom I hung out two or three times following our first meeting. She is a nice person, very good at studying, and we could talk about various things. It's enjoyable to talk with her. But perhaps I was not in the right mindset ... I was very busy with my work after a date with that woman, and I didn't send her any message for one or two weeks. When I had time, I thought in my mind: 'It's tiring, do I have any reason to ask her out?'

As Wade seemed to run out of words, I changed the direction of my questions by asking him whether he had had any romance. He recalled how his relationship with a woman ended several years ago; this was not because he had lost his passion for the woman (as might have happened in the foregoing case) but because his ex-girlfriend thought that they 'did not share the same plan for the future'. Wade could not accept this explanation initially and had a very hard time getting over her. Because of this tough experience, Wade said that his mentality became stronger and he could now maintain a positive attitude towards developing a new romance, without trying to erase his memories of his ex-girlfriend and the women with whom a romance was impossible to establish.

Hovering between Different Prospects of Life

Like Wade, Heidy (born in the mid-1980s) initially did not plan to return to Kinmen when studying at a university in Taiwan. But because of her lack of interest in working in the field in which she had studied, she decided to become a civil servant, which her parents fully supported. After graduation, Heidy returned to Kinmen to prepare for the civil service examination. As she gradually became impatient and bored with studying for the examination, she found a job in a local university, where she has been working for some years on projects that she finds very interesting. In answering my question of whether she still wanted to become a civil servant, Heidy admitted that this was a tough question for her.

> I like my current job very much but, you know, this is a contract job and unstable. We don't have the various welfare benefits that civil servants have and this is a big difference. I am therefore caught in a dilemma at the moment. To be honest, I paid money to take the civil service exam every year, but I never attended it. I am in a dilemma: one voice in my head says that I will enjoy a better salary, welfare and stability if I pass the exam; and the other voice says that I may not like what is involved in working as a civil servant. So, I don't really know … Moreover, if I plan to establish a family in the future, if I have children, public employment would be a better option. But for now, I tend to avoid making a decision because I am satisfied with my current job, including its flexibility, content and pay. Given that I am single at present, I am fine with my current state, but considering the long-term future, this job may not be good.

As Heidy's parents expected her to become a civil servant, I asked how they responded to her current conditions and single status. Heidy said that her parents are fine with her work but had started asking about her marriage after she passed the age of thirty. 'But they are not like many other parents in Kinmen, who constantly pressure their children to get married', Heidy added. Heidy also dismissed her relatives' enquiries and suggestions of marital candidates because she preferred to find a partner herself. But as illustrated by our conversation below, she did not make strong links between her ideal partner, marriage and childbirth.

> Heidy: I don't have concrete criteria for an ideal partner. What is important is the people-to-people interaction; what matters is whether we can *chude-lai* [have good interaction with each other].
> Hsiao-Chiao: How about a man's economic capacity, house ownership, etc.?[3]
> Heidy: I think I will see whether a man has a stable job, whether he is a diligent and reliable person. As for the house, if he has none, we can work together to buy one.
> Hsiao-Chiao: Do you think that marriage is something you must have in your life?
> Heidy: I think I should give birth to a child but marriage is not that necessary [laughs]. Do I sound too radical? [laughs] I don't dare to tell my mother about this.
> Hsiao-Chiao: It sounds ok to me.
> Heidy: I am saying so at this moment [as I haven't prepared for having a child]. If I really become a mother, from the child's perspective, it may be better to have a complete [*wanzhengde*] family.
> Hsiao-Chiao: Why do you want a child?
> Heidy: Because kids are so cute.
> Hsiao-Chiao: Would you mind adopting a child?
> Heidy: I think that is different ... my thoughts are that only if a girl [*nühaizi*] becomes a mother [*muqin*] will her life become complete [*wanzheng*].
> Hsiao-Chiao: How about marriage?
> Heidy: As far as I have observed the people around me, I think that marriage and having a happy life are two different things ... Though marriage is an element that constitutes a woman's complete life, it cannot guarantee a happy life. My life will still be complete if I have my own child without a marriage, though I may have some regrets about the absence of a marriage.

Towards the end of our interview, Heidy said that she might get married to fulfil her desire to give birth to a child, but she has not made any plans to do so. Building a family is not something that she can think through for the time being for various reasons: she has not yet met a suitable partner; she is hesitating about changing her career; and she has witnessed several unhappy marriages and divorces.

Expecting A Partner for Mutual Care in Old Age

Unlike Heidy, Tina does not include childbirth in her considerations about marriage. Tina was born in Kinmen in the late 1970s, but grew up in Taipei. When she was about thirty years old, she came to Kinmen to recover her health after breaking up with a man. Her paternal uncle in Kinmen helped her to find a short-term job in a government department. Tina originally thought that she would return to Taipei after one or two years of good rest, but her job contract was extended and soon she had been in Kinmen for several years. She bought a house as her own residence, which was also an investment because she can let it out if she decides to leave Kinmen some day. In reply to my question about her thoughts of marriage, Tina noted the difficulties of meeting a marital partner on the island:

> Tina: Frankly speaking, it became difficult for me to find a boyfriend when I came here. Many men around my age were either preparing to get married or were already married with two children. Moreover, everything was new to me here. I didn't have friends but relatives; I barely knew any local people at that time. Also, most of my colleagues are women...
>
> Hsiao-Chiao: Haven't your relatives tried to introduce any men to you?
>
> Tina: They did indeed, but I rejected them. Not because I didn't want to meet new people, but because they always pushed a man at me without trying to know what kind of a person that man is.
>
> Hsiao-Chiao: But as far as I know, local elderly people always judge whether a man is a good match by looking at his education, work, economic capacity, etc.
>
> Tina: Yes, they only looked at those things ... but they never considered whether or not that man and I could *hedelai* [get along well or feel compatible with each other]. My aunt once phoned me about this kind of thing and I responded angrily [laughs]. I said, 'Never do this again! Don't create this kind of trouble for me. I will find a boyfriend myself'.

Though Tina has not been able to meet a suitable person in Kinmen, she prefers to stay on the island because it is hard to find a new job in Taipei and easier to save money in Kinmen. She has used her savings to travel around the world and she developed romantic relationships with some Taiwanese men she met during her trips, though none of these relationships lasted.

> Tina: One uncle of mine is a fortune-teller, who told me that all my ex-boyfriends treated me well and loved me; the problem was one Chinese character in my name, which was not good for my relationship to last, however

good the relationship was. 'That's alright', I thought. I decided to buy into my uncle's words and changed my first name. I also thought that I will still be picky [*tiao*] even though I am getting old. Some people said that I should not be picky now because I am getting old. I objected and said, 'Of course I should be picky, because I want to have a partner who will look after me in my old age and I will look after him too'.

Hsiao-Chiao: Do you think that marriage is something that you must have in your life?

Tina: Not really … what I think now is it would be good if I can find a man with whom I can get along well [*hedelai*].

Hsiao-Chiao: How about having a child?

Tina: Because I don't like children, I don't consider it at all. But I feel a bit sorry for my dad. [Tina is an only child.]

Hsiao-Chiao: Have you always thought like that?

Tina: This thought emerged in recent years because I found … perhaps I have been enjoying the freedom of being single; I can go anywhere whenever I feel like it. Having a child would occupy so much of my time … [She described the case of her female cousin.]

Hsiao-Chiao: But if your partner wants a child…

Tina: It's almost impossible because of my age. It will be very difficult for me to bear a child. I will therefore let a potential partner know this before going further. I am also fine with a divorced man and even a divorced man who has a child with him. What matters is whether I and that man can *hedelai* or not. It's OK for me to take care of his child … I think, in retrospect, my low expectations about marriage and establishing a family are linked to my family background. My parents did not get along well with each other and therefore, since my childhood, I have never had experiences of a harmonious family, such as parents playing happily with their children. Though this did not affect my developing a romantic relationship, sometimes, perhaps my temper and ideas about many things were influenced by my family background…

Despite her several unsuccessful romantic relationships, Tina appears to remain positive about finding a lifelong partner for mutual care in old age while excluding childbirth. Her freedom and financial ability to travel around the world have provided her with opportunities to meet a partner, instead of marking her rejection of marriage. She has been undergoing a testing process of identifying what factors (e.g. her previous first name and her parents' unhappy relationship) might have led to her failed romantic relationships, and in the meantime, making her single life enjoyable while waiting for the appearance of a suitable partner.

Individual Configurations of Marriage and Temporality

In reply to my questions, my three informants moved between different stages of their lives, reflecting on how their past experiences, present conditions and imaginings about the future have affected their actions and ideas about marriage. Their testimonies show that marriage for them is not about socially recognized adulthood and filial duty to parents and ancestors, nor simply an expression of love and freedom. Their responses were reflective and, as they admitted, they had considered most of my questions for a while because they encountered questions of marrying on a daily basis. The notion of temporality helps to illuminate the imaginative work that marriage incites about the ways of life and futures that these young people desired and sought to create in relation to their past experiences and current conditions. This imaginative work, therefore, involved a constant process of self-transformation in which the actors reflected, changed their ideas and made adjustments with time in order to pursue their desired futures. For Wade, a long recovery from a failed romance probably influenced his perceptions of marriage as just one possible outcome of a relationship. For Heidy, her current job and uncertainties about the future prevented her from any serious consideration of establishing a marriage and family despite her desire to give birth to a child. For Tina, thoughts of excluding procreation from her future marital life emerged after she reached a certain age and observed the effort involved in childrearing.

These three informants, as well as my other young interlocutors who have university degrees and experiences of the outside world, did not directly draw on the criteria of education, occupation and economic capacity to describe the image of their ideal partner. Though their descriptions of those whom they had affection for previously or whom they might find attractive suggest that their ideal partner would tend to have similar levels of cultural and economic capital as they did, they emphasized the actual interaction with a potential partner. An ideal partner is a person with whom they feel compatible and have something in common – *liaodelai*, *chudelai* or *hedelai*. My interlocutors' portraits of an ideal partner echo many other scholars' findings across different contemporary Chinese societies in which a transnational ideal of companionate marriage that is based on a couple's mutual affection and commonalities has been widely espoused by younger generations (e.g. Cheng 2014; Nakano 2016; Zavoretti 2017).

Childbirth is traditionally closely connected to marriage not only through the idea of continuing the family line (*chuanzong jiedai*) but also relating to a couple's concern about their own life in old age. Notably, most of my younger interlocutors reject the conventional idea of raising children to provide for one's old age (*yanger fanglao*), and many are considering how to support themselves in later life (for example, by buying a long-term care insurance programme). Among my younger interlocutors, women were more likely to mention childbirth in relation to marriage than their male counterparts because of the biologically restricted reproductive timing that has posed challenges to women globally (see Inhorn 2020; San Román 2020; Vialle 2020 for discussions of women's reproductive temporality in Euro-American societies). The case of Heidy suggests a paradoxical feeling that many other women may also have: while viewing childbirth as essential for fully realizing womanhood, she was unsure about whether she wanted to have a child out of wedlock because she cared about her parents' feelings and thought that a complete family was better for a child (see Papadaki 2021 for a similar paradox in Athens). Heidy's concerns were arguably related to the social prejudices against single-parent families (and the connection between low marriage rates and low fertility rates as noted at the beginning of this chapter). Her hesitation was present in the absence of any action towards marriage and childbirth, and she may change her ideas as time passes and as her conditions change.

By seeing young people's prolonged delay in marrying as an ongoing process of reflection and trial, I want to highlight a significant generational difference. Most of my older respondents, whether their marriages were arranged by parents or their own choice, tended to view marriage as an indispensable part of a person's life, and therefore a mingling of individual and social (and conservative) visions of life and the future. This view is also shared by many younger people, like Wade's colleagues, as noted earlier. But the growing trends of later and less marriage in Kinmen (including Kinmen natives residing elsewhere in Taiwan) imply that young people increasingly have different visions of life and the future inconsistent with normative or conservative visions. For these young people, marriage is not an approach to create the life a person desires, but an option enfolded into the way a person works out the kind of life they want now and for the future.

Balancing Personal Desires and Familial Duties

Studies of family change in Taiwan and across East Asia usually underscore young adults', especially women's, ability to be economically independent as the key to their autonomy in their marital decisions, including the options of postponing marriage and non-marriage (e.g. Chen and Chen 2014; Jones and Gubhaju 2009; Raymo et al. 2015; Yang and Yen 2011). But what has happened to these young people's relations with their families and intimate social circles regarding their deviation from the normative track of life has been underexplored. Following the above analysis of young people's experiences of postponing marriage as a testing and transforming process, this section considers how these young people dealt with the potential clash or conflicts between personal desires and familial expectations, and how their relations with their family members were reconfigured.

As we have seen, young single people dismissed or expressed resistance to any enquiries about their marriages and suggestions of marital candidates from their parents and wider social networks. Their responses were arguably related to their ability to be economically self-reliant, but notably, they do not detach themselves from their familial circles. Like most of their single or married coevals in Kinmen, Wade and Heidy live with their parent(s) partly to save money and partly out of filial sentiment. While Tina moved from her grandparents' house (where her uncle's family also resides) to her own house a few years ago, she keeps in touch with her relatives, from whom she had received considerable support in finding a job and settling down in Kinmen. In many other respects, my single interlocutors are also on the track of family-based morality. Wade, especially, suppressed his ambition to pursue a different career in another place out of concern for his divorced mother, who had worked hard to bring up her son by herself. He was also responsible for a mortgage and other regular expenditure of his family, including his mother's insurance. By being emotionally and financially supportive of his mother, Wade proved his maturity and was able to be assertive in dismissing his mother's and other relatives' questions about marriage.

For several of my unmarried informants who have two or more siblings and live with their parents and their married siblings' families in the parental home, their single status may in certain respects be beneficial to family members. They themselves may also receive emotional and other support from such co-residence. Cherry, whom we met in Chapter 3, lives with her parents, a married brother and his family in her natal home since returning to Kinmen in 2016. Though she preferred city life and liked her former job in Taipei, which she found interesting but also stressful, she decided to quit because she did not want to sacrifice her health and quality of life for work. Despite the clash between her lack of interest in marriage and social and family expectations for her to marry, Cherry said that she still wants to live in Kinmen, where her 'home' – the place providing her with a sense of belonging – is. She developed close ties with her two co-resident nephews and shared the parenting roles of her brother and sister-in-law by teaching her nephews English and supervising their schoolwork. She also followed her mother's and sister-in-law's advice to manage her money efficiently so as to ensure her financial security in old age. By being economically independent and nurturing emotional ties with her family members, Cherry made her life in Kinmen enjoyable and her single status acceptable to her parents for the time being.

In the story of Ya-Fen described in Chapter 3, we saw that she came back to Kinmen because of her parents' reliance on her, as their eldest child, to assist with various family matters, including her younger siblings' weddings. After an unfortunate accident leading to her ex-boyfriend's lifelong injury, Ya-Fen has stayed single because of her complicated relations with him and her devotion to her work and to her natal family. She enjoys good relations with her married siblings and their children; she has especially close ties with her youngest, unmarried brother who once offered to take care of his sister in her old age. But, as noted previously,

Ya-Fen was trying to secure her own mental and material well-being by rejecting her parents' overt demands. She made up her mind to try different possibilities for her career and life by moving to Taipei for a new job a few months after our interview. While the case of Cherry shows challenges to the conservative vision of marriage and gendered futures co-produced through individual autonomy and familial support, the case of Ya-Fen shows strong individual volition to make changes to her own life and relations with her family.

The stories of Cherry and Ya-Fen also call for a reconsideration of the association between singlehood and being alone, which has been compellingly unpacked by Allerton (2007) in her discussion about single women in Indonesia. Allerton argues that the single women in her fieldsite are not really 'alone' despite their singlehood, because they lived with their natal families and keep close ties with their family members. But she noted that being alone is a complexly gendered notion and understood differently in different sociocultural contexts. For the group of people that she studied, women who remain unmarried are not the subject of ridicule within the village and can inherit land from their fathers to sustain themselves financially. In contemporary Kinmen, Taiwan and China, though women are not necessarily excluded from inheritance of family property as they were previously, they tend to attain economic independence through paid employment outside the family (thanks to their parents' investment in their education). Nevertheless, single women with higher education and well-paid jobs are pejoratively labelled 'leftover women' in China. In Kinmen, though my single female informants enjoy their current lives, their parents are still worried about their daughters' potential 'loneliness' in old age if they remain unmarried. Notably, these parents' articulation of worries shows growing attention to, and care for, daughters compared to the early twentieth century when parents usually sacrificed their daughters' well-being in order to focus resources on raising their sons.

While I know some middle-aged never-married women who were commended by their families and neighbours for their thoughtful care of elderly parents, none of my younger interlocutors, female or male, mentioned such caring responsibilities as a factor contributing to their deferral of marriage. My older research participants who are pleased to have their single children's company still expect their children to get married in the near future. Though patrilocal co-residence remains a dominant pattern in Kinmen, I observed that many married women have greater freedom and mobility to visit their natal home and provide care for their parents, whether or not the latter have support from married sons. I also heard of several cases of married sons who resigned from their jobs in Taiwan and returned to Kinmen to look after their ill parents. In other words, a person's marital status does not affect his or her care of parents as much as in the past because elderly support is not only a conventional filial duty but is also linked to children's emotional ties with parents.

Respect for parents and for seniors in wider social circles is widely regarded by my younger interlocutors as part of one's moral personhood. But respect does not mean total obedience and the repression of one's own emotions and desires. Young single people express respect and care for their parents while rejecting unwelcome advice and intervention from parents regarding their life and future, including marriage. Despite worries about their single children's long-term well-being, parents try to accommodate their children's non-normative behaviour following numerous failed interventions and efforts at persuasion.

Conclusion

Drawing on material about young single people's everyday living experiences in Kinmen, this chapter has unravelled a paradox that they confront: it is difficult both to find a partner and to stay single. Their deferral of marriage is entangled with wider social changes and a resilient cultural repertoire, which have generated different and gendered impacts on their marital prospects. A woman's higher education and reputable career may be emphasized in order to ask for a higher bridewealth from the groom, but may also reduce her chances to meet men who do not have similar levels of cultural and social capital. Men in manual jobs and factory work are disadvantaged in the local marriage market even though they may have a stable and decent income. The persistent association of marriage with the reproduction of the patrilineal family in this close-knit society also intrudes on young people's private lives through incessant questioning about their prospective marriages and suggestions of marital candidates. Though young people tend to refuse these suggestions of marital partners, their restricted mobility in day-to-day experiences prevents them from getting to know new people.

These young single people are aware of the social constraints on their marital options, but they also challenge the conventional understanding of marriage in their ongoing 'testing' processes of figuring out the meaning and place of marriage in their lives. In these testing and transforming processes, their past experiences, present conditions and imaginings about the future have intertwined with each other and shaped their thoughts about marriage, childbearing and the family. Unlike the senior generations and married cohorts who view marriage as an indispensable part of a person's life, these single women and men constantly reconfigure their views in relation to their shifting, individual circumstances and visions of life and the future. As they usually have experiences of living in urban Taiwan from several years of advanced studies and work there, they tend to be more open to new discourses of gender and marriage equality that have rapidly proliferated following Taiwan's democratization. Most of them openly supported the legalization of same-sex marriage in the debates and national referendum in 2018 in stark contrast to other opposing opinions within local society (see this book's Conclusion). None of these young informants mentioned new options of legalized intimate relations and family constitution, such as civil partnerships – whose legalization is currently being promoted by an NGO in Taiwan – as something they wanted. But their own experiences of deferring marriage have already challenged the conservative patriarchal vision of marriage and the family, signalling increasingly diversifying imaginings of intimate futures, such as childbearing out of wedlock or marrying a divorced man while excluding childbirth.

The stories of my single informants also illustrate their efforts to balance personal desires and familial duties. They safeguard their autonomy in making their own decisions about their lives and marriages not only through their economic independence but also through realizing family-based morality. They keep amicable ties with their families and intimate social circles while firmly rejecting any unwelcome intervention in their private lives. Despite worries about their single children's long-term well-being, parents have gradually learned to accept their children's visions of life and the future that are inconsistent with the normative visions that they themselves uphold. The growing trends of later and less marriage are thus not merely reflections of wider socioeconomic changes but enfold possibilities of reconfiguring intergenerational relations as well as exploring new forms of intimate relations. In the next two chapters, examining cross-border marriage and marital lives in patrilocal households, we will see how the generational hierarchy intrinsic to traditional patriarchy is also questioned or unsettled by young couples', especially women's, attempts to assert their autonomy and authority about their own lives.

Notes

This chapter is a revised version of my article in an edited volume, *Marriage in Past, Present and Future Tense* (Carsten et al. 2021).

1. The notion of waithood was first proposed by the political scientist and ethnographer Diane Singerman (2007, 2013) to describe young men's difficulties in attaining adulthood through marriage due to frustrating political and economic situations across the Middle East and North Africa region (Smith-Hefner and Inhorn 2020: 2–3). Smith-Hefner and Inhorn consider this kind of waithood engendered by wider politico-economic constraints as unintentional, while expanding the application of waithood to other situations involving actors' intentional deferral of their marriage in order to pursue other personal desires.
2. Howlett (2020) presents an interesting angle into women's education and marriage. His ethnography shows how, rather than an obstacle to a woman's marriage, higher education is perceived as a means for her to escape parental pressure to marry while improving her own situation and searching for a suitable partner (see also Zavoretti 2017 on how young women in urban China seek to prepare themselves for the appearance of 'Mr Right').
3. I asked whether or not a man's house ownership was one of the criteria that my female respondents considered in their choice of mate because several studies in post-reform China have shown that house ownership matters greatly to a man's success in finding a

spouse, and this was also emphasized by my interlocutors in China. However, most of my younger female informants in Kinmen did not emphasize their (potential) marital partner's house ownership as a key reason for their agreement to marriage, though their partners might inherit housing from their parents in the future.

5

CROSS-BORDER MARRIAGE ON THE BORDERLAND

During a conversation with several elderly men on the island of Lieyu (Little Kinmen) in 2018, they immediately responded to my research on changing marriage by mentioning the significance of marriages between local men and women from China. One man who had retired from the local governmental bureau of civil affairs was introduced to me as an expert on this issue. This man said that the number of brides from abroad, especially China, had rapidly increased following the end of military rule in 1992. He commented, 'Frankly speaking, local men in cross-border marriages were all from economically vulnerable families, so were their wives. If this channel for marriage had not existed, this society would have become very chaotic'. Another man added, 'If the government had not allowed local men to marry foreign spouses in earlier times, half the schools on this island would have been closed now. Children whose mothers are foreign women constitute at least half of the total primary school students'. Nevertheless, as they noted, the number of Chinese brides has declined in recent years because of the surge in China's economy, particularly in the southeast coastal region from which Kinmen received many brides (see Figure 5.1).

These men's remarks reflect their views of cross-border marriage as a solution to saving local society where many men engaging in low-skilled or factory work faced greater difficulties in finding a spouse. One female interlocutor said, 'the young women in Kinmen are too picky (*tiao*), so my younger brother and several men in this village [some of them working in the sorghum distillery] all went to China to look for a bride [around the mid-2000s]'. These comments appear to validate the theory of a 'marriage squeeze' that relates to women's hypergamy in explaining the rise of cross-border marriage in Taiwan, Hong Kong, South Korea and Japan – the receiving sides for brides from Southeast Asia and China since the late twentieth century (Goodkind 1997; Ishikawa 2010; Lee et al. 2016; So

---

Endnotes for this chapter begin on page 127.

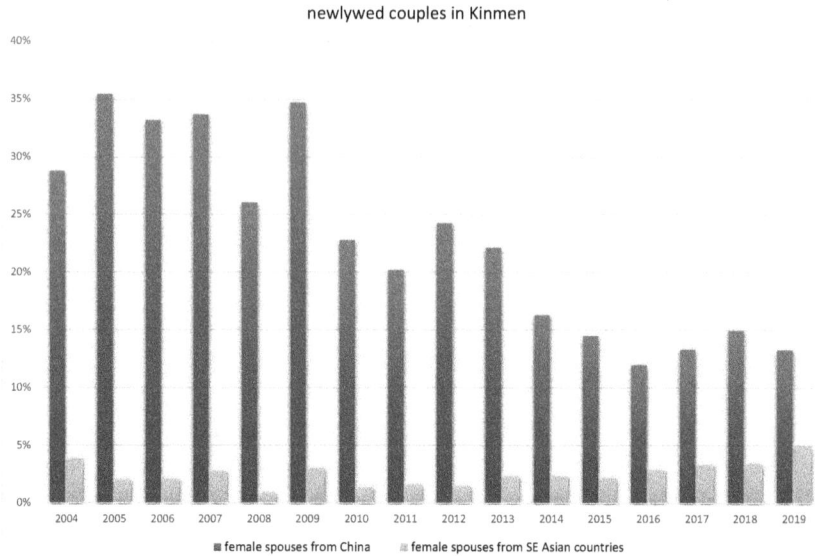

Figure 5.1. The significant proportion of female marriage migrants from China in Kinmen and its recent decline. Source: The Department of Household Registration, Ministry of the Interior, Taiwan (https://www.ris.gov.tw/app/portal/674).

2003; Yang and Liu 2013). They also echo the bride-receiving societies' official and popular emphasis on foreign brides' reproductive roles in child-bearing and childcare (Faier 2009; Friedman 2015; Kim 2013; Lan 2008; Yu 2020). This conservative vision of a patriarchal family-based social order appears to be persistent and is supported by the Taiwanese government and many individual islanders in Kinmen.

However, my interlocutors' comments did not capture the recent dynamics in cross-border marriage relating to Kinmen's status as a borderland, which has had convenient access to China by ferry since 2001. Thus, I knew some young male and female islanders who met their Chinese spouses during periods of work or study in China, and who resided in Kinmen or China, or maintained two residences across the border after marrying. An employee in a government agency supporting foreign spouses in Kinmen told me that she had seen several cases in recent years of divorced, widowed and economically active older men marrying Chinese women who tended to be much younger than themselves, and whom they had met during sightseeing visits to China. These emerging phenomena began to alter the earlier pattern centring on working-class men in Kinmen and their brides from rural China. This chapter will not discuss these new patterns, but they illustrate the constantly shifting ways in which marriage, human mobility

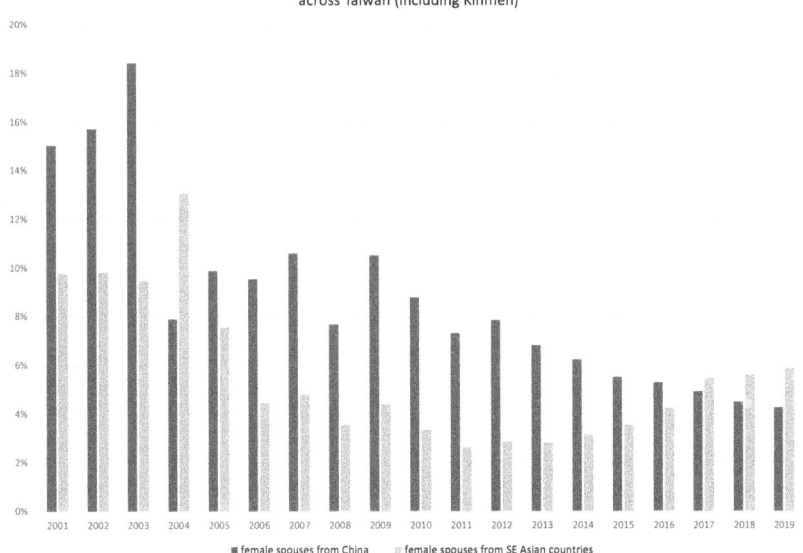

Figure 5.2. The changing dynamics of cross-border marriage in Taiwan in the last two decades. Source: Department of Household Registration, Ministry of the Interior, Taiwan (https://www.ris.gov.tw/app/portal/674).[1]

and economy intersect in the age of globalization and changing regional political economies, as well as the dialectics between the local and the global (Constable 2005, 2009).

What was also missed by my interlocutors was the importance of Kinmen's borderland status in contributing to the rise and dominance of cross-border marriage between Kinmen and China – a local pattern apparently different from the national one, in which the percentages of brides from Southeast Asia are also considerable (comparing Figure 5.1 and 5.2). The border, in its territorial sense of marking the boundary of Taiwan's exercise of sovereignty and separating Kinmen from the Chinese mainland, emerged as a result of the Chinese Civil War in 1949 and restricted the islanders' maritime activities during the period of military rule (Szonyi 2008: 94–95). As my ethnography below demonstrates, this border became porous and permeable in the early 1990s following the waning of military tension between Kinmen and China. I argue that kinship, including marriage, played a significant role in the initiation and restoration of contact between ordinary people on the two sides. Unlike most studies of cross-border marriage between Taiwan and China, which focus on the links between sex and commodification, citizenship and the sovereignty question of Taiwan (e.g. Chao 2004a, 2004b; Friedman 2015; Lu 2005), this chapter explores the role of kinship in animating this phenomenon. I highlight how kin ties and Kinmen's borderland status jointly promoted cross-border matchmaking, and how this arrangement of marriage might not be subject to patriarchal control because of conflicting elements arising from the differences between Kinmen and China formed under opposing regimes after 1949.

Drawing on ethnographic material collected from people living in Kinmen and China who are related to cross-border marriage in varying ways, this chapter explores the emergence, processes and consequences of marriages between Kinmen and China that have been occluded in the scholarship on cross-border marriage in Taiwan. My ethnography foregrounds experiences of Chinese women who married into Kinmen between the late 1990s and early 2010s, and whom I interviewed or had conversations with during my two periods of fieldwork. The ways in which I came to know these women to a large extent frame the ethnography presented here and its insights. During my first fieldwork in 2013–2014, when my research focus was not on marriage, I carried out interviews with foreign spouses in order to understand family change in relation to Kinmen's post-Cold War circumstances. I approached the local governmental agency which supported foreign spouses for help with recruiting research participants. An employee in that agency invited me to attend a handicraft workshop for female *xin zhumin* (lit. new residents, referring to foreigners married to Taiwanese citizens and living in territories under Taiwan's governance). Through this workshop, I gained consent to interview two women originally from Indonesia and China, and through their introduction, I subsequently interviewed women from China, Vietnam and Myanmar.

I tried using similar methods to recruit Chinese women as research participants during my second fieldwork in 2017–2018. Some attempts succeeded and some failed. One woman introduced by a friend of mine rejected my enquiry immediately by saying that she could not stand any more questions about her marital life from different governmental agencies (as one way to check the 'authenticity' of her marriage) and researchers like me. Another woman whom I met at an event organized by the local government answered, 'You should ask those women whose husbands came along with them because they *bijiao hui shuo* (are more capable of talking). I don't want to talk about my private life'. Indeed, some women who agreed to be interviewed confirmed that they had good marital experiences compared to some traumatic stories they knew. Some stated clearly that they were sharing their stories with me because they were annoyed by prejudiced views of them as greedy and morally questionable shaped by the Taiwanese government and the mass media (Hsia 2007; Lu 2008; Shih 1998). But this does not mean that some of the women I interviewed did not have a difficult time in their marital lives. Through my experiences of finding interviewees and conducting the interviews, I gained insights about how these women perceived and reacted to local social environments and to bureaucratic measures regulating their marriages.

In what follows, I initially describe how the border between Kinmen and China became permeable in the early 1990s, and how cross-border marriages mushroomed as a consequence of reconnecting kin across the waters. I then delineate how the parents of Kinmen grooms participated in their sons' cross-border matchmaking, and how Chinese women made the decision to marry in Kinmen. This is followed by personal stories of my Chinese female informants, which demonstrate how they reacted to the bureaucratic and social boundaries which distinguished them as a special group subject to suspicion and pressured them on a daily basis. Though some of my informants had traumatic experiences in their everyday marital lives, they have stayed in their marriages, mostly for the sake of their children, while navigating ways through which to pursue their personal interests and happiness. The rapid growth of China's economy in the last decade and Kinmen's borderland status have also been used by many Chinese women to negotiate their power and autonomy in their marital families. Their stories reveal the possibilities of unsettling or transgressing the patriarchal norms created by the women themselves, and in some cases, together with their husbands. This chapter argues that the rising number of cross-border marriages between Kinmen and China was an aspect of the transformative capacities of kinship serving to reproduce the patrilineal family, but the conflicting elements involved in these marriages have led to challenging forces, also generated from the intimate sphere of kinship, against this patriarchal institution.

Border-Crossing and Reconnecting Kin

Some weeks after I settled in Kinmen in 2013, I joined a one-day shopping trip organized by some elderly villagers to Xiamen, China, where they bought various goods including dried food, daily necessities and fishing tools to sell back in Kinmen. We travelled between Kinmen and Xiamen via *Xiao San Tong* (as noted in this book's Introduction, local people use this term to refer to the ferry service linking the two sides since 2001). I only realized the problems that these villagers often faced when I helped to put the goods that they had purchased on the X-ray inspection machine for the customs to check in Kinmen's port. One inspector warned one of the villagers not to bring so many things back next time, otherwise he might charge duty or fines for bringing dried food exceeding the permitted amount, which might harm Taiwan's market and food security. This villager appeared to be familiar with the situation. After we came back to the village, he told me that it had become much harder for him to profit from this trade route today than in the 1990s, when smuggling across the waters was very profitable. What struck me later were the links between this informal trade, kinship and cross-border marriage.

Informal trade or smuggling between Kinmen and coastal China emerged immediately following Kinmen's demilitarization and flourished throughout the

1990s (Juan 2003; Yang 2011). Initially, people from the two sides only traded on the waters but gradually more and more people from China landed on the shores of Kinmen to conduct transactions. A wide range of products from China, from fresh fish and fruits to crafted objects and daily necessities, filled the small, licensed and unlicensed, grocery shops and stalls in market towns and tourist sites throughout Kinmen in this period (Szonyi 2008: 216–18). What was communicated between people from the two sides was not, however, only goods but also kin ties and marriage.

Ray, a Chinese man in his mid-sixties living on the island of Dadeng (opposite the north side of Kinmen) whom I met in 2017, told me that he had taken part in *zousi* (a term he used, meaning smuggling) in the 1990s. He said that his elders on Dadeng often recalled their mobility across the sea prior to 1949 and many families were connected with Kinmen by kinship and marriage in very recent generations. These intimate memories and economic incentives motivated unauthorized border-crossing adventures by Ray and his fellow islanders. Ray started his trade together with a friend in another village on Dadeng whose mother had married there from Kinmen, and who resumed contact with his maternal uncle in Kinmen to enable his business. Through some tips from his elders and help from his trading partners in Kinmen, Ray reconnected with his distant kin in Kinmen who had preserved their lineage's written genealogy, which suggested that Ray's ancestors had moved from Kinmen to Dadeng about two centuries ago. Ray ceased his informal trading in the late 1990s, but he maintains regular contacts with his distant kin in Kinmen. He also served as a matchmaker, brokering two marriages between women from Dadeng and his male relatives in Kinmen.

I heard about another scenario reflecting the direct connection between smuggling and matchmaking during my attendance at a handicraft workshop in 2014 as I sat around a table with a number of Chinese women. At one point, one woman asked where I was from. I said that I was from Taiwan and asked her the same question. She replied that she was from Weitou, a village in southeast China, opposite the east side of Kinmen. She continued, 'You probably don't know where it is, but many residents of Kinmen know because they went there to smuggle seafood and fruit, even drawing alongside the shore to trade with us previously'. Another woman asked her whether she had married in Kinmen because of that business connection. She answered yes, and said that many women from her village also married in Kinmen, including her younger sister.

The informal trade between ordinary residents in Kinmen and China eventually encountered the Taiwanese state's shift to stricter control of its borders in the form of two laws regulating activities in Taiwan's territorial waters.[2] Since July 1998, in light of the new laws, the local police in Kinmen, allied with the military, have seized dozens of intruders from China. Ray was once arrested and jailed for several months before being deported back to China. This tightening control of the border and the launch of the *Xiao San Tong* ferry service in 2001 made informal trade no longer profitable for people on both sides. Nevertheless, the restoration of connections by people on the two sides continued and has facilitated the establishment of many cross-border marriages in the following decade, posing new challenges for the Taiwanese state.

The above-described practices of border-crossing resonate with the conceptualization of borders as processual from the standpoints of different actors (the state, NGO, ordinary people, etc.) in the growing interdisciplinary literature on border studies (e.g. Johnson et al. 2011; Newman 2006; Paasi et al. 2018; Wilson and Donnan 2012). Scholarly attention has been paid to the changing conditions of national and international political economy of borderlands, and to the forms of migration, commerce and smuggling that pose challenges to the sovereign power of states. At the same time, researchers have investigated how states try to retain the rigidity of borders through various new measures, such as the employment of technical devices and biometrics, in a performance of sovereignty. These bordering practices by states are familiar in the form of the Taiwanese government's regulation of cross-border marriages, for example, in a border-interview system for Chinese spouses which was set up in 2004 in order to filter out 'fake marriage' (Chen 2015; Friedman 2010a).

Recent scholarly discussions note the overlap between the concept of the border and the concept of boundary (Fassin 2020; Fischer et al. 2020). The concept of boundary is usually traced back to Barth's (1998 [1969]) discussion of ethnicity, and has been expanded to encompass a multiplicity of potential criteria, such as race, language, religion, class, gender and sexual orientation, which are used to distinguish between groups. 'Boundary work' concerns how similarities and differences are produced and is not necessarily related to states, while bordering has to do with states and the exercise of their sovereignty. As Fassin notes, though these two concepts can be theoretically differentiated, recent developments across the world suggest that 'borders cannot be thought of without the boundaries they establish or reinforce, and boundaries have to be analyzed in relation to the justifications they provide for the control or even the shifting of borders' (2020: 19).

This entanglement between border and boundary is palpable in the Taiwanese government's different treatment of spouses originally from China and those from other countries. As several studies have shown, due to Taiwan's special relationship with China, the Taiwanese government's policies of pre-entry interview, residency and citizenship for Chinese spouses are different from those for spouses from other countries (Cheng 2017; Friedman 2010b, 2015; Lan 2008; Momesso and Cheng 2017). Friedman's (2010b, 2015) work, especially, pertinently captures the interrelated anxieties of the Taiwanese state's exercise of sovereignty and dealing with Chinese spouses' 'similarity' to Taiwanese citizens through differentiated legal and political treatment. Recent research on marriage migrants has moved beyond a focus on this state-individual nexus in conceptualizing citizenship to the family as a primary site where citizenship is negotiated and contested (Chiu 2020; Chiu and Yeoh 2021). The focus of this chapter is not on citizenship; instead, I unpack how kinship and practices of bordering and making boundaries, especially in the intimate sphere of the family, significantly shaped my Chinese female informants' marital experiences and their attitudes to Taiwanese citizenship.

Kinship Networks and Matchmaking across the Border

Cross-border marriages between Kinmen and China significantly increased in the early 2000s when many islanders from Kinmen went to China to visit their distant kin, to do business, and to invest in real estate using the convenient *Xiao San Tong*. These intensive communications between the two sides appeared to return to levels seen in the era prior to 1949 when Kinmen was part of Minnan (southern Fujian province) where people shared a common dialect (Hokkien) and cultures, and were connected by marriage. These cultural similarities and social networks based on kinship and economic ties encouraged cross-border matchmaking. There were people in Kinmen and China who were called 'professional matchmakers' (*zhuanyie meiren*) as they earned profits through organizing matchmaking tours for Kinmen men to China – a popular way of transnational matchmaking across Asia (Freeman 2011; Lu 2005, 2008; Yamaura 2015a). But these professional matchmakers mostly operated within their own social networks and under the guise of helping kin or friends, unlike the commodified matchmaking often seen in Taiwanese-Vietnamese marriages (Tseng 2015, 2016). For example, I heard from several villagers in Kinmen that a man in their village had been detained in Xiamen in 1949 when transportation between the two sides was suddenly interrupted.[3] This man visited Kinmen soon after travel became possible and, probably after being asked by his kin and acquaintances on both sides, he started an informal business of matching Kinmenese men and Chinese women. He passed away some years ago, and before that, he had successfully brokered numerous cross-border marriages for his natal village. As I demonstrate below, the salience of social networks in cross-border matchmaking enabled parents in Kinmen to easily intervene in their sons' marriages on the one hand, and mitigated the uncertainties of marrying across the waters faced by Chinese women on the other.

Parental Intervention

The numerous anecdotes I heard from various interlocutors, including Chinese spouses, suggest varying degrees of intervention from the grooms' parents in cross-border marriages. The most impressive story was from a local friend's uncle, Mr Huang, who had arranged his eldest son's marriage to a Chinese woman in the early 2000s. In my friend's company, I visited Huang's modern four-storey house in 2017 where he resides with his wife, married eldest son and his family, and his unmarried second son. My friend did not try to introduce me to the eldest son when we met, as he looked shy and seemed to prefer not to be too visible. During a short conversation with the second son (who was friendly but shy of talking with me), I learned that his father had made great efforts to get his older brother married. I then shifted to their father for the details.

Unlike his two sons, Mr Huang was talkative and, thanks to my friend's presence, open in sharing with me how he had found a bride for his eldest son. Huang said that he was worried about his eldest son, who was in his late twenties and did not have a stable job at that time, so he took action to help him settle down. He consulted his relatives in Kinmen and was recommended to contact a female matchmaker in China. He paid for a first visit to China to meet her and chose a woman from a list prepared by the matchmaker. He then took his eldest son for a second visit to China to meet the selected woman. After meeting each other, the Chinese woman took the young man on a two-day sightseeing tour in the neighbouring area. The two young people felt comfortable with each other, and kept in touch by international phone calls for some months before they decided to marry. My friend added that the expensive charges for international calls were all paid by her uncle.

The marriage followed common customs on both sides in terms of paying bridewealth and hosting wedding feasts. As described in Chapter 3, parents in Kinmen usually spend a great deal on their sons' weddings; Mr Huang was no different. As requested by his affines, he paid RMB 86,000 (about USD 10,000 in the early 2000s) as bridewealth – an amount that was not too demanding by Kinmen standards but generous at the time in China. Mr Huang also prepared additional money for monetary gifts (*hongbao*) for various people on the bride's side. The bride's parents hosted a small-scale wedding feast to entertain their relatives and some guests from Kinmen whom Huang invited as witnesses. After his daughter-in-law completed the bureaucratic procedures imposed by the Taiwanese government for Chinese spouses and arrived in Kinmen, Huang hosted a large wedding feast and invited all the households in his village to the celebration.

Chinese Women's Motives for Marrying in Kinmen

Although Mr Huang appeared to intervene seriously in his eldest son's marriage, it was his son's decision to marry the woman who initially had been chosen by his father. Similar phenomena also occurred in other cross-border marriages in which the groom's personal preference mattered most in his choice of spouse. On the side of the bride, the stories that I collected suggest that the bride's own decision also mattered most there, and this decision was usually inseparable from the social networks in which the woman was embedded.

Cultural similarities between people in Kinmen and Minnan have no doubt contributed to the popularity of cross-border marriage. Most of my Chinese informants were born in the rural parts of Minnan and speak the dialect of Hokkien also used in Kinmen. The economic conditions of their hometowns were on average less good than the conditions in Kinmen in the early 2000s. They tended to give up education early either of their own volition or due to their family's financial difficulties, and usually started working in their early teens. Several women became migrant workers in the factories or service sectors in Xiamen, Shenzhen and Hong Kong, and some of them met their husbands in their workplace (see also Binah-Pollak 2019). Other studies have pointed to the future-making and relational aspects of marriage that this book focuses on. They document how many women's motives for transnational marriage were linked to their imaginings of upward mobility and a materially better life elsewhere. Moreover, these imaginings were often extended to include better futures for their children from their current or an earlier marriage (Binah-Pollak 2019; Freeman 2011). But these desires might be balanced or compromised by other concerns. Many Chinese women explained their preference for marrying within East Asia by articulating their desire to live closer to their homeland so that they could often visit their natal families and also perhaps children from a first marriage (Freeman 2011; Yamaura 2015b). For most of my Chinese informants, one key factor affecting their decision was the 'similarity' they felt in relation to Kinmen.

Like their Kinmen husbands and parents-in-law, for my Chinese interlocutors, similarity was not merely about shared cultures and dialect but about familiarity built on the social networks and intensive contacts between Kinmen and their homeland. Several informants recalled that they were called to matchmaking meetings with men from Kinmen by a relative who had married in Kinmen or who had connections with people in Kinmen. For example, Shu-Ting's meeting with her future husband was arranged by her cousin who had a business partnership in the tourism industry with this man's father. Shu-Ting agreed to marry after only five or six meetings with her partner (whose mother was mostly present too) because she thought that she already knew enough about her future marital family. She also emphasized that, after marriage, she did not find any difference between her pre-marital knowledge and the actual conditions of her marital family.

As most of my Chinese informants have relatives or acquaintances who married in or often visited Kinmen, they already knew before marriage that Kinmen was not as advanced and prosperous as urban Taiwan. By contrast, some women from Southeast Asia, who had married in Kinmen through commercial matchmaking services, told me that they were deceived into thinking Kinmen was a developed place. But Kinmen's rural environment still shocked some of my Chinese informants upon arrival. One informant said that though she had some preliminary understanding about Kinmen, such as its size and number of residents, she was still surprised by the reality when she came in 2001. She described Kinmen as '*xiangxia* (countryside) that was even more like *xiangxia* than my natal village'. Despite this kind of initial shock, my informants generally accommodated to life in Kinmen which is slow-paced and lacks entertainment and, as they claimed, they can always have fun by simply going to the prosperous city of Xiamen. This geographic proximity to China, as well as the generous benefits and social welfare provided by local government as noted in this book's Introduction, were said to still make marrying in Kinmen an attractive option for Chinese women who have witnessed their country's surging economy in the last decade.

Among my Chinese informants, Xiao-Yun's story is particularly intriguing and illuminates the common pressure on women to marry early in post-reform China and the nature of cross-border marriage as a gamble in a woman's life. Xiao-Yun was born in rural Minnan and started working in childhood because she had no interest in studying. At one stage, she became a migrant worker in Xiamen and was then summoned back home to help in her brother's fishing business. One day when Xiao-Yun was about twenty-four years old, her sister's friend, whose daughter had just married in Kinmen, asked if she would like to meet a man from Kinmen. Xiao-Yun was initially a bit resistant but her sister (who was married in a neighbouring town) encouraged her strongly because the sister had longed to marry in Taiwan but had not had the chance. Xiao-Yun said that her sister did not really know the difference between Kinmen and urban Taiwan, but she herself had heard about Kinmen's resemblance to rural Minnan. But, given that she was approaching the local upper limit of marriageable age of twenty-five and had not yet found a suitable local man, she decided to give herself a chance by meeting the man.

Xiao-Yun consented to marry within one week after the first meeting, not because of her satisfaction in the man's appearance or his economic situation. As she described it, 'He was quite reticent and we barely talked with each other. His appearance was ok for me and I didn't care about appearance very much. I knew he worked in construction, but I thought I could earn a good living as long as I worked hard'. Pressured by the matchmaker who had spent too much time on this trip, Xiao-Yun went to a local temple to ask for the god's advice by drawing lots. The lot, with a written message on it, suggested that Xiao-Yun marrying in Kinmen would be fine though there might be a tough period in her marital life. Xiao-Yun deemed it acceptable advice and made up her mind to marry. As she remarked, 'Anyway, it's my fate. If I didn't have a good fate, my life would not be good wherever I went. So, I decided to take this gamble (*duzhu*)'. Like Xiao-Yun, most of my Chinese informants did not initially intend to marry abroad, and some of them mentioned pressure to marry before they were 'too old'. Given that they had not found a good match locally, marrying in Kinmen seemed a viable alternative in spite of the risks of living and marrying under a different political regime.

Chinese Women's Post-Marital Experiences of Difference and Differentiation

Though many marriages of Chinese women in Kinmen involved being introduced by their relatives or acquaintances, their feelings of similarity and familiarity in relation to Kinmen usually faded soon after they settled. Shock and disappointment arose not only because of Kinmen's rural landscape and dullness but also because of differences in ways of life between Kinmen and China. While the gendered division of labour within households in post-reform China still tends to be patriarchal (Hu and Mu 2021; Liu 2004; Xie 2021), studies have shown how young married women have taken active roles (usually with their husbands' cooperation) in maximizing their conjugal interest and challenging generational hierarchy. Yan's (2003, 2006) ethnography in rural China in the late 1990s revealed the rise of conjugal power through demanding an earlier division of family property and the establishment of a nuclear household, usually at the cost of the husband's parents' interests. However, with increasing pressures from marketization and state policies, nowadays young couples and their parents(-in-law) seek to cope with housework and childcare with restricted time, resources and space by emphasizing intergenerational cooperation and emotional intimacy (Xie 2021; Yan 2016, 2021; Zavoretti 2017).

In contrast to the above shifts in family relations in post-reform China, my Chinese informants found Kinmen to be far more patriarchal, traditional and conservative than they could imagine before marriage. Though we have seen changing intergenerational relations and young people's growing emphasis on personal desires in present-day Kinmen, in local patrilocal joint households, the everyday organization of household chores could be very patriarchal and traditional, especially from the standpoint of outsiders from abroad, including in-married Chinese women. Almost all of my informants took patrilocal residence after they arrived in Kinmen, living together with their parents-in-law and even their married and unmarried siblings-in-law. Several women faced parents-in-law's demand for total obedience and their responsibility for all the household chores. The amount of work and frequency of preparing rituals of ancestor worship in local households were commonly mentioned by my informants as demands that they found difficult to adapt to – this was also true for young married women who are native to Kinmen or from Taiwan (see next chapter). Despite the religious and ritual revival in post-reform China and growing up in Minnan where ancestral rituals are performed on certain important dates, in-married Chinese women were shocked by the number of rituals and the details of preparation (of food offerings in particular) which they had to learn from their mothers-in-law (see Chiu 2017). During a talk with my neighbour who had married in from China, she said that she once asked her husband jokingly, 'Is it because your life in the past [the period of military rule] was too hard that you [Kinmen islanders] performed so many rituals so that you could eat more and better than usual (as the offerings usually become the worshippers' lunch afterwards)?' Her husband just answered her impatiently, 'You said it'.

Some of my Chinese informants admitted that their marital experiences were generally good compared to many sad cases they knew of in which Chinese women suffered verbal abuse from their husbands and in-laws, and even physical violence from their husbands. Indeed, I observed and heard about local elderly people's different attitudes towards daughters-in-law from China. Some elders, like Mr Huang who had actively intervened in his son's marriage and visited China several times, tended to be open and less demanding of their Chinese daughters-in-law. Shu-Ting, whom we met earlier, said that her pre-marital knowledge about her in-laws and her post-marital experiences were consistent. Her parents-in-law treated her well, and she was asked to 'help' her mother-in-law to prepare food offerings for ancestor worship, not to do it all by herself. Moreover, she told me that her parents-in-law gave in when her husband rejected the idea of having a second child after she gave birth to a daughter, despite their hopes of having a grandson. This flexible response, as Shu-Ting explained, may have been related to her parents-in-law's prior experiences of living in Taiwan for years. Interestingly, several of my Chinese interlocutors linked their parents-in-law's open attitudes to their previous residence in Taiwan, whereas studies focusing on Chinese spouses living in Taiwan have described the prejudices and unjust treatment of parents-in-law (Chao 2004b; Friedman 2015; Lu 2008). This kind of opinion of my Chinese interlocutors, as well as my neighbour's remarks on rituals in Kinmen as described above, suggest that they treat Taiwan (specifically the Taiwanese mainland) and Kinmen as two distinct places subject to comparison with each other. The homogenization of Kinmen is related to its nature as a borderland far from the Taiwanese mainland and earlier experiences of military rule, which in their perceptions, have made Kinmen more traditional and conservative than 'Taiwan'.

Some of my Chinese informants had bitter experiences of interacting with parents-in-law who financially supported their sons' cross-border marriages but had limited knowledge about China and recent developments there. These elders tended to have prejudiced views about Chinese brides as women intent on taking money back to China. Fuelled by media discourse and local rumours, they established a social and moral boundary marking Chinese women as 'questionable others'. They sought to prevent their daughters-in-law from *bianhuai* (becoming rebellious) by restricting their contacts with other Chinese women and the world outside. This was made worse by the Taiwanese government's earlier policy of strict regulation of Chinese spouses' rights to work. Before modification of the relevant laws in 2009, Chinese spouses faced an eight-year passage to citizenship and typically a two-year delay in obtaining residency and work permits compared to other foreign spouses who obtained residency and the right to work immediately upon arrival. As several studies have documented, Chinese spouses generally expressed strong criticisms of this earlier policy and many had to work 'illegally' because their husbands did not earn enough to feed the family (Chao 2004b; Friedman 2015; Lu 2008). Often when Chinese women could apply for a work permit, they encountered difficulties from their husbands or parents-in-law who questioned their motives in earning money and demanded that they stay at home for housework and childcare. Several of my Chinese informants had similar experiences, and I was told that this restriction of Chinese spouses' rights to work had resulted in several divorces because the in-married women felt hopeless in such an underdeveloped and enclosed environment.

Yue-Hua, who met her future husband and decided to marry him during his matchmaking tour in the late 1990s, shared with me her tough experiences in the early period of her marital life. She admitted that her quick decision to marry was taken because she had wanted to change her environment, and because of her husband's strong interest in her after meeting several women during the trip. Yue-Hua's parents, uninformed about this matchmaking meeting and anticipating that their daughter would marry nearby, agreed to the marriage, but told Yue-Hua that she would have to be responsible for this decision whatever the consequences might be. Though Yue-Hua had heard about the differences between Kinmen and urban Taiwan, she was surprised by the underdeveloped nature of Kinmen when she arrived, especially compared to her hometown, a coastal city in Minnan that was economically advanced and is even more prosperous now. After she arrived, Yue-Hua and her husband, the eldest son of his parents, lived with his parents in a village far away from the market towns in Kinmen, which further prevented her from having contact with the outside world. During the initial few years, constrained by her in-laws' demanding that she do all the housework, childbirth, and her lack of the right to work, Yue-Hua lost almost all communications with people outside of her marital family and became depressed. This was worsened by her husband's frightening short temper and frequent verbal abuse. Yue-Hua was afraid that her husband's temper might lead to physical violence against her and their children, and she had returned to her natal home in China. She stayed there for two to three months and eventually returned to Kinmen because of her husband's constant phone calls and pleas for her to return.

When I interviewed Yue-Hua in 2014 (and met her again in 2018), she looked confident, beautiful and in great spirits. She told me that after the above incident in which she 'left home' (*li-jia-chu-zo*), she tried to communicate with her husband who did not earn much as a fisherman and may have felt strong pressure to feed the large family. She began to ignore some of her parents-in-law's demands and to go outside with her children by taking a bus tour around Kinmen. She happened to get to know some women who were also married from China at the bus station, and they became friends and often organized meetings afterwards, which served as a helpful channel for Yue-Hua to release the pressure and negative emotions accumulated in her marital family. After her two children entered public kindergarten, Yue-Hua went out to work in the service sector to share her husband's burden of providing for the family and, more importantly, to allow her to have a disposable income of her own. She told me, 'Women must be economically independent, otherwise they have to ask money from their husbands for anything they want. I don't like this kind of dependence'. Similar remarks were made by several of my Chinese informants who resorted to work so as to break through the intersecting barriers set up by the Taiwanese government and their marital families regarding their places of origin.

Pursuing Personal Happiness beyond Patriarchal and Territorial Boundaries

The story of Yue-Hua shows that her gainful employment outside the home was an important way to rebuild her confidence, autonomy and independence threatened by government policy and her marital family's excessive demands on her 'free' labour. During my two meetings with her, she emphasized that she now only cares about her own and her children's well-being and happiness. She has probably stayed in the marriage for the sake of her children whom her husband does love and help to take care of. After completing our interview in 2014, I accompanied her to a new shopping mall which had just opened in Kinmen (which targets Chinese tourists through duty-free luxury goods) where she bought some bread and sweets for her children and husband. The prices of these were much higher than the products sold in local bakeries but Yue-Hua said that she now felt alright about spending money that she had earned. She also said that she now spends money on things that make her happy.

Xiao-Yun, who had drawn a lottery and received a message from a god that she would encounter some difficulties in her marital life, found that her widowed mother-in-law (who was in her late forties when Xiao-Yun married) had a huge debt because she was addicted to gambling. Moreover, her mother-in-law, who did not work despite her relatively young age, asked her eldest son, Xiao-Yun's husband, for money for gambling and alcohol. Xiao-Yun initially did not know about the debt but when the monthly allowances she received from her husband constantly shrank and she could hardly buy food and necessities, she interrogated her husband to get at the truth. She then told him that she would help to clear the debt by working 'illegally' (because she had not obtained a work permit yet) while her mother-in-law helped to look after her new-born son. However, her mother-in-law still drank a lot and often left her child unattended. Xiao-Yun was ultimately relieved when her first child was old enough to enter kindergarten and her mother-in-law started to work part-time. It took ten years for Xiao-Yun to clear the debt; after that, she tended to ignore all affairs related to her mother-in-law even though they still live under the same roof. Xiao-Yun now focuses on her own work and a small business selling sorghum liquor, trying to save money for a house – a dream that was sacrificed due to her mother-in-law's debt.

Both Yue-Hua and Xiao-Yun barely talked about their husbands and their relationships during interviews. This might have been because they had very limited knowledge about their husbands before marriage and their husbands did not provide support and care for them when needed. They stayed in the marriage, as they said, for their children and because their experiences of going out to work at a young age had trained them to be strong. When they regained their confidence and autonomy through working outside the home, they were able to dismiss the socio-moral demands of wholehearted devotion to their marital families and obedience to their parents-in-law. While Yue-Hua and Xiao-Yun single-mindedly carved out ways to pursue personal happiness, the story of Xin-Ru shows that her alliance with her husband based on their mutual affection enabled them to counter unjust accusations from the husband's family.

Xin-Ru was one of the very few Chinese women whom I interviewed who spontaneously talked about her husband, with only affection and praise, and showed me her husband's photo on her smartphone. She and her husband have only a one-year age gap; both married early and then divorced, and each has a child from their previous marriage. When Xin-Ru was in her mid-thirties in the early 2010s, she was called back from Xiamen to her hometown nearby to meet her future husband who was introduced by a relative's friend. She initially resisted the meeting because she was enjoying her single status, but her parents wanted her to remarry because she was still young. The same pressure was applied to her husband, who was pushed by his parents in taking this matchmaking trip. Eventually they met and found that they got along with each other. They stayed in contact through QQ (a Chinese instant messaging app) and then decided to marry. Xin-Ru told me that she thought that her husband would be a man who *thiànn-bóo* (in Hokkien, lit. indulgent to his wife) so she agreed to the marriage. She also stated several times during the interview that her husband is very *thiànn-bóo*.

Xin-Ru initially lived with her parents-in-law, her younger brother-in-law's family, and divorced elder sister-in-law after arriving in Kinmen. She told me that her parents-in-law treated her and her brother-in-law's wife (who was from Taiwan) unequally as she was asked to do most of the housework and cook dinner for the entire extended family every day. Xin-Ru initially accepted these demands for her husband's sake, even during the difficult times of her pregnancy. However, her husband's attempts to assist her with household chores were obstructed by her parents-in-law who said that their son was tired from working all day outside. Similar situations occurred time and again, and ultimately Xin-Ru started to challenge her in-laws' requests. For example, she suggested that she and her brother-in-law's wife could take turns in cooking dinner, but her parents-in-law and sister-in-law rejected this and said that Xin-Ru had more time because she did not work outside. When Xin-Ru said that she could also work, her in-laws refused and insulted her by saying, 'You Chinese women only care about money and want to take money from us back to China'. Her husband defended her and answered back, 'My wife's natal family is much wealthier [than us], and do we have money for her to take?'

As the conflicts between the couple and their family members escalated, Xin-Ru's husband finally decided to give up his share of family wealth and move out. On the first Chinese New Year after they moved out, they visited the parental home for ritual ancestor worship. However, they were questioned about whether they still hoped for a share of the family property. After this they avoided visiting the parental home and taking part in the ancestral rituals. Xin-Ru said that she was pleased with her current life with her beloved husband and son in their nuclear household, and she has a job which has allowed her to make several good friends, also married from China. But she has not applied for Taiwanese citizenship, which requires her to cancel her household registration in China (see Cheng 2017). This is because she has housing in China and a first son, who lives in China with his father. Moreover, keeping her household registration in China gives her power and freedom as she can choose to go back whenever necessary. Indeed, her connections and property in China were her backup when she started countering her in-laws' unjust treatment and verbal abuse as she could simply return to China with her husband and son.

Xin-Ru's decision not to apply for Taiwanese citizenship is not rare, as confirmed by an employee in Kinmen's agency supporting foreign spouses, because many marriages between Taiwanese (including Kinmen natives) and Chinese citizens were connected to the couples' pre- and post-marital economic activities across the border. But Xin-Ru is indeed different from most of my Chinese informants who had no valuable personal assets in China before marriage, and had married before the surge of China's economic power. Nevertheless, the opening of *Xiao San Tong* in 2001 contributed to the growth of the tourism industry linked to duty-free shopping focusing on Chinese visitors, which provided Chinese women with economic opportunities. There are numerous guesthouses in Kinmen operated by Chinese women, who use social media, such as QQ and WeChat (a Chinese multi-purpose messaging, social media and mobile payment app), to attract Chinese tourists and provide customized tours and services. For example, they take their Chinese customers to various stores in Kinmen to purchase items such as milk powder, nappies and skincare products made in foreign countries such as Australia, Japan or South Korea because they are safer and cheaper than those sold in China. They create comfortable tourist experiences for their customers by assisting in packing their customers' purchases and delivering them to the port. Mr Huang's daughter-in-law had engaged in this kind of business for some years before I visited their home. She was absent when I visited, and we saw her husband washing a new car outside the house. Mr Huang told me that this car had been bought by his daughter-in-law who has earned remarkable profits from her tourist business and had just recently expanded her business. He seemed proud when describing to me his daughter-in-law's ability to establish and manage a successful business.

Xin-Ru's unwillingness to apply for Taiwanese citizenship and many Chinese women's tourism businesses building on *Xiao San Tong* appear to challenge and even undermine the Taiwanese state's bordering measures. These businesses' reliance on social media used by the vast Chinese population to attract customers also suggests the power of technology and China's huge consumer market to penetrate Taiwan's border. Chinese women may have been disappointed by the undeveloped environment of Kinmen's borderland upon arrival, but now make use of this borderland status for its economic possibilities. Rather than realizing their own visions of a good life directly through marriage, they created their desired lives through hard work and their abilities to absorb and use knowledge of new trends and technology. They were no longer bounded by the local society and the Taiwanese state's demands of their reproductive roles within the home.

Conclusion

The cases of cross-border marriage in Kinmen, in various regards, resemble those on the Taiwanese mainland that have been scrutinized in a growing interdisciplinary scholarship. They all show how the Taiwanese state's bordering practices are entangled with its bureaucratic and discursive boundaries separating Chinese spouses from other foreign spouses and from Taiwanese citizens. This entanglement is also tied to a vision of a patriarchal, family-based social order that the Taiwanese state still supports, as shown in other policies encouraging heterosexual marriage and childbirth. Though the laws regulating Chinese spouses' residency, work rights and citizenship have been relaxed in the last decade, official discourses reveal the persistent emphasis on Chinese women's reproductive capacities not only for their families' well-being but also in the national interest (Friedman 2015). Chinese women's post-marital lives in Taiwan also reveal demands for their reproductive capacities and the boundary work of marking them as 'questionable others' from their husbands, in-laws and surroundings, mirroring state and media discourses. This chapter contributes to this scholarship by highlighting a local perspective, showing how kinship and Kinmen's borderland status have jointly produced marriages between Kinmen and China that have also challenged the Taiwanese state's power of bordering.

Ethnographic material on cross-border marriages between Kinmen and China has shown how changing forms of kinship have enabled the reproduction of the patrilineal family in a post-Cold War context featuring an increasingly individualized and commercialized pursuit of intimate relations. The economic asymmetry between Kinmen and rural China in the 1990s and the memories of close ties between the two sides before 1949 encouraged informal trade as well as cross-border matchmaking. The establishment of the *Xiao San Tong* made it easier for people on both sides to further their communications through kinship-based activities, including collaboration in restoring ancestral rituals and investment in real estate in China, and matchmaking. Nevertheless, this cross-border matchmaking was different in nature from the old pattern of matchmaking across the region of Minnan prior to 1949 because of the long-term separation of the two sides under mutually opposing political regimes. These different lived experiences were the source of tensions (e.g. in practices of ancestral rituals, and perceptions of generational and gender hierarchies) in these cross-border marriages which, together with the Taiwanese government's bordering practices, significantly affected the marital lives of Chinese women, often in a negative sense.

Kinmen's borderland status and close ties with the Chinese mainland prior to 1949 meant that kinship ties were a prominent motor for arranging marriages between Kinmenese men and women mostly from the Minnan region of China. Nevertheless, not all Kinmenese men and their family members had close contact with people in China or up-to-date knowledge about China before they married a woman from China. This resulted in divergent marital experiences among the Chinese women married in Kinmen. Some women whose marital families had contacts with China said that their husbands and in-laws treated them well, though they were often expected to take on the gendered work of childbirth, childcare and managing the household.

By contrast, some women were not only required to do all the housework in a large joint household but were also constantly subjected to their in-laws' suspicion and verbal abuse. There were numerous cases of divorce and domestic abuse telling of Chinese women's traumatic marital experiences, although the stories of my informants also show their resilience in overcoming hardship and pursuing their personal interests and happiness. Many Chinese women make use of Kinmen's borderland status, the expanding market of Chinese consumers, and technology to establish their own enterprises as well as to build their confidence and independence. Through their resilience and agency, they have the capacity to challenge and overcome the Taiwanese state's and local patriarchal society's attempts to confine them within the home and the territorial borders of Taiwan.

Chinese women's interactions with their parents-in-law within patrilocal households also provide a critical lens onto the problems in intergenerational and in-law relationships within extended families. These in-married women's twofold 'outsider' status (Oxfeld 2005) – as an outsider to her marital family and as an outsider from China – put them in very difficult positions when their in-laws have strong, prejudiced views about 'Chinese brides'. The stories of Yue-Hua and Xiao-Yun show how, by behaving as 'obedient' sons to their parents, their husbands did not help them. These men's 'ignorance' of their wives' suffering may have been related to a socialization suffused with gender inequality and a lack of affection in their marriages.

In contrast, Xin-Ru's story illustrates her husband's disobedience of his parents and renouncement of his share of family property because his parents' excessive demands and verbal abuse of his wife endangered his marriage, and probably his dignity as well. Leaving his parental home would have been a very tough decision for Xin-Ru's husband, or he could have moved out years earlier (though Xin-Ru's endurance may also have deferred the decision). The emotional alliance and cooperation in pursuing conjugal well-being between Xin-Ru and her husband resembles the nuptial intimacy that Yan (2003) highlights in young people's marriages based on romantic love in post-reform China. These cases suggest the significance of the couple's affectionate ties with each other in reconfiguring hierarchical intergenerational relationships between the young couple and the husband's parents in Chinese families (especially for the wife and her in-laws). Although I interviewed few younger married men in Kinmen, the foregoing stories also illuminate my observation about local men's relationships with their parents, which are complicated by their personal ties, the social-moral norms of filial piety, and their rights to inherit family property.

These Chinese women's stories demonstrate challenges to the conservative visions of marriage and the family of many Kinmen islanders in the local patriarchal context. While many of these women's marriages were associated with kinship-based networks in which they were embedded, they sought to create their own lives through their own choices and actions without being bound by expectations and restrictions from their marital families and the Taiwanese government. Their efforts to pursue their desired lives and futures, with or without the support of their husbands, have contributed to the growing reconfiguration of the generational and gender hierarchies in local patriarchal families discussed in the previous chapters.

The experiences of my Chinese female informants are similar to those of Chinese women marrying Hong Kong men. They also maintain physical and emotional attachment to the Chinese mainland because of its geographic closeness, and try to secure personal freedom and autonomy in the face of patriarchal demands (Binah-Pollak 2019; Chiu and Choi 2020). The comparison of cross-border marriages in Kinmen and in Hong Kong is theoretically and politically suggestive, especially regarding the interconnectedness between these marriages and the political positions of these two borderlands alongside their changing relations to China. Binah-Pollak (2019) notes how the pursuit of a new political subjectivity in Hong Kong in recent years has led many Hong Kongers to emphasize the separation of themselves from residents originally from the Chinese mainland, including marriage migrants. Though my Chinese informants also encountered prejudice due to their places of origin, they generally feel comfortable about living in Kinmen and can openly ask for their rights and entitlements to be met because local government and society in general prefer to maintain amicable relations with China, as noted in this book's Introduction. This comparison brings to the fore how kinship and marriage are also political processes that have important effects beyond the control of formal politics. Given recent rising tensions between Hong Kong and China and Taiwan and China, which are closely linked to the growing assertion of political subjectivity among the populations of Hong Kong and Taiwan, which is at odds with the expectations of China, further research and comparison of cross-border marriage in Kinmen and Hong Kong may provide fresh insights into these political entanglements.

Notes

1. The available data for Kinmen for Figures 5.1 and 5.2 starts from the year 2004 but cross-border marriages emerged in Kinmen many years before. The original official data already distinguished foreign spouses by gender and by nationality or place of origin. Female spouses from China mean those from the Chinese mainland, with spouses from Hong Kong and Macau excluded. Female spouses from Southeast Asian countries mean those from Indonesia, Malaysia, Singapore, Philippines, Thailand, Myanmar, Vietnam, Cambodia or Laos.
2. These two laws are the Law on the Territorial Sea and the Contiguous Zone of the Republic of China (1998) and the Law on the Exclusive Economic Zone and the Continental Shelf of the Republic of China (1998) respectively.
3. There are many stories about this kind of displacement in Kinmen and Xiamen. I also heard from my informants in Kinmen that they knew some men who were residents of Dadeng and were recruited by the Chinese Communists to be boatmen to ship their soldiers to Kinmen for an attack in late 1949. These boatmen tried to hide after landing, and then married local women and stayed in Kinmen.

6

THE WORK OF MARRIAGE
An In-Married Woman's Perspective

Despite the increasing expression of individual-focused lifestyles, the patrilocal joint household remains common in Kinmen today. This residential pattern is not merely a reflection of persistent patriarchal norms, including continuing male-focused transmission of family property and filial duties, but is also closely related to the financial constraints faced by young couples amid economic changes in Taiwan as a whole. Wage stagnation and recession in some industries on the Taiwanese mainland since the beginning of this century have created a growing inverse flow of young people, from fresh graduates to experienced workers, back to Kinmen to seek other possibilities and to save money by living in their parental homes. Young couples' attempts to purchase housing of their own are obstructed by the rapid rise in local property prices since the establishment of the ferry service between Kinmen and Xiamen in 2001, which attracted many Taiwanese businessmen to invest in Kinmen's real estate. On the other hand, many parents have built modern three- or four-storey houses on their unused family farmland in which they have reserved rooms for their married and unmarried children – in a mixture of care for their children and expectation of their children's company in old age. This has further encouraged their married sons and their wives to accept patrilocal co-residence.

    The above phenomena illustrate the dilemma between personal desires and familial obligations that many young people in Kinmen experience today, as I have elaborated in the foregoing chapters. Recent anthropological scholarship has documented similar situations across many Asian societies where conservative gendered norms and patrilocal residence remain the norm. While recognizing the increasing emphasis on conjugal ties and intimacy in these societies, resonating with a global rise of individualism for self-consciously modern or middle-class

---

Endnotes for this chapter begin on page 145.

subjects, this scholarship highlights the emphasis that young people place on their familial ties and obligations. This sustaining of kin ties may serve as a safety net or ensure continued upward mobility, or both, in the era of what Beck (1992) has termed 'risk society' (Hu and Mu 2021; Maqsood 2021a, 2021b; Yan 2016, 2021). But, in light of conservative aims to reproduce the family or preserve a given social order, kin ties may also continue to constitute structural constraints and processes within which individuals have to negotiate between personal and collective interests (Donner and Santos 2016; Santos and Harrell 2017).

Building on this scholarship, this chapter traces the interaction between conjugality and wider kin bonds with a focus on in-married women's experiences. While young couples in Kinmen live patrilocally out of filial sentiment, financial constraints and access to help with childcare from paternal parents, tensions or conflicts between family members, especially between female in-laws, can arise. In the preceding chapter on cross-border marriage, we have seen how in-married Chinese women suffered excessive demands for their domestic labour and verbal abuse from their in-laws. Though these Chinese women's difficult experiences were related to their places of origin, the tensions between daughters-in-law and mothers-in-law are a well-documented feature of societies with patriarchal traditions across the world (Brown 2004; Gallin 1986; Kandiyoti 1988; Vlahoutsikou 1997; Wolf 1972). This chapter considers the complicated interaction between multiple dyadic relations – wife-husband, parent-child and in-law relations – within patrilocal households over an extended period of time. I demonstrate how my longitudinal study in Kinmen provides insights into the future-making and relational aspects of marriage, illuminating how changes to unequal and oppressive elements of patriarchy could be generated from the intimate spheres of kinship and marriage.

My ethnography centres on a woman called Shu-Hui – a Kinmen native in her late thirties when we met in 2013 – as well as members of her marital family. The family was one of several joint families in a large patrilineal village that I visited frequently between 2013 and 2020. I focus on this family because I interacted with several members across three generations in their extended family, including those who reside outside the village and in Taiwan, and their family stories instantiate how people live their lives within a tight kinship web in Kinmen. My observation of the shifting circumstances of their family over the past several years has enabled me to explore the relational aspects of marriage, especially how both the positive and negative effects of kinship practices resulted in kin ties, including conjugal ties, being thickened or thinned over time (Carsten 2013, 2019; Das 2007; Lambek 2011). It also allowed me to probe into the future-making aspect of marriage by examining what the couple do to maintain their marriage while creating their preferred lives and desired futures. Inspired by their stories and by a theoretical horizon provided by new kinship studies, I use an inclusive and expansive term, 'the work of marriage', to denote the reciprocal effects that the couple's investments of various kinds in their marriage had on their conjugal ties.

The significance of my use of the term 'the work of marriage' is two-fold. First, it refers to the actual work that people do in everyday marital lives, including physical labour, emotional input and ethical struggles. Second, it denotes the immediate results as well as the cumulative effects that the mundane work of marriage have on people, moulding their subjectivities and perceptions of their nuptial relationships over time. These effects are part of what kinship does and how (Carsten 2013) – rather than what kinship is – which has become the focus of enquiry in new kinship studies. Relatedness, a key notion in this scholarship, is used to sidestep the biological/social dichotomy which has bedevilled definitions of kinship (Carsten 2000, 2004), and its inclusive qualities encompass what marriage does as part of people's experiences of kinship or intimate relations. Nevertheless, the blurring between experiences of kinship and marriage under the concept of relatedness risks passing over the distinctive status that marriage entails for a person in a given culture. In this regard, Margery Wolf's (1972) concept of uterine family is helpful to allow intersectional analysis of culture and gender in my discussion of the work of marriage.

Based on her nuanced observation of family lives in rural Taiwan in the late 1950s, Wolf (1972) argued that sustaining a patrilineal family was inseparable from an informal sub-group created by a mother and centring on her ties with her children, especially sons, which she called a 'uterine family'. The emphasis on mother-son ties reflects the in-married woman's vulnerable position in her husband's family in traditional settings because marriage did not directly make her a member of that family. She had to give birth to a son to solidify her position, and, through nourishing ties with her son, she hoped to secure her son's support to her in old age. While confirming Wolf's conceptual breakthrough, Stafford (2000a, 2000b) notes that Wolf seemed to downplay the significance of the uterine family by viewing it as 'only a way of accommodating to the patriarchal family' (Wolf 1985: 11; see Stafford 2000a: 52). He therefore proposed the cycle of *yang* (care and nurturance) to foreground women's crucial and positive roles in Chinese kinship. However, this emphasis on the positive effects of *yang* in making kinship or relatedness may overlook the darker side of kinship in terms of conflicts and rupture between female in-laws. It is at this point that I return to Wolf's discussion on the interactions between an in-married woman, her husband and her mother-in-law, in light of her concept of uterine family, which reveals the negative impact of the patriarchal structure on a woman's marital experiences.

In Wolf's ethnographic account of the uterine family, women's strategies in coping with the gender inequality inherent in the patriarchal structure led to the damage, marginalization or thinning of conjugal relations. Not only might a woman's relationship with her husband be negatively affected by her focus on rearing her son but also, after her son grew up and married, his relationship with his wife might be threatened by this mother-son bond. Wolf pertinently captured how the tensions between female in-laws engendered by the patriarchal structure arose in the forms of open disputes and tacit emotional mistreatment in everyday interactions between the older and younger women. Both women tried to draw the son/husband to her side, and it was usually the mother who won the game (Wolf 1972: 158–60). Besides the structural suppression of conjugality (conventionally through parental control over children's marriages and moral emphasis on filial piety), the strong mother-son ties also worked against the daughter-in-law's interests and her nuptial relationship, even in the case of marriage by choice.

As Wolf's ethnography was situated in a context where women had only recently begun to gain some autonomy through working outside the home, this raises the question of how the suppression or marginalization of conjugality might change with wider social transformations that weakened the patriarchal family's control of its members' labour, income and desires. Moreover, while Wolf portrayed what a married woman's life in old age would be like (1972: 215–29), she did not touch on how an aging woman's illness and need of care might affect the relations between members of her extended family. In what follows, I examine these questions through the double significance of the work of marriage, on the basis of my ethnographic material centred on Shu-Hui's marital experiences over the past several years. This longitudinal study of family lives, I argue, brings to light how kinship and marriage not only create pressure for individuals to fulfil the conservative aim of preserving the patriline but also generate transformative challenges to the patriarchal order – though this is often unremarked and occurs at a gradual pace in everyday lives.

Conjugal Intimacy and Patrilocal Co-Residence

It has been widely documented in contemporary non-Western societies that 'love marriage' has been associated with people's self-shaping as modern or middle class, and the rise of the individual who actively pursues personal feelings and desires (Cole and Thomas 2009; Donner and Santos 2016; Hirsch and Wardlow 2006). Though none of my interlocutors in Kinmen, whose family backgrounds, education and careers vary, used *xiandai* (modern) or *zhongchan jieji* (middle class) to describe who they are or want to become, the lifestyles that they pursued appeared congruent with those described as 'modern' or 'middle-class' across the globe. Romantic love is indeed significant in many of the marriages of young people whom I interviewed or met in Kinmen.[1] Notably, 'love' is not always the term that my informants used to express their intimate feelings towards their partners. Maqsood (2021a, 2021b) observed in urban Pakistan that women described their husbands' love for them using English words such as 'caring'. Similarly, my interlocutors used other registers to describe their conjugal relations and intimacy, such as *hedelai* (get along well or feel compatible with each other) or *thiànn-bóo* (in Hokkien, lit. indulging one's wife). Members of the younger generation are obviously different from their parents in their espousal and open expressions of their nuptial intimacy.

Yan's (2003) ethnography of changing private lives in post-reform China has compellingly shown how the rising pursuit of 'love marriage' among young people has involved materially securing conjugal privacy and intimacy. They may demand an individual room specifically for themselves in the patrilocal joint residence, or take a further step and ask for early division of family property in order to establish their own nuclear household. In Kinmen, as explained at the beginning of this chapter, many couples take patrilocal joint residence for various interlinked reasons. But there were several cases in which young couples received housing or support to buy a new residence from the wife or the husband's resourceful parents upon marriage and formed nuclear households. I also knew several couples who decided to move out of the paternal parental home by renting a residence with a view to securing their spatial privacy and freedom.[2]

Young couples who live in the husband's parental home also find ways to ensure conjugal privacy and happiness. Usually, it is not a problem for the young couple to have an independent room for themselves and another room(s) for their children, but the entire stem or joint family tends to use the same kitchen and eat together. Similar to young couples' behaviour in Pakistan (Maqsood 2021a, 2021b), my informants resorted to consumption to gain private space and time for themselves or for their nuclear family by eating outside and by booking a trip to Taiwan or to other countries. For example, Wan-Rong, a woman who was originally from Taiwan and moved to her husband's parental home after marriage, arranged a trip, with her husband's help, to Taiwan for several days during the Chinese New Year holidays every year just for her nuclear family. This is significant because the Chinese New Year is a time for family reunion and there are various rituals in Kinmen which take up women's time and labour in preparing food offerings, and Wan-Rong does not go to visit her parents (who are no longer living). Wan-Rong and her husband just want to find a time when the husband and children can take a longer break from work and school, and enjoy themselves together far away from home.

In the case of Shu-Hui – the female protagonist of this chapter – in addition to eating out and having fun outside of Kinmen, she and her husband created a space for their nuclear family by reconstructing his family's old house. Shu-Hui's husband, Jia-Cheng, was the youngest of five sons and the only one who lived with his widowed mother in the parental home. When I moved to Shu-Hui's marital village in 2013, their house was under reconstruction. The old house was a traditional-style building, consisting of two single-storey living spaces originally separated by a small courtyard between them, plus an external kitchen. Shu-Hui had been living with her mother-in-law in the front part of the house after her marriage and after giving birth to two daughters. The reconstruction was to turn the courtyard into a roofed space for a living room, and to renovate the rear part as a work and study space and two bedrooms for the couple and their school-age children. Shu-Hui's nuclear family moved into the new living space after the reconstruction was completed, but they still used the old kitchen to cook everyday meals and came to the front common room to dine with the grandmother. However, this balance between her desire for a space for her nuclear family and the norm of patrilocal co-residence involved Shu-Hui in a compromise.

In a conversation in their new living room, Shu-Hui once told me that, instead of reconstructing the old house with the money that she and Jia-Cheng had saved after several years of hard work, she originally wanted to buy a new modern house in a neighbouring village. But she eventually went along with Jia-Cheng's wish to stay in his beloved natal village and look after his mother, who would never agree to move away. It was for the same reasons, as well as Jia-Cheng's lack of money when he married, that Shu-Hui accepted patrilocal co-residence. Though Shu-Hui did not say so explicitly, my familiarity with the couple suggests that her affection for Jia-Cheng contributed to her compromise. When I talked about my new research on marriage on a visit to their home in 2017, Jia-Cheng said in front of his wife and children that his marriage with Shu-Hui was out of *ai* (love), and it was Shu-Hui who made the first move.[3] Back in the early 2000s, Shu-Hui happened to see Jia-Cheng in her uncle's workplace and she asked her uncle to introduce them to each other. Jia-Cheng said that he was a poor man without money and higher education, but Shu-Hui, a woman with a university degree and from a good family background, was still willing to marry him and had endured hardship in their early marital life. The following sections depict how this couple's mutual affection and Jia-Cheng's appreciation of Shu-Hui's compromise or sacrifice are objectified in their work of marriage, informing their actions and shaping their shared sense of their union.

Rupture between Female In-Laws in Mundane Daily Lives

I became familiar with Shu-Hui much later than with her mother-in-law, husband and children. My participation in the village's voluntary group, mainly composed of female villagers between the ages of fifty and eighty, led me to befriend Shu-Hui's mother-in-law, Ming-Yu, who was in her late sixties in 2013. As I volunteered in numerous village activities, such as cleaning the village's public spaces and assisting with preparing food for participants in village funerals, I soon gained positive recognition from Jia-Cheng who was a young leader in managing the village's affairs. I was often invited by Ming-Yu or Jia-Cheng to have lunch or dinner at their home, and I thus became close to Jia-Cheng's two daughters as well. Shu-Hui was almost absent in these public village events and during my visits to their home because she looked after her clothing shop in the market town from morning to late evening almost every day. Shu-Hui's absence from daily activities in her marital household fuelled Ming-Yu's negative judgements about this daughter-in-law and the obvious rupture between them.

The rituals of ancestor worship carried out at different levels in Kinmen – by an individual family, a patrilineage branch, or a patrilineage as a whole – manifest the resilience of patrilineal values in organizing local lives (Chiu 2017). Most old and middle-aged female homemakers I know arranged their daily and annual schedules by prioritizing the numerous dates for worshipping ancestors and local gods for which they had to prepare food offerings. For various reasons, the total number of ancestral rituals that Ming-Yu's family attended to in a year was much greater than those of other families. Ming-Yu prepared food and carried out the rituals mostly by herself until 2017 when illness seriously affected her ability to remember the duties of worship. When I lived in the village in 2013–2014, I often helped Ming-Yu by laying out the offerings on the table and burning the ghost money for ancestors or gods. Ming-Yu was not a talkative person and was rather shy and reserved. But, like other old village women, as she became accustomed to my presence, she volunteered various things about herself and her five sons.

Gradually I learned about Ming-Yu's married sons' families – apart from Jia-Cheng, three sons live in Taiwan and one lives in a market town in Kinmen. I also heard Ming-Yu's commendation of or complaints about specific sons and daughters-in-law. Her fourth son – whom Ming-Yu deemed to have a similar personality to herself – and daughter-in-law appeared to be her favourite. Ming-Yu proudly told me that this couple were both school teachers in Taiwan and, despite their heavy workloads, managed to give birth to four children – two boys and two girls. She also emphasized that this couple were very *guai* (well-behaved and filial) because they, especially the daughter-in-law, always assisted Ming-Yu with ritual preparations when they came home for the Chinese New Year holidays and other festivals. Ming-Yu's praise of her fourth daughter-in-law was often articulated along with her critique of Shu-Hui, who, Ming-Yu asserted, 'doesn't know anything about cooking and ancestor worship because she was spoiled by her natal family'.

As we have seen throughout this book, the preservation of patrilineal traditions in Kinmen has sustained a vision of a patriarchal family-based social order which serves as the framework in reference to which people take action and make moral judgements. For local women of Ming-Yu's generation, it was normal for the work of marriage for a woman to extend far beyond the unit of the conjugal family. A woman was evaluated by the extent to which she fulfilled patrilineal duties, including daily dutiful care of her parents-in-law and dead ancestors (through ritual) and procreation of male offspring to continue the agnatic line. It appeared that Ming-Yu's preference for her fourth son and his wife was built on a combination of specific mother-son ties and this couple's individual achievements and compliance with traditional patrilineal obligations. By contrast, Ming-Yu's negative judgements about Shu-Hui focused on the young woman's failure to fulfil this extensive work of marriage.[4]

The ways in which Ming-Yu judged her daughters-in-law by reference to patriarchal gendered roles were common among other senior village women. I often heard these women's evaluations when volunteering with them – implying that these women tried to find moral support for themselves by extending a personal judgement into a social one. For example, during a volunteering activity, I once heard a woman in her early seventies ask a middle-aged woman next to her whether she was afraid of her mother-in-law. When the younger woman answered yes, the older one remarked immediately: 'That's it. When I entered my marital household, I was very afraid of my mother-in-law. I followed her every instruction and worked hard every day. Now, look at my daughter-in-law, she always stays in their [conjugal] room'.

As older women often implicitly or explicitly critiqued their daughters-in-law at gatherings of village women of different ages, it was very likely that a daughter-in-law living in the same village would know how her mother-in-law talked about her. Despite this, Shu-Hui admitted openly several times that she had no interest in learning how to do the rituals and that she was bad at cooking. Though Jia-Cheng might sometimes become angry at Shu-Hui because of her lack of care over household chores, as I heard from Ming-Yu, the couple have maintained a mutually understanding and supportive relationship. They have supported each other's decisions about their careers, such as Shu-Hui's small shop in the market town and Jia-Cheng's investment in various business projects. Wolf (1972) suggests that the strong mother-son ties produced by the oppressive patriarchal structure might lead a son to align with his mother and against his wife when he had to take sides. But she did not consider how a mother's unequal treatment of her children might affect the ties between the mother and a specific child as well as other relationships. Ming-Yu's preference for her fourth son was obvious from her talk about him, and was recognized by Sui-Hui who felt that Ming-Yu had not paid due attention to Jia-Cheng. I never heard Jia-Cheng comment on this matter; rather, I observed him protecting his ties with Shu-Hui by assisting his mother in cooking and ritual preparation whenever he could, and dismissing potentially harmful questions about Shu-Hui from his mother and close villagers.

However, Shu-Hui was not unaffected by the male-focused living environment and associated expectations. During my first fieldwork, both Shu-Hui and Jia-Cheng claimed that 'it's enough to have two children' (*sheng liangge jiuhaole*), even though they were daughters. But, when I paid a visit to them in late 2015, I was surprised to find that Shu-Hui had just given birth to a third child. Shu-Hui said that she had long felt the pressure from others to produce a son, so she discussed it with Jia-Cheng and they decided together to give it a try. Their decision to have a third child resembles a case in China that Santos (2021: 5–8) describes, in which childbirth was not a couple's 'free choice' but an 'intimate choice' that involved complex moral negotiations between multiple actors and their values, such as the expectations to have a grandson from the husband's natal family.[5] Though the birth of their third daughter understandably disappointed Shu-Hui and Jia-Cheng, as well as the grandmother, to some extent, they explicitly expressed their love for the baby. Shu-Hui became a stay-at-home mother engaged in full-time childcare afterwards, and started learning how to cook from other young mothers in the village, with support from her husband and two school-aged children.

Predicaments of Elderly Care and Ethical Struggles

Shu-Hui closed her clothing shop in early 2014 because the profits were lower than predicted, and she then found an administrative post in an acquaintance's company. Shu-Hui seemed realistic about closing her business (she also persuaded her husband to give up some unsuccessful business projects) and appeared not to be particularly ambitious about her career. This might explain her acceptance of becoming a homemaker after giving birth to her third child, and in the face of her mother-in-law's worsening health condition. During my stay in the village in 2013–2014, Ming-Yu had occasional serious headaches that prevented her from getting enough sleep, and her ability to remember things was declining. In my visits over the years between 2015 and 2020, while Ming-Yu was physically able to move around and could converse with others fluently, her loss of short-term memory worsened noticeably. She almost immediately forgot what she had just said and done, and this caused numerous minor and more major problems. Her waning short-term memory eventually prevented her from doing most housework, including cooking and routine worship of ancestors and gods, which she had carefully attended to for decades. Though Shu-Hui had been trying to take over this work – which she had intentionally avoided before – and look after her mother-in-law, the tensions between these two women had not eased but were becoming more severe, as demonstrated in a scene below.

On one of my visits to Shu-Hui's family in 2017, I was invited to have dinner in their home as usual. As Jia-Cheng had a business appointment that evening, he asked Shu-Hui to save time by buying takeaway food and bringing it home. After Shu-Hui brought the food home, I helped to set the table and chairs for dinner in the old common room. Ming-Yu then entered the room and greeted me enthusiastically but frowned when seeing the takeaway food on the table, without saying a word. Shu-Hui showed Ming-Yu the bowl of noodle soup intended for her. Ming-Yu took the bowl quietly and retreated to a chair a bit away from the table, though I asked her to sit beside me. Over dinner, conversation between the three adults and two school children was rather limited as Shu-Hui was busy feeding her baby daughter while Ming-Yu focused on slowly eating her noodles. Shu-Hui's two elder daughters finished their meals quickly and, with their little sister, went to the new common room in the rear part of the house. Ming-Yu then claimed that she was full and put her bowl on the table, with nearly half her portion remaining. As Shu-Hui responded that she would clean up the table, Ming-Yu left the house to go somewhere else.

I stayed with Shu-Hui, who had just started to enjoy her noodle soup. Regarding Ming-Yu's behaviour, Shu-Hui sighed and said, 'It's not that she didn't like the noodles but she just dislikes anything I do. She doesn't like the food I cook either'. Shu-Hui gave me some examples of her daily predicament in coping with her mother-in-law's resistance to her provision of care. Though Ming-Yu disliked Shu-Hui's cooking, she usually ate the food at dinner time when Jia-Cheng was present. But things became very difficult in the daytime when Jia-Cheng was at work, as Shu-Hui described: 'During weekdays when only mom, me and my baby were at home, I often had to buy takeaway food as lunch. I couldn't cook because mom was unwilling to help me take care of the baby. But mom barely ate the food I brought back'. Initially, Shu-Hui thought that Ming-Yu might simply dislike takeaway food, but this was not the case. One time Shu-Hui and her friends – a number of young mothers in the village – conducted a test. One of Shu-Hui's friends delivered the takeaway food to Ming-Yu without revealing the truth that the food had been bought by Shu-Hui. Ming-Yu happily received the food and finished all of it. With this example, Shu-Hui concluded: 'She is determined to be against me (*ta jiushi gen wo zuodui*)'.

The predicament and pressure that Shu-Hui faced came not only from her mother-in-law's direct rejection of care but also from her siblings-in-law's suspicions about the appropriateness of care. As Ming-Yu gradually lost her ability to manage household chores, sometimes her sons and daughters-in-law living in Taiwan were unable to properly judge her condition on their occasional return visits. There was a period during which Ming-Yu was able to cook several dishes of food to welcome the return of her sons, daughters-in-law and grandchildren, though she barely cooked in daily life. These sons and daughters-in-law thus did not find Ming-Yu's health condition particularly worrying until Jia-Cheng and Shu-Hui told them about their mother's troubles. In a conversation between me and Shu-Hui about a serious problem caused by Ming-Yu in 2018, Shu-Hui said that though her brothers-in-law did not criticize her or her husband directly, they blamed them for not paying sufficient attention to their vulnerable mother. 'But, was it possible for us to restrict her movement or to keep an eye on her all the time? They [her brothers-in-law and their wives] were not here so they didn't know what really happened here and how much trouble we have gone through', Shu-Hui complained bitterly with her voice raised. She then remarked in a distressed tone: 'Things are very tough for those who are left behind to look after their parents'.

Shu-Hui's feelings of distress and bitterness generated by her failure to earn her in-laws' recognition of her efforts are shared by many of my older and younger female interlocutors in Kinmen. This problematizes a tendency to understand the notion of *fengyang* (respectfully caring for the elder) through its positive aspects (Stafford 2000a, 2000b), without due attention to negative responses from the care-receiver which result in tensions between the care-receiver and care-provider, and between the care-provider and third parties. Veena Das's (2012, 2018a, 2018b) discussion of ordinary ethics considered in Chapter 1 provides a window onto these female care-providers' emotional suffering and ethical striving in their everyday persistence of caring for their parents-in-law. Their strength to endure the challenges of elderly care are continuously complemented by their ethical struggles with social norms and personal feelings and by relatedness-making with others from whom they receive support in carrying out the work of marriage.

Reconfiguring Relations within and beyond the Nuclear Family

After Shu-Hui closed her small enterprise in 2014, her relations with her two school children became notably closer. Though she still had a full-time job, she came home to dine with her family every evening and became more involved in her children's lives. A young village woman who is close to Shu-Hui told me that, when Shu-Hui revealed her pregnancy with a third child, her second daughter became unhappy and even cried and patted her mother's belly. My interlocutor interpreted this girl's reaction as her realization that there would be one more child sharing her mother's love and attention, which she had only recently begun to receive. Fortunately, the baby girl's birth was eventually welcomed by her two elder sisters, who assist their mother with housework. Moreover, because Shu-Hui's second daughter is very close to her grandmother who had looked after her earlier when her mother ran the small shop, Shu-Hui usually relied on this daughter to attend to Ming-Yu, for example, by calling her to dinner and reminding her to take her medicines. I witnessed on several occasions how Shu-Hui looked relieved when she could rely on her daughter to conduct these minor tasks of care, which saved her from confronting rejection or silence from her mother-in-law.

With the birth of her third daughter, Shu-Hui appeared to enhance the solidarity of her uterine family, and she and her daughters have deepened their emotional bonds with each other. In Wolf's conceptualization, the father is not quite a member of this informal group and may even be 'the enemy'. From what I observed, Jia-Cheng, the husband and father, is not excluded but is rather an important source of physical and emotional support for Shu-Hui and his three daughters. At my numerous dinners in their home in recent years, Shu-Hui did the cooking, sometimes with Jia-Cheng's help. Several times, over the dinner table, Jia-Cheng told me with a smile of pride on his face that Shu-Hui had made significant progress in cooking. While Jia-Cheng, currently the only breadwinner of his family, was very busy with his work, I witnessed that he shared the work of caring for the baby and attending school events of their two elder daughters whenever he could. Jia-Cheng's involvement in housework and childrearing may be less connected to his recognition of gender equality than to his affectionate ties with his wife and children, but his input in the work of marriage did signal certain changes in family relations in the younger generation. He and some young married men I knew in Kinmen illustrate new expressions of masculinity, which emphasize both a man's ability to provide for his family and his emotional and physical engagement in strengthening the bonds between members of his nuclear family (see Wong 2020 on similar phenomena in China). With all the family members' input to maintain the course of everyday life, Shu-Hui's nuclear family has become much more solid than before.

Shu-Hui's transition to becoming a homemaker has not limited her social life but rather expanded her circle of friends within the patrilineal village. During my first fieldwork in 2013–2014, while Shu-Hui had good interactions with some women who were wives of her husband's friends and agnates, she was rather detached from these social networks because of her full-time occupation. Things changed after Shu-Hui gave birth to her third child. In my numerous visits to Shu-hui in recent years, I observed that she had befriended more young mothers in the village – again, wives of Jia-Cheng's friends and agnates – and had frequent meetings with them. They routinely took an after-dinner walk around the village together with their children, and often had a chat over afternoon tea in Shu-Hui's home. As Shu-Hui told me, she has received much emotional and practical support from these friends, who had taught her how to cook, helped to care for her baby girl, and advised her on how to interact with her mother-in-law – as described earlier, when Shu-Hui and her friends conducted a test to see Ming-Yu's reaction to takeaway food.

The social circle involving Shu-Hui and her friends on the surface resembles the women's community described by Wolf (1972: 37–40) but has distinctive differences. The female community that Wolf observed decades earlier was built on in-married women's sharing of space and time together when doing domestic chores outside the house, such as washing clothes on the riverbank and cleaning vegetables at a communal pump. Similarly, Ming-Yu became especially close to some women whom she met regularly when serving food offerings to the common ancestors in the ancestral buildings of her marital village. In other words, the women whose husbands belong to the same lineage branch (i.e. the same circle of ancestor worship) tend to be closer to each other, and thus there are several women's communities within the village, and the boundaries between them are blurred.

With women's increasing employment outside the home after marriage and childbirth, the space and time for the formation of women's communities were much reduced. In Shu-Hui's case, her new social circle was formed on the basis that most women are currently full-time homemakers because they had preschool children, and some women's husbands preferred them to stay at home to attend to the heavy household chores, including caring for aging parents-in-law. But, unlike the older women's communities in which their husbands were barely involved, these younger women's husbands are important in bringing their wives together initially, and now and then take part in their wives' sociality. These young couples also create a larger community, with their children included, by holding various joint entertainments (e.g. barbecues) in their leisure time. In so doing, these young couples manage to increase intimacy between members of their nuclear families but also maintain good relations with wider social networks, which are essential when they are in need of help.

Shu-Hui's energy for the difficult work of caring for her mother-in-law is arguably inseparable from her enhancement of ties with members of her nuclear family and wider social networks. Though disputes and ruptures occurring within these circles upset Shu-Hui from time to time, she continuously engaged herself in activities that sustain these ties and bring her joy. She made significant changes to herself through trying to fulfil the normative roles expected of an in-married woman in this patrilineal community, i.e. by being a full-time homemaker taking care of children, parents-in-law and household chores. Her self-adjustment was difficult and her female companions in the village have served as a cushion to tolerate and soothe her negative feelings generated from domestic work. But these female companions also reminded Shu-Hui about avoiding making 'complaints' publicly, and that all women in Kinmen endure the same pressure and burden of work. Rather than simply drawing on the patrilineal framework to restrict Shu-Hui, these women advised her to respond to the normative expectations pragmatically so as to maintain her marriage and her life in this patriarchal community as smoothly as possible. But these pragmatic responses did not occur without Shu-Hui's ethical striving to maintain a lifeworld including people she cares about (Das 2012), for whom she has made changes to herself and compromises (see Papadaki 2021 on similar scenarios of women's self-change and compromise in marriage in Athens).

The Work of Marriage and Time

I do not know how Shu-Hui and Jia-Cheng imagined their conjugal relationship before they decided to marry based on their affection for each other. As shown in previous sections, Shu-Hui made several compromises from the beginning of her marriage by accepting patrilocal co-residence, then giving up the purchase of a new modern house, and learning to cook and taking care of her ill mother-in-law. Though I use the term 'compromise' several times in this chapter, Shu-Hui did not use the Chinese terms for compromise or sacrifice in her narratives about her marital life. When describing a situation or result related to her husband that diverged from her original plans or desires, Shu-Hui always said, '*meibanfa* ("I could not do anything" or "it was not up to me"), because that's what he [Jia-Cheng] wanted'. While this short phrase suggests Shu-Hui's suppression of her individuality and submission to Jia-Cheng's desires, it does not mean that her thoughts and desires were not recognized and valued by her husband.

In updating the family news from Shu-Hui, Jia-Cheng and their children in the past several years, I noticed that they often mentioned how a decision was made collectively by Shu-Hui and Jia-Cheng. The children talked about how family trips to Taiwan or abroad involved the opinions of both their mother and father, and the plan sometimes suited their mother's preferences more, and sometimes their father's. Both spouses mentioned how Shu-Hui's previous enterprise and Jia-Cheng's several business projects were established and terminated through the couple's discussion and joint decision. Though Shu-Hui tended to go along with Jia-Cheng's plans when she had doubts, her advice was listened to and followed by Jia-Cheng when things did not go as well as expected. Jia-Cheng told me several times that his investment in various new projects, with Shu-Hui's support, was not aimed at immediate material gains but at material security for their three daughters in the future. The relational aspect of marriage suggests the potential challenges to the two persons in a conjugal relationship to assert their individuality as they may sometimes make compromises for one another or take decisions together to attain a collective aim – which is linked to the future-making aspect of marriage.

Magee (2021) notes that in marriage counselling in the US, where individualism and the association of marriage with religious and social ties are both valued, the question of how spouses can retain their individuality in a long marriage frequently came to the fore. People were advised that some degree of personal transformation and enduring individualism are both necessary to make their marriage work. The term 'individualism' (translated as *ge-ren-zhu-yi* in Chinese), which may be narrowed and equated to egoism as Yan (2003) observed in China, is not a term that my young informants used to refer to themselves, but their growing demonstration of individuality through referencing personal rights and desires is palpable. Rather than suggesting repression of their individuality, the deep participation in each other's lives that I describe for Shu-Hui and Jia-Cheng reflects how their words and actions marked their solidarity as a marital union. When Shu-Hui remarked that 'things are very tough for those left behind to look after their parents', she viewed herself and her husband as a union in facing together the problems, suspicions and blame of others. When Jia-Cheng commended Shu-Hui's significant progress in cooking, he appeared to take on the burden of Shu-Hui's numerous failed attempts and eventual achievements. This couple demonstrates how their marital union is strengthened through their engagement in each other's lifeworlds, viewing each other's desires, problems and feelings as their own.

Just as clients of marriage counselling in the US were advised to make certain personal adjustments to keep their marriages going, such self-change, as part of the work of marriage and the time involved, are also significant in Shu-Hui's experiences. The patriarchal environment of Jia-Cheng's natal community which Shu-Hui married into and lived in presented more challenges for Shu-Hui than for Jia-Cheng in their marital lives. For the first decade of her marriage, Shu-Hui did not submit to the patriarchal norms demanding that she concentrate her labour and time on housework. Despite the tensions with her mother-in-law due to her avoidance of housework, Shu-Hui had her husband's support. At the same time, Shu-Hui supported Jia-Cheng's ambitions in his career and investment of time, labour and money in his natal village's affairs. It was this mutual support through a decade that sustained their marriage and encouraged Shu-Hui to make significant changes to herself by focusing her labour and time on her family and household chores when her mother-in-law had an increased need of care. We see the work of time (Das 2007) in generating changes in actors in a marriage and their relationships with others, not through open conflicts or rebellion but through the mundane work of caring, tolerating and tinkering with injury through mutual help and pursuing shared happiness in life. As suggested in Carsten's (2019) discussion on the gradations of kinship and temporality, the thickening or thinning of marital ties over time has much to do with the extent to which a couple engage themselves in the actual everyday work of marriage.

The processual character and potential for change implied in the idea of relatedness or gradations of kinship help to enrich our understanding of people's marital experiences, including both bright and dark moments in their marital lives, all of which together are important to the survival or end of their marriages. The story of Shu-Hui illustrates the work of marriage and time in her self-change and her endeavour to take on the roles and work expected of an in-married woman in the local patriarchal setting. Through their involvement in each other's lives, Shu-Hui and her husband shared the burden that a marriage entails in their society but also the joy that they themselves create through family trips and joint entertainment with wider networks. Their marital experiences cannot simply be evaluated by the criteria of how they divide housework or share family decision making, or whether they have prioritized conjugal interest over familial obligations. However, as demonstrated in the course of Shu-Hui's marital life, it is also important to note how patriarchal norms remain resilient and powerful in shaping gendered expectations that are unequally experienced by women today. But it is also important to detect how a couple collaborate innovatively and ethically to maintain their marriage while upholding familial duties and wider social bonds.

Conclusion

The rapid global expansion of a neoliberal economy and marketization since the late twentieth century has had two seemingly contradictory consequences, which are particularly prominent in Asia: the dominant trend of 'love marriage' manifesting personal freedom and emotions on the one hand, and the continued popularity of joint living arrangements in both urban and rural settings on the other. Recent scholarship has explained these intriguing phenomena as ordinary people's agency and pragmatic responses to the intersection between the weak provision of social welfare under neoliberal governance and ordinary families' joint efforts to tackle resource constraints and to secure upward mobility (e.g. Donner and Santos 2016; Ochiai and Hosoya 2014; Maqsood 2021a, 2021b; Yan 2016, 2021). Ethnographic evidence from different social settings shows how young couples try to pursue conjugal intimacy and desires, which are potentially threatened by the lack of privacy in stem or joint households. Consumption, which implies the powerful penetrative force of marketization, appears to be a common means employed by people across the world to attain and materialize their conjugal intimacy and happiness as well as to mark their modern or middle-class subjectivities. While joint households are usually driven by economic concerns, family members also emphasize their emotional intimacy, which is important not only for the harmony of extended households but also for individual members' moral personhood and fulfilment of their familial obligations.

The instances of young people's marital lives described in this chapter can be understood as part of a wider new dynamic between practices of kinship and intimacy and neoliberal economy and governance as sketched above. In revisiting Wolf's theorization of the uterine family, this chapter has explored the inherent tensions between multiple dyadic relations in a patrilineal extended family from the perspective of an in-married woman. Wolf's ethnography echoes a Chinese idiom, '*xifu ao cheng po*' (even a submissive daughter-in-law will one day become a domineering mother-in-law), which captures the changes that marriage potentially involves for a woman and the shifting power dynamics between female in-laws. This conventional assumption of an in-married woman undergoing a long-term linear transition from being a powerless young bride to a powerful old woman in the patrilineal family is no longer generally applicable today as families have lost absolute control of its members' labour and desires. Nevertheless, Shu-Hui's marital experiences and the stories in the previous chapters indicate that young people's exercise of personal autonomy and pursuit of personal desires are very often entangled with their gendered upbringing, their emotional ties with their parents, and their ethical struggles.[6]

Set against the tensions between female in-laws noted by Wolf, my longitudinal study in Kinmen has highlighted the relational and future-making aspects of marriage through focusing on an in-married woman's marital stories over the past several years. I have used the phrase 'the work of marriage' to encompass the process and a wide range of work and relationships that an in-married woman is expected to engage with in patrilocal households, but also to grasp their impact on the woman herself and her conjugal ties. During this process, the relational aspect of marriage requires the woman to constantly interact with others, including her husband, children and kin, which may involve her compromise or collaboration with others in order to sustain her marriage and make her marital life compatible with her desires. The work of marriage is inseparable from a woman's visions of desired futures for herself and those whom she cares about, and for which she may make compromises or changes to herself over an extended period of time, but this also creates challenges for the patriarchal order.

As we have seen, Shu-Hui was not a docile and submissive bride after entering her husband's family and her mother-in-law Ming-Yu could barely control her. But Ming-Yu's resort to moral judgements, which earned her social support from other villagers to some degree, harmed Shu-Hui's reputation in the village. While Shu-Hui made a compromise by accepting patrilocal co-residence, she and her husband Jia-Cheng pursued in various ways their conjugal intimacy and desires in order to maximize their nuclear family's well-being. The later changes, with Shu-Hui becoming a full-time homemaker caring for her baby girl and ill mother-in-law, were therefore striking. Shu-Hui's failed attempt to give birth to a son suggests the persistent power of patrilineal ideology in Kinmen which constantly pressures young couples to redraw their visions of a good life to fit the conservative vision. Her mother-in-law's illness seemed not to weaken the latter's mobilization of moral accusations from other villagers and of her non-co-resident sons and daughters-in-law against Shu-Hui. But Shu-Hui's third pregnancy and her adjustments were supported by her alliance with her husband in the work of marriage over time that has solidified their marital union, as well as their relatedness in wider social circles. Shu-Hui and her husband have worked together to sustain their family and to seek secure and promising futures for their daughters.

While Shu-Hui's marital experiences were shaped by various circumstances that were particular to them, what she encountered was by no means unfamiliar to other in-married women in patrilocal households in Kinmen and Taiwan. In the numerous marital stories that I heard in Kinmen, such as those described in Chapter 5, it was not uncommon for in-married women to become depressed due to harsh treatment by their co-resident in-laws and their husbands' ignorance of their suffering. Shu-Hui and her female friends in the village (some of whom married in from China) were perhaps fortunate in that they could form a mutually supportive community via their husbands, and include their husbands and children in pleasurable activities together which constantly revitalized ties within and beyond their nuclear families. Though Shu-Hui and her female companions tended not to straightforwardly challenge patriarchy, they enabled certain changes in their marital and parent-child relations. In Shu-Hui's case, the mutual affection and support between her and her husband in the first decade of their marriage encouraged her to invest more time and labour in deepening her ties with her husband and children, who have also made a physical and emotional input. This involvement of the entire nuclear family in pursuing shared happiness and well-being is very different from the family lives and parent-child relations envisioned in traditional Chinese patriarchy. While the oppressive and unequal patriarchal elements may not be obliterated in the short-term, new dynamics within and beyond individual families have increasingly unsettled the hierarchical and unequal relations of patriarchy. Children learn from their parents that gender stereotypes in local patriarchal environments can be challenged and changed, and that wider kin and social ties can be supportive of their creation of new ways of life and new futures.

Notes

1. Throughout this book, I have used the term 'marriage by choice', instead of 'love marriage', to describe the younger generation's marriages. This is because several of my younger informants, in cases of cross-border marriage and marriage between two citizens of Taiwan, highlighted their 'volition' rather than 'love' for their partners in the decision to marry. Nevertheless, they also mentioned that their decision of marriage was inseparable from pressure from their families and surroundings as discussed in the previous chapters.
2. These couples tended not to buy a new residence of their own because the husbands may inherit housing from their parents in the future and, as mentioned at the beginning of this chapter, they may be dissuaded by the high prices of local property.
3. Jia-Cheng actually emphasized the term '*ai*' intentionally when speaking because '*ai*' was not a term he and his coevals usually used and, in so doing, he expressed his trust in me as we often talked to each other jokingly. But, immediately following this phrase, he described how he and Shu-Hui had got married and his feelings of affection for and appreciation of Shu-Hui.
4. Ming-Yu's strict judgements of Shu-Hui were also arguably related to their co-residence. Based on her semi-structured interviews with married women and men on Taiwan, Chung (2021) notes that a couple that forms a nuclear family away from the husband's parental home is more likely to have a fairer share of housework due to much less intervention from the husband's parents. The physical distance between a mother-in-law and her daughter-in-law not only reduces the former's intervention in the latter's marital life but also shields the young woman from constant examination by the older woman on a daily basis. Moreover, this physical distance allows a daughter-in-law to more easily comply with her mother-in-law in their meetings but disobey her when they are apart, as described by Shih and Pyke (2009) for Chinese immigrant families in the US.

5. Santos (2021) links these negotiations regarding a couple's intimate choices around childbirth to the wider contexts of the Chinese government's campaigns targeting the eradication of the custom of son preference since the 1990s, in resonance with the global advocacy (for example, through the United Nations) of gender equality and son-daughter equality. The Taiwanese government proposed similar policies of family-planning and son-daughter equality from the 1970s onwards. According to current health-related laws in Taiwan, gender selection during pregnancy is prohibited.
6. Despite differences in our theoretical and methodological approaches, my ethnographic material from Kinmen and Kung's (2019) findings in urban Taiwan both suggest that the power dynamics between female in-laws are not simply determined by the resources, such as education, income and occupational status, available to the young and older women respectively. Kung argues that a daughter-in-law is usually affected by the traditional filial norms emphasized by her husband and mother and thus behaves respectfully towards her mother-in-law. I agree with this argument while also highlighting a daughter-in-law's daily ethical struggles and feelings of frustration, bitterness and resentment resulting from her mother-in-law's negative response to her provision of care.

Conclusion

This book has explored the intersection and interaction between personal lives and dramatic political changes in Kinmen – a geopolitically salient archipelago located between Taiwan and China – over the past century, a period of rapid modernization in Asia. Marriage has been highlighted in mainstream theories of modernity, mainly grounded on Euro-American experiences, as an index of wider social changes enabling individual men and women to become independent of familial bonds and assert their personal freedom and autonomy. This has been challenged by a significant body of literature in Asian studies showing how 'traditional' familial or patriarchal norms remain effective in shaping individual life. While this scholarship compellingly argues that Asian governments have created or reinforced familial or patriarchal prescriptions of gendered roles through their policies, very often kin ties and the patrilineal family are treated as zones of conservatism demanding the individual's compliance with unequal gendered expectations. Building on new kinship studies in anthropology, I have moved beyond the oft-posited dichotomy between individual autonomy and familial bonds, and a hypothetical practice which circumscribes kinship as a 'private domain' in theses of modernity. Exploring the future-making and relational aspects of marriage in the life stories of multiple generations in Kinmen, I argue that, rather than zones of conservatism, kinship and marriage engender new futures and changes in society at large.

Mid-twentieth-century anthropological studies of kinship, including those of Chinese kinship, have pointed out the constitutive power of kinship and marriage in forming political structures and processes. In theses of the lineage paradigm or the corporate model of Chinese kinship, patrilineal descent was the politico-jural principle of social organization (Cohen 1976; Freedman 1958 1966; Watson

---

Endnotes for this chapter begin on page 158.

1982). In this earlier scholarship, kinship's constitutive power was associated primarily with preserving the patriline ideologically and materially. But this conservative reproduction of the patrilineage required a group's capacities to make, or adapt to, changes over time, for example, by investing in male offspring's upward mobility and expanding alliances through marriage. It is in this regard that we can first identify the transformative capacities of kinship.

However, the formalist approach to Chinese kinship of earlier scholarship tended to sidestep the day-to-day interactions between kin living under the same roof, and their emotions, desires and clash of interests. Building on a number of pioneering studies of Chinese kinship (e.g. Stafford 1995; Wolf 1972; Yan 2003) and new kinship studies (Carsten 2000, 2004), I have explored another dimension of kinship's transformative capacities by focusing on processual and performative aspects of kinship. This not only illuminates how kin ties are established and nurtured over time but also directs attention to how transgressions or changes may arise from everyday unremarkable acts of kinship (Carsten 2013, 2019; Das 2007; Lambek 2011). The positive and negative effects generated by day-to-day interactions in the intimate sphere of kinship may lead to kin ties being thickened or thinned out over time, and they may also encourage transgressions or changes which challenge the given norms, such as the patriarchal order of the Chinese case. Examining marital change in Kinmen, I have unpacked two dimensions of kinship's transformative capacities by considering the future-making and relational aspects of marriage.

Highlighting the future-making aspect of marriage, I have traced how new visions of personal and collective futures held by an individual, the family and the state emerged under different conditions of modernity in Kinmen which were shaped by constantly shifting politics at domestic and international levels. Equal attention to the relational aspects of marriage facilitated my investigation of the relations between spouses, between generations, between groups and between ordinary people and the state that were contested and negotiated both in the intimate and political realms. I have singled out gender, generation and temporality as three main themes to explore the links between personal biographies, family histories, and shifting national and transnational politics. The themes of gender and generation have brought to the fore how kinship practices have conservative or transformative effects, reconfiguring the gender and generational hierarchies of Chinese patriarchy amidst the transition into contemporary modernity with democratization and expansive marketization. The conservative and transformative qualities of kinship were not only experienced and contested in the intimate sphere of the family but also animated or appropriated in the political sphere through making or lobbying for relevant laws and policies. My discussion has highlighted the temporalities inherent to the imaginative work that marriage involves, showing how the challenges and changes to gender and generational hierarchies arose from actors' reflections on familial experiences and imaginings of new futures. Considering marital stories across multiple generations in Kinmen through these three themes, this book shows a shift of emphasis in kinship practices from the goal of preserving the patriline in earlier times to the goal of attaining emotional and material well-being for kin across different generations in the face of increasing uncertainties.

The ethnography of this book began with the 1920s, a time when Kinmen's economy relied heavily on men's labour migration abroad and when a new regime, the Republic of China, had just been established. The conditions of modernity that Kinmen islanders confronted for the first time mixed the material modernization brought about by the remittance economy and new visions of marriage closely tied to new visions of a modern Chinese nation-state advocated by young, Western-educated intellectual migrants. Parents of young migrants, who remained in the communities built around patrilineal ties and values, were anxious about their sons' long-term absences and sought to tie their sons to the home through arranging their marriages to local women. Kinship and marriage worked to preserve the patriline, which involved remarkable gender inequality and pressure on left-behind wives to stay loyal to their marital families physically and sexually – despite their husbands' absence and infidelity abroad. However, I have argued that the patrilineal family was reproduced not just through replicating what the ancestors had done but through finding new ways to ensure the family's growth, such as by sending sons to receive a Western education using money earned abroad. These transformative capacities of kinship were also evident in the case of a patrilineage in Kinmen that collected funds from wider kin networks to support the modern enterprises of a village school and a publishing house.

Relations between the Chinese mainland and the islands of Taiwan and Kinmen were further complicated after the outbreak of the Chinese Civil War and amidst Cold War geopolitics. Kinmen's status as an anti-communist frontline in the Cold War era meant the island being always readied for war, and military and geopolitical concerns being prioritized in every facet of modernization. This constant state of war mobilization with the aim of retaking the Chinese mainland led to unequal access to marriage and family lives among soldiers retreating from China, and between them and the Taiwanese population. On Kinmen, however, the enlarged presence of soldiers from China and Taiwan was a threat to local men's marital prospects but stimulated local women's alternative imaginings of marriage and futures outside of Kinmen. The prosperity of micro-businesses catering to the necessities of soldiers, largely dependent on women's labour, created new dynamics of gender and economy within local households. The local patriarchal order of sex-gender and generational hierarchy was undermined by women's newfound economic and intimate agency. Many women pursued their desires for new futures by marrying a soldier from outside or establishing lives in

Taiwan, whereas many others accepted parental arrangements to marry local men. Whatever route they took, these women's economic contribution to their natal and marital families supported their younger male and female siblings' and children's advanced education and upward mobility outside of Kinmen, earning them an authority that was recognized by their husbands and children.

Changing diplomatic relations between Taiwan, the US and China in the 1970s contributed significantly to the vibrant social movements for democratization in Taiwan and the eventual transition of Taiwan from one-party rule to multi-party democracy in the late 1980s. Nevertheless, Kinmen remained under martial law and military rule due to lingering military tensions with China, until 1992. Despite these political constraints, the average living standards of local families had improved remarkably, with increasing numbers of male and female teenagers pursuing higher education in Taiwan. As several of my ethnographic examples have shown, mothers played an important role in shaping their children's life paths through their economic power to initiate changes to the male-focused transmission of family wealth. While many mothers still privileged sons in their allocation of available resources, including housing, the growing investment in daughters' education and material security has diversified their options, and they can be confident about creating their desired futures, with or without marriage. Changes to intergenerational transmission since the 1970s were not only materially important but also occurred in an emotional register. As shown in several instances, mother-daughter and father-daughter ties are close and increasingly expressive in contrast to formal father-son filiation as emphasized in the patrilineal system.

While kinship's resources remained associated with preserving the patriline (embodied in the persistence of rituals and male-focused transmission of family property), its transformative capacities could be identified in processes of parenting. My ethnographic examples have shown how mothers with the authority to decide family matters and fathers with less patriarchal attitudes instantiated alternative images of gender, distinct from the images of traditional patriarchy, to their children in long-term parent-child interaction. With Kinmen's transition in the context of political and economic liberalization since the 1990s, young islanders with long-term experiences in Taiwan tend to pursue a lifestyle similar to what can be found in urban Taiwan. This often included an emphasis on personal (and conjugal) privacy and desires, and a middle-class style of consumption, such as a larger budget for leisure activities and the objectification of affective ties, for example, in commoditized celebrations of marriage, birthday and other events. Local elderly people have responded to enlarging generational differences in ways of life flexibly and creatively by simplifying traditional marital rituals and tolerating, or joining in, their children's enthusiasm for creating memorable moments of marrying through new commodities. The mixture of old and new elements in marital celebrations today embodies the creative conservatism supported by both generations' emotional ties with each other and care of wider social bonds in the face of increasingly uncertain and precarious conditions of life.

Growing parental investment in the higher education of children of both sexes has had implications for class differences in marital choice: many well-educated women and men postponed their marriages while their male coevals with working-class jobs were squeezed out of the local marriage market. I have argued that this emerging phenomenon of deferring marriage is not simply a reflection of young people's assertion of personal freedom and autonomy but a trial or a testing process in which they are creating their desired lives and futures while maintaining close ties with their families. Moreover, this testing process is also a transforming process in which young people move between different temporalities, reflecting on their past experiences and envisioning alternative life options. This imaginative work opens up their horizon for diverse expressions of sexuality and intimacy as well as diverse family forms beyond conservative visions based on marriage of a heterosexual couple with children. Imaginings of childbearing out of wedlock or marrying a divorced man while excluding childbirth have become possible for young women.

While my young single informants were able to dismiss questions of their marriage from their parents, they still experienced the pressure to marry in gatherings of kin and in the workplace. However, it was not easy to find a marital partner in their day-to-day lives within the limited space of Kinmen. Some local working-class men, pressured by these trials of marrying, eventually found a spouse from abroad, particularly from southeast China. Though these cross-border marriages are similar to those in several Asian countries where working-class men found their spouses from the economically weaker countries nearby, I have shown that the pattern in Kinmen was unique because most marriages were established through kinship ties rather than the commercialized matchmaking often seen in other places. More importantly, the rise of cross-border marriages between Kinmen and China since the 1990s not only reflected the mitigation of military tensions between Taiwan and China but also signalled Kinmen's autonomy in defining its relations with China, being not fully subject to the control of the Taiwanese government.

Scholarship on cross-border marriages in Asia usually focuses on how the governments of bride-receiving countries have asserted their control of state borders through strict laws and policies regulating marriage migrants' entrance and citizenship, and how these measures have involved inequality and discrimination among migrants from different places. Instead of this state-individual nexus, my discussion has foregrounded the significance of kinship in the cross-border matchmaking between Kinmen and China and how in-married Chinese women interacted with their marital families. I have demonstrated how the spontaneous restoration of contacts and kinship ties between ordinary people in Kinmen and in coastal China, initially through informal maritime trade and then through marriage, has challenged Taiwanese control of its borders. Stories showing in-married Chinese women's varying relations with their marital families point to the negative effects of everyday interactions between kin in patrilocal joint household, which led to Chinese women's resistance to their in-laws' unjust treatment. With or without their husbands' support, my Chinese informants sought to create a better life for themselves and their children by making themselves economically independent. Their strategies of negotiation included not applying for Taiwanese citizenship and using Kinmen's borderland status to sustain their ties with China and establish businesses targeting Chinese tourists in Kinmen, which posed new challenges to the Taiwanese government's control of its border.

Stories of in-married Chinese women showed their individual struggles with their marital families that were patriarchal and oppressive, and how these struggles had relational effects for their husbands and children. In other words, they were redefining their relations with their husbands, children and in-laws. The marital story of a woman that I focused on in the last chapter of this book also exemplified how this woman created her family by making changes to herself and her relations with her family members over time. Her story illustrated how patriarchal structures and values remain effective in present-day Kinmen, where women in patrilocal joint households often experience intense pressure to comply with traditional gendered roles, under the surveillance of their mothers-in-law and wider kin networks. But her story also showed how an initially disobedient daughter-in-law (as described by her mother-in-law), made significant changes to herself by engaging more in household chores after the birth of her third daughter. These changes, as I showed, were encouraged by her affective ties with her husband, and their mutual support, over the initial several years of their marriage. The later changes she made to herself were also changes made to her relations with her two elder daughters and her mother-in-law as she spent more time, energy and attention on these persons in the joint household. While her relationship with her mother-in-law appeared not to improve, her efforts, together with her husband's contribution, have strengthened her nuclear family. The couple are co-creating their desired family lives through, for example, mutual support of each other's career decisions and various activities that enhance bonds with their children and wider circles of friends. They are also seeking to provide secure and promising futures for their three daughters through various business ventures. Their stories illustrate how, despite negative effects that were difficult to avoid, kinship and marriage could encompass positive changes to intimate relations, and gradual enhancement of equality and equity between the sexes through new futures for children.

Alternative Imaginings of
Intimate and Social Futures in Kinmen and Taiwan

In line with my argument about the transformative capacities of kinship, I conclude this book with a discussion of recent developments in LGBT rights in Taiwan and Kinmen. My fieldwork began soon after Taiwan's constitutional court's ruling in May 2017 that the legalization of same-sex marriage should be completed within two years. This temporal coincidence allowed me to reflect on the roles of kinship and the agency of individual actors in pursuing new visions of personal and social futures. Though I did not recruit any LGBT people as research participants in Kinmen, I asked my local friends who are cisgender and open to LGBT issues whether they knew people who did not conform to local heterosexual norms. They usually did not refer to any queer friends but, interestingly, they all mentioned the story of Hsu Chih-Yun (a gay man in his thirties), a Kinmen native and psychiatrist practising in Kinmen and Taipei, to suggest the extreme difficulties of 'coming out' in their homeland. Whether my informants knew Hsu personally or not, they maintained that Hsu was only able to come out 'publicly' after his father passed away and that he does not stay in Kinmen all the time. Hsu himself said in a press interview, however, that he had revealed his sexual identity to his parents at the age of twenty-seven, two years before his father died.[1] This suggests that Hsu felt able to become more publicly engaged in pro-LGBT rights activities, such as serving as the general-director of Taiwan Tongzhi (LGBTQ+) Hotline Association, after the death of his father who would not be harmed by gossip about or criticism of his son.[2]

In Kinmen's patriarchal and tight-knit communities, LGBT people's concerns about gossip that could harm themselves and their families are all too imaginable. The uncertainties and fear of exposing one's sexual nonconformity have become one main driving force for queer people to stay away from Kinmen, as shown in the life stories of four gay men discussed in a recent Master's thesis (Lee 2018). These four men, between the ages of twenty and forty, all went to Taiwan for further studies after senior high school and prefer living there. In this way, they not only achieved greater freedom but also became positively and openly identified with their sexual orientation in Taiwan. Despite the support of the constitutional court's ruling in favour of gay marriage, they doubted that Kinmen as a whole would become LGBT-friendly within a few years, as one of them put it, before 'our generation fully take over our parental generation' (see Lee 2018: 47). What was implied in this pessimistic outlook is Kinmen's relatively delayed process of democratization closely linked to its previous status as a militarized frontline and its relatively closed social system revolving around kinship ties and patrilineal values.

The above examples echo Amy Brainer's (2019) findings on the Taiwanese mainland, where 'coming out' has become a predominant concern for young gay people today, who desire to settle their sexual and self-identity by revealing 'the truth' to their families but are afraid of the deep harm this might engender. But, as Brainer emphasizes, her data, which includes stories of LGBT people ranging in age from their twenties to their seventies, shows that 'coming out' is not a crucial issue for older gay people. Her older queer informants, unlike younger people, are not anxious about whether and how to disclose their sexual identity to their families. Instead, they sidestep this issue in their everyday lives and strive to manage their various family roles and relationships. This does not mean that their families of origin are unaware of their sexual nonconformity; their families' 'silence' actually signals tacit acceptance or even support (Brainer 2018). Women's painful experiences of being pressured to enter marriage, including lesbian women's marriages to heterosexual men because of housing insecurity resulting from the male-focused transmission of family property, and being exploited in patriarchal households, has helped to forge their support for their children's nonconformist behaviour and sexuality. Queer mothers and divorced mothers of gay children are critical of the sex-gender inequality intrinsic to patriarchal structures, and endeavour to become the anchor providing financial and emotional support for their children (Brainer 2017b).

Brainer's findings resonate with my discussion of kinship's transformative capacities in this book, especially the important role of mothers – with resilient power and flexibility despite their vulnerable position in the patriarchal structure – to tolerate or accept the transgressions of their children and seek to protect them. Rather than being passive, such parental tolerance or acceptance is crucially supportive of LGBT children's creative pursuit of their desired personal and social futures. The aforementioned psychiatrist Hsu recalled that it took him ten years to make up his mind to reveal his sexual identity to his parents, and he struggled to find the right moment for disclosure. Though he was surprised by his parents' rather calm response, his professional experience suggested that they might be too shocked to respond. He later checked with his parents again and found that his father viewed his sexual nonconformity as an illness that could be cured, whereas his mother accepted it quietly and said that she would find excuses for him to dismiss his grandfather's questions about his marriage. Hsu recognized that his mother's calm reaction had much to do with the hardship and difficulties that she had been through; she had her own way of facing her son's deviation from the norms of masculinity. This encouraged Hsu to further his efforts to improve the public understandings of LGBT people.

While Hsu and his parents got along with each other after his disclosure, he witnessed how many young queer people were in great tension with their parents. Brainer (2017c) also notes that the social expectations and women's own recognition of their primary responsibility for childrearing, in tandem with new parenting discourses that emphasize constant attentiveness to children's physical, intellectual and emotional development, have created emotional burdens for heterosexual mothers in relation to their queer children. In spite of the difficulties, many parents have adopted various approaches to deal with their relationships with their queer children and their needs. Some mothers went further and created new narratives to counter mainstream discourses of gender, sexuality and parenthood. This suggests that intergenerational ties are protected and thickened not through parents' hierarchical control of children but through a reciprocal exchange of thoughts and feelings between generations. These processes of exchange potentially engender changes to parents' own visions of social world and futures, which may move closer to those of their children.

Moreover, transformations in relations between heterosexual parents and their queer children have also been supported by democratization and the surge of civil movements advocating LGBT rights since the late 1990s (Brainer 2019; Chu 2003; Liou 2005; Pai 2017). Within only two decades, the LGBT rights movement has gained several path-breaking achievements, including building an alliance with parents of LGBT children. Taiwan is the first among East Asian countries to pass laws banning discrimination based on sexual orientation in education (since 2004) and at work (since 2007), and where a large-scale LGBT Pride parade has been held annually since 2003. The establishment of Asia's first organization for parents of LGBT children, Loving Parents of LGBT Taiwan, in 2011 by the mother of a transgender child marked the cross-generational support of new intimate and social futures. In Kinmen, which had been a place that many queer people were afraid to return to, fresh voices and innovative actions supporting LGBT rights emerged in the midst of the 2018 referendum on marriage equality.

I did not touch on LGBT issues much during fieldwork, but there were significant new developments after I left Kinmen in August 2018. The 2017 constitutional court's ruling to legalize same-sex marriage incited a series of protests from conservative groups and eventually led to a set of referenda related to LGBT issues in November 2018.[3] Conservative groups proposed to protect the rights of same-sex couples through enacting special legislation,[4] rather than by amending the Civil Code, while the pro-LGBT groups demanded the institution of gay marriage through the Civil Code.[5] Though the referenda concerned the preferred route to legalize gay marriage, it was not easy to clarify this point at the level of mobilizing votes among the general public. Conservative activists used rhetoric in their campaigns and print materials that suggested that their proposal, seemingly to protect same-sex marriage by a special law, was in fact a call to deny the possibility of marriage to same-sex couples.[6] It was also reported that conservative groups were accused of spreading misinformation about LGBT rights and demonizing LGBT people as a bad influence on children.[7] Around one month before the referendum, I began to see these conservatives' campaign messages disseminated among my Kinmen informants on LINE (an app for instant communications on smartphones). I am a member of a chat group on LINE which is composed of people from a Kinmen village, mostly aged fifty and above, and I saw an increasing number of messages against gay marriage forwarded by some villagers. Although these messages usually did not elicit any response within the chat group (partly because most elderly female users have limited literacy), they signalled the presence of conservative audiences in Kinmen. My local young friends told me that they saw even more virulent messages against LGBT people circulating in chat groups on LINE composed mainly of middle-aged and elderly users.

On the other hand, through some local friends, I saw a new Facebook page called *Caihong Piao Piao Gua Kinmen* (lit. hanging up a rainbow flag in Kinmen), with the English name 'Queermoy' (a combination of Queer and Quemoy, the Hokkien spelling of Kinmen), that promotes LGBT rights in Kinmen.[8] The page displayed photos of two or three people unfurling a large rainbow flag, shot on the site of various tourist attractions in Kinmen, to show their support for marriage equality. I learned later from Andy, a local activist, who had coined the word Queermoy earlier in 2017, that this Facebook page had initially been established by two cisgender men and one gay person who came from Taiwan to work in Kinmen. Andy joined them when they became more active in promoting marriage equality around one month before the referendum. They continued to photograph people with the rainbow flag at various sites, and gained permission from a couple of local shops to display the rainbow flag outside their businesses, such as *Houpu Paochajian* (lit. teahouse in Houpu – the downtown area in west Kinmen).[9] The managers of this teahouse had been supportive of the campaigns for marriage equality from the very beginning, for example, by being a site for collecting petitions to set up pro-LGBT referendum proposals against those proposed by the conservative groups. The Queermoy activists also distributed LGBT-friendly leaflets acquired from Taiwan and tried to talk to people on the street and in shops. They got permission from some shopkeepers to display leaflets in their shops, whereas some others asked them not to talk about LGBT issues inside their shops. In general, their gentle, small-scale campaigns usually went peacefully and without serious conflict or attacks from people on the streets, which they had originally anticipated.[10]

In the end, conservatives succeeded in their three referendum proposals related to LGBT issues. However, the central government and the legislature then followed both the court ruling and the referendum results by passing the Enforcement Act of Judicial Yuan Interpretation No. 748, which legalized same-sex marriage on 17 May 2019. This Act was celebrated as a great success in defending LGBT rights. On 24 May 2019, the first day the Act came into effect, around 500 same-sex couples registered their marriages throughout Taiwan, including two couples registered in Kinmen. While pleased with these major achievements, Jennifer Lu (2020), the chief executive director of the Taiwan Equality Campaign (TEC), notes that the Act fails to address several issues concerning same-sex couples' marital rights, including joint adoption rights and access to artificial reproduction. Moreover, conservative groups continued their strong protests against this Act before and after it passed into law. Three days after the Act came into force, a privately published local newspaper (*Kinmen Shibao*) ran a discriminatory headline suggesting the impossibility of same-sex couples procreating biologically. In the face of these conservative attitudes, the TEC sought to develop effective messaging strategies and platforms to encourage public understanding of LGBT people and marriage equality. They also attempted to strengthen their political alliances, for example, by publicly expressing their support for LGBT-friendly political candidates in the 2020 elections. They continue to highlight the legalization of gay marriage as a significant index of democracy, freedom and the universal values of human rights in Taiwan, as well as being diplomatically beneficial to Taiwan's reputation in the international community.

Though the TEC's various measures may not change conservative minds in the near future, its persistent advocacy of respect for, and protection of, diverse sexual identities and family forms may have a profound influence on Taiwanese society at large. Just as the legalization of same-sex marriage was the result of thirty years of continuous democratic development and the dedication of previous LGBT activists, the emergence of innovative advocacy of LGBT rights in Kinmen in late 2018 was built on the cornerstone laid by previous work in Taiwan. My local interlocutor Andy told me that though Queermoy activists had forwarded campaign messages from pro-LGBT groups in Taiwan on their Facebook page, their activities were spontaneous, without any formal alliance with or advice from these groups. Andy has continued to promote LGBT rights since then through several spontaneous activities. For example, he paid for the design and production of flags printed with a map of Kinmen in rainbow colours in 2019, and got support from some owners of local shops to display the flag in their shops.[11] Together with some friends in Kinmen and Matsu (another group of islands that served as an anti-communist frontline in the Cold War era), Andy took their new rainbow flags printed with maps of Kinmen and Matsu to the annual LGBTQ Pride parade in Taipei in 2020. Based on his experience of studying in Taiwan and his acute observation of political differences between Kinmen and Taiwan, Andy has been anxious about the growing hostility of *Tai-pai* (people in favour of Taiwan's independence) towards Kinmen – this has also been a worry for several of my younger local interlocutors. His efforts to link his pro-LGBT rights movement in Kinmen to those in Taiwan were partly driven by this political anxiety.[12] He wanted to show publicly that there are also those in Kinmen who support cultural diversity and believe in the values of democracy and civic communication.

Overall, rapidly growing public acceptance of new conceptualizations of sex-gender, marriage and family since Taiwan's democratization in the late 1980s has been mainly driven by civil society forces. While Kinmen was behind in this progress of democratization, there have recently been new forms of expression of these diverse values and desires. The outburst and rapid growth of this civic power has been inseparable from the changing intergenerational transmission and interactions described in this book, where parental investment in children's long-term well-being may, instead of reproducing the patrilineal family, encourage different articulations of a good life and possible futures. Parents may also be moved by their children's new imaginaries to shift their positions closer to those of their children. This generative power of the family and civil society has reconfigured the state's vision of the social order and of the future through directly participating in policy- and law-making and accumulating political alliances. The current democratic government seeks to gain support from citizens with divergent views and social imaginaries by proposing policies responding to different demands, rather than imposing a singular vision as the imperial governments and the KMT did in the past.

While LGBT-friendly laws and policies have been proposed, other policies pertaining to the idea of heterosexual, monogamous marriage and the conjugal family are also promoted to deal with the worrying trends of later and less marriage and the sharp decrease in fertility rates in Taiwan. In this way, the democratic polity enables the participation of civil forces with diverse interests in drafting laws and policies related to marriage and family. Although sometimes contentious and even chaotic, democratic debates over marriage and the family are also debates over different visions of the social order and possible futures of society and of the state. These debates illuminate underlying inequalities and injustices, and stimulate joint efforts to seek creative change. In these transforming processes of mutual constitution of family and state, kinship and marriage, rather than zones of conservatism, have been important sources of change for alternative visions of the future.

Notes

1. See the article about the interview, *Up Media*, 23 October 2018, retrieved 15 March 2023: https://www.upmedia.mg/news_info.php?SerialNo=50251.
2. Hsu had been a volunteer in the Tongzhi Hotline Association during his medical studies in Taipei. In 2015, he set up an outpatient service providing psychological counselling to LGBT people in a Taipei hospital, and in 2018 he published a book which includes fourteen stories from his patients to improve public understanding of LGBT people and their families.
3. There were ten referenda held in Taiwan in 2018; among these three questions related to LGBT issues were proposed by conservatives and two questions were proposed by pro-LGBT rights groups. See an English translation of these referendum questions online, retrieved 15 March 2023: https://rfrd-tw.github.io/en/#page-top.

4. See Ho (2019, 2020) for further discussion of the rationale and organization of campaigns of the conservative groups.
5. Feminist legal scholar Chao-ju Chen (2019) critically points out that the pro-LGBT activists' emphasis on formal equality (i.e. legalizing gay marriage via the Civil Code) had been intensified during their navigation of a legislative lobbying strategy in the face of rising pressure from the conservative counter-movement. But this strategy endorsed marital supremacy and left aside a feminist critique of marriage as an institution of male dominance.
6. Legal scholar Hsiao-Wei Kuan published a newspaper article discussing the problems and confusion caused by conservative referendum proposals and campaign strategies that might mislead voters. See the article on *Apple Online*, 9 November 2018, retrieved 10 October 2022: https://tw.appledaily.com/forum/20181109/PQP36KHVN3OHXIRPEVUQDFMXYU/.
7. See the news report on the website of *The Washington Post*, 23 November 2018, retrieved 15 March 2023: https://www.washingtonpost.com/world/2018/11/23/taiwan-was-supposed-be-first-asian-country-legalize-gay-marriage-then-things-got-complicated/.
8. Facebook page of Queermoy, retrieved 15 March 2023: https://www.facebook.com/lgbt.quemoy/.
9. This local teahouse was established by my two young local friends in a space constructed by the military in the Cold War era and owned by the management committee of a neighbouring Daoist temple in 2018. The teahouse opened to display creative ways of revitalizing old spaces of historical value, and served as a civic space welcoming discussion and advocacy on various public issues. The teahouse was closed in 2020 because the temple's committee had other plans for the space.
10. On the Taiwanese mainland, the coalition campaigning for marriage equality faced attacks on their campaign workers, including hate speech and even physical attacks, by certain religious opponents (Lu 2020).
11. This idea of making a rainbow flag specific to Kinmen generated from disputes during the referendum campaign in 2018, when some people questioned why they should hang up a rainbow flag with only the image of the Taiwanese mainland, with Kinmen and Matsu excluded, outside the *Houpu Paochajian*. See the Facebook page of Queermoy for the rainbow flags with the maps of Kinmen and Matsu respectively, retrieved 15 March 2023: https://www.facebook.com/lgbt.quemoy/photos/pb.100063969783673.-2207520000../2389370318038238/?type=3.
12. Andy revealed that he was quite nervous about taking his rainbow flags, highlighting Kinmen and Matsu, to the Pride parade in Taiwan because the political image of Kinmen as a whole in recent years has been quite negative in LGBTQ circles in Taiwan. This negative image largely relates to an impression of Kinmen's closeness to the KMT, which has been associated with the conservative groups in anti-LGBT campaigns. Andy was afraid of being called *lan-jia* (an abbreviation of gay people who politically support the KMT), which he is definitely not, when attending the Pride parade.

References

Adrian, Bonnie. 2003. *Framing the Bride: Globalizing Beauty and Romance in Taiwan's Bridal Industry*. Berkeley, CA: University of California Press.
Allerton, Catherine. 2007. 'What Does It Mean to Be Alone?', in Rita Astuti, Jonathan Parry and Charles Stafford (eds), *Questions of Anthropology*. Oxford: Berg, pp. 1–28.
Baas, Michiel and Brenda S.A. Yeoh. 2019. 'Introduction: Migration Studies and Critical Temporalities', *Current Sociology Monograph* 67(2): 161–68.
Barber, Pauline Gardiner and Winnie Lem (eds). 2018. *Migration, Temporality, and Capitalism: Entangled Mobilities across Global Spaces*. Cham: Springer International Publishing.
Barth, Fredrik (ed.). 1998 [1969]. *Ethnic Groups and Boundaries: The Social Organization of Culture Difference*. Long Grove, IL: Waveland Press.
Beck, Ulrich. 1992. *Risk Society: Towards a New Modernity*. London; Newbury Park, CA: Sage Publications.
Beck, Ulrich and Elisabeth Beck-Gernsheim. 2001. *Individualization: Institutionalized Individualism and Its Social and Political Consequences*. London: SAGE Publications.
Binah-Pollak, Avital. 2019. *Cross-Border Marriages and Mobility: Female Chinese Migrants and Hong Kong Men*. Amsterdam: Amsterdam University Press.
Birge, Bettine. 1995. 'Levirate Marriage and the Revival of Widow Chastity in Yüan China', *Asia Major*, Third Series, 8(2): 107–46.
Brainer, Amy. 2017a. 'Patrilineal Kinship and Transgender Embodiment in Taiwan', in Howard Chiang and Yin Wang (eds), *Perverse Taiwan*. London; New York: Routledge, pp. 110–28.
———. 2017b. 'Materializing "Family Pressure" among Taiwanese Queer Women', *Feminist Formations* 29(3): 1–24.
———. 2017c. 'Mothering Gender and Sexually Nonconforming Children in Taiwan', *Journal of Family Issues* 38(7): 921–47.
———. 2018. 'New Identities or New Intimacies? Reframing "Coming Out" in Taiwan through Cross-Generational Ethnography', *Sexualities* 21(5–6): 914–31.
———. 2019. *Queer Kinship and Family Change in Taiwan*. New Brunswick, NJ: Rutgers University Press.
Brandtstädter, Susanne. 2009. 'The Gender of Work and the Production of Kinship Value in Taiwan', in Susanne Brandtstädter and Gonçalo D. Santos (eds), *Chinese Kinship:*

Contemporary Anthropological Perspectives. Milton Park, Abingdon, Oxon: Routledge, pp. 154–78.
Bray, Francesca. 1997. *Technology and Gender Fabrics of Power in Late Imperial China*. Berkeley, CA: University of California Press.
Brown, Judith K. 2004. 'Transitions in the Life-Course of Women', in Carol R. Ember and Melvin Ember (eds), *Encyclopedia of Sex and Gender*. New York: Kluwer Academic-Plenum, pp. 163–74.
Bruckermann, Charlotte. 2017. 'Caring Claims and the Relational Self across Time: Grandmothers Overcoming Reproductive Crises in Rural China', *Journal of the Royal Anthropological Institute* N. S. (23): 356–75.
———. 2019. 'Why Do Grandparents Grumble? Chinese Children's Birthdays between Kinship, Market, and State', *Ethnos* 85(1): 145–67.
Carsten, Janet. 1995. 'The Substance of Kinship and the Heat of the Hearth: Feeding, Personhood and Relatedness among Malays of Pulau Langkawi', *American Ethnologist* 22(2): 223–41.
——— (ed.). 2000. *Cultures of Relatedness: New Approaches to the Study of Kinship*. Cambridge: Cambridge University Press.
———. 2004. *After Kinship*. Cambridge: Cambridge University Press.
———. 2013. 'What Kinship Does – and How', *HAU: Journal of Ethnographic Theory* 3(2): 245–51.
———. 2019. 'The Stuff of Kinship', in Sandra Bamford (ed.), *The Cambridge Handbook of Kinship*. Cambridge: Cambridge University Press, pp. 133–50.
———. 2021. 'Marriage and Self-Fashioning in Penang, Malaysia: Transformations of the Intimate and the Political', in Janet Carsten et al. (eds), *Marriage in Past, Present, and Future Tense*. London: UCL Press, pp. 140–59.
Carsten, Janet, et al. (eds). 2021. *Marriage in Past, Present, and Future Tense*. London: UCL Press.
Chan, Shelly. 2018. *Diasporas Homeland: Modern China in the Age of Global Migration*. Durham, NC: Duke University Press.
Chang, Doris T. 2009. *Women's Movements in Twentieth-Century Taiwan*. Urbana, IL: University of Illinois Press.
Chang, Kyung-Sup. 2010. *South Korea under Compressed Modernity: Familial Political Economy in Transition*. London: Routledge.
Chang, Lung-chih. 2014. 'Colonialism and Modernity in Taiwan: Reflections on Contemporary Taiwanese Historiography', in Susanne Weigelin-Schwiedrzik (ed.), *Broken Narratives: Post-Cold War History and Identity in Europe and East Asia*. Leiden: Brill, pp. 133–64.
Chao, Antonia Yen-Ning. 2004a. 'Gongmin Shenfen, Xiandai Guojia yu Qinmi Shenghuo: Yi Lao Danshen Rongmin yu "Dalu Xinniang" de Hunyin wei Yanjiu Anli' [The Modern State, Citizenship, and the Intimate Life: A Case Study of Taiwan's Glorious Citizens and their Mainland Wives], *Taiwanese Sociology* 8: 1–41.
———. 2004b. 'Xiandaixing Xiangxiang yu Guojing Guanli de Chongtu: Yi Waiji Peiou Yimin wei Yanjiu Anli' [Imagined Modernities, Transnational Migration, and Border Control: A Case Study of Taiwan's 'Mainland Brides'], *Taiwanese Journal of Sociology* 32: 59–102.
———. 2008. 'Qinmi Guanxi zuowei Fansi Guozuzhuyi de Changyu: Lao Rongmin de Liangan Hunyin Chongtu' [Nationalism and its Moral Struggles in Intimate Relationships: A Case Study of Old Veterans' Cross-Strait Marriage], *Taiwanese Sociology* 16: 97–148.

Chau, Adam Y. 2004. 'Hosting Funerals and Temple Festivals: Folk Event Productions in Rural China', *Asian Anthropology* 3(1): 39–70.
Chen, Changching. 2006. *Kinmen Teyue Chashi* [Special Assignation Teahouses on Kinmen]. Kinmen: Kinmen xian wenhuaju.
Chen, Chao-ju. 2019. 'Migrating Marriage Equality without Feminism – Obergefell v. Hodges and the Legalization of Same-Sex Marriage in Taiwan', *Cornell International Law Journal* 52(1): 65–108.
Chen, Da. 2011 [1939]. *Nanyang Huaqiao yu Min Yue Shehui* [Overseas Chinese in Southeast Asia and Fujian and Guangdong Society]. Beijing: The Commercial Press.
Chen, Mei-Hua. 2015. 'The "Fake Marriage" Test in Taiwan: Gender, Sexuality, and Border Control', *Cross-Currents: East Asian History and Culture Review* 15: 82–107.
Chen, Yu-Hua. 2012. 'Trends in Low Fertility and Policy Responses in Taiwan', *Japanese Journal of Population* 10(1): 78–88.
Chen, Yu-Hua and Hsinmu Chen. 2014. 'Continuity and Changes in the Timing and Formation of First Marriage among Postwar Birth Cohorts in Taiwan', *Journal of Family Issues* 35 (12): 1584–1604.
Cheng, Isabelle. 2017. 'Reality or Pretense? Renouncing Nationality and Organized Hypocrisy of the Sovereignty of Taiwan', *Asian and Pacific Migration Journal* 26(4): 436–58.
———. 2018. 'Saving the Nation by Sacrificing Your Life: Authoritarianism and Chiang Kai-shek's War for the Retaking of China', *Journal of Current Chinese Affairs* 47(2): 55–86.
Cheng, Tun-Jen. 2001. 'Transforming Taiwan's Economic Structure in the 20th Century', *The China Quarterly* 165: 19–36.
Cheng, Yen-hsin Alice. 2014. 'Changing Partner Choice and Marriage Propensities by Education in Post-Industrial Taiwan, 2000–2010', *Demographic Research* 31: 1007–42.
Cheng, Yen-hsin Alice and Chih-lan Winnie Yang. 2021. 'Continuity and Changes in Attitudes toward Marriage in Contemporary Taiwan', *Journal of Population Research* 38: 139–67.
Cherlin, Andrew J. 1978. 'Remarriage As An Incomplete Institution', *American Journal of Sociology* 84: 634–50.
———. 2004. 'The Deinstitutionalization of American Marriage', *Journal of Marriage and Family* 66(November): 848–61.
Chiang, Bo-wei. 2010. *Xingzhou Wumin: Xinjiapo Kinmenren de Zongxiang Huiguan* [Kinmen Migrants in Singapore: Kinmen Migrants' Associations in Singapore]. Kinmen: Kinmen Cultural Bureau.
———. 2011. 'Hybrid Modernity: A Study of Cultural Imagination and Practice of the Overseas Chinese in Modern Kinmen', *Journal of Chinese Ritual, Theatre and Folklore* 174: 185–257.
———. 2016. 'The Relationship between Translocal Chinese and Their Hometowns (1920s-40s): The View from "Shining" Monthly of Jushan, Quemoy', *Translocal Chinese: East Asian Perspectives* 10: 259–92.
Chiu, Hsiao-Chiao. 2017. 'An Island of the Floating World: Kinship, Rituals, and Political-Economic Change in Post-Cold War Jinmen', PhD dissertation. London: London School of Economics and Political Science.
———. 2018a. 'Cooperation in Funerals in a Patrilineal Village in Jinmen (Taiwan)', in Charles Stafford, Ellen R. Judd and Eona Bell (eds), *Cooperation in Chinese Communities: Morality and Practice*. London: Bloomsbury, pp. 81–100.
———. 2018b. 'Women's Labour, Kinship, and Economic Changes in Jinmen in the Era of Authoritarian Rule', *Journal of Current Chinese Affairs* 47(2): 193–218.

Chiu, Tuen Yi. 2020. 'Everyday Mixed Status: Spillover Effects of State Power in Mainland China-Hong Kong Cross-Border Families', *Gender, Place & Culture* 27(5): 643–59.
Chiu, Tuen Yi and Susanne Y.P. Choi. 2020. 'The Decoupling of the Legal Migration and Spatial Migration of Female Marriage Migrants', *Journal of Ethnic and Migration Studies* 46(14): 2997–3013.
Chiu, Tuen Yi and Brenda S.A. Yeoh. 2021. 'Marriage Migration, Family and Citizenship in Asia', *Citizenship Studies* 25(7): 879–97.
Chou, Miao-chen. 2009. *Zhandi Shiqi Kinmen Funü yu Xingxiang, 1949–1978* [Women and their Images in Militarized Kinmen, 1949–1978]. Kinmen: Kinmen xian wenhuaju.
Chow, Tse-tsung. 1960. *The May Fourth Movement: Intellectual Revolution in Modern China*. Cambridge, MA: Harvard University Press.
Chu, Wei-cheng. 2003. 'Tongzhi Taiwan: Xing-gongmin, Guozu Jiangou huo Gongmin Shehui' [Queer(ing) Taiwan: Sexual Citizenship, Nation-building or Civil Society], *Journal of Women's and Gender Studies* 15: 115–51.
Chung, Wei-Yun. 2021. 'Gendering Distance, Gendered Housework: Examining the Gendered Power Dynamics through Housework Allocation in Taiwanese Homes', *Gender, Place & Culture*, DOI: 10.1080/0966369X.2021.1974355
Chyn, Yu-Rung. 2019. 'Zhaogu, Laodong yu Xingbie Pingdeng: Cong Funü Xinzhi Jijinhui de Changyi Jingyan Tanqi' [Care, Labour and Gender Equality: A Talk on the Experiences of Advocacy of Awakening Foundation], *Forum in Women's and Gender Studies* 110: 40–47.
Cohen, Myron L. 1976. *House United, House Divided: The Chinese Family in Taiwan*. New York: Columbia University Press.
Cole, Jennifer and Lynn M. Thomas (eds). 2009. *Love in Africa*. Chicago; London: The University of Chicago Press.
Constable, Nicole (ed.) 2005. *Cross-Border Marriages: Gender and Mobility in Transnational Asia*. Philadelphia: University of Pennsylvania Press.
———. 2009. 'The Commodification of Intimacy: Marriage, Sex, and Reproductive Labor', *Annual Review of Anthropology* 38: 49–64.
Croll, Elisabeth. 1978. *Feminism and Socialism in China*. London; Henley; Boston: Routledge & Kegan Paul.
———. 1984. 'The Exchange of Women and Property: Marriage in Post-Revolutionary China', in Renée Hirschon (ed.), *Women and Property-Women As Property*. London: Croom Helm, pp. 44–61.
Cruz, Resto. 2019. 'An Inheritance That Cannot Be Stolen: Schooling, Kinship, and Personhood in Post-1945 Central Philippines', *Comparative Studies in Society and History* 61(4): 894–924.
Das, Veena. 2007. *Life and Words: Violence and the Descent into the Ordinary*. Berkeley, CA; London: University of California Press.
———. 2012. 'Ordinary Ethics', in Didier Fassin (ed.), *A Companion to Moral Anthropology*. Chichester; Malden, MA: Wiley-Blackwell, pp. 133–49.
———. 2018a. 'Ethics, Self-Knowledge, and Life Taken As A Whole', *HAU: Journal of Ethnographic Theory* 8(3): 537–49.
———. 2018b. 'On Singularity and the Event: Further Reflections on the Ordinary', in James Laidlaw, Barbara Bodenhorn and Martin Holbraad (eds), *Recovering the Human Subject: Freedom, Creativity and Decision*. Cambridge: Cambridge University Press, pp. 53–73.
Davis, Deborah S. and Sara L. Friedman (eds). 2014. *Wives, Husbands, and Lovers: Marriage and Sexuality in Hong Kong, Taiwan, and Urban China*. Stanford, CA: Stanford University Press.

Davis, Deborah S. and Sara L. Friedman. 2014. 'Deinstitutionalizing Marriage and Sexuality', in Deborah S. Davis and Sara L. Friedman (eds), *Wives, Husbands, and Lovers: Marriage and Sexuality in Hong Kong, Taiwan, and Urban China*. Stanford, CA: Stanford University Press, pp. 1–38.

Diamond, Norma. 1975. 'Women under Kuomintang Rule: Variations on the Feminine Mystique', *Modern China* 1(1): 3–45.

Ding, Yuling. 2004. 'Transnational Networks and Social Change in An Emigrant Village in Fujian', PhD dissertation. Hong Kong: The Chinese University of Hong Kong.

Donner, Henrike and Gonçalo D. Santos. 2016. 'Love, Marriage, and Intimate Citizenship in Contemporary China and India: An Introduction', *Modern Asian Studies* 50(4): 1123–46.

Ebrey, Patricia Buckley. 1993. *The Inner Quarters: Marriage and the Lives of Chinese Women in the Sung Period*. Berkeley, CA; London: University of California Press.

Evans, Harriet. 2008. *The Subject of Gender: Daughters and Mothers in Urban China*. Lanham, MD.: Rowman & Littlefield Publishers.

Evans-Pritchard, Edward E. 1951. *Kinship and Marriage among the Nuer*. Oxford: Oxford University Press.

Faier, Lieba. 2009. *Intimate Encounters: Filipina Women and the Remaking of Rural Japan*. Berkeley, CA; London: University of California Press.

Fan, Yu-Wen. 2006. 'Hunyin yu Jundui Zhandou Shiqi: Guojia Guanzhi xia Daluji Shiguanbing de Nanzhixing (1950–1970)' [Marriage and Military Morale: Masculinity of Soldiers from the Chinese Mainland under State Governance, 1950–1970], *The Annual Meeting of Taiwanese Sociological Association*, 25–26 November 2006. Taichung: Tunghai University.

Fan, Yun. 2019. *Social Movements in Taiwan's Democratic Transition: Linking Activists to the Changing Political Environment*. Abingdon, Oxon; New York: Routledge, Taylor & Francis Group.

Fassin, Didier (ed.). 2020. *Deepening Divides: How Territorial Borders and Social Boundaries Delineate Our World*. London: Pluto Press.

Faure, David. 2007. *Emperor and Ancestor: State and Lineage in South China*. Stanford, CA: Stanford University Press.

Fischer, Carolin, Christin Achermann and Janine Dahinden. 2020. 'Editorial: Revisiting Borders and Boundaries: Exploring Migrant Inclusion and Exclusion from Intersectional Perspectives', *Migration Letters* 17(4): 477–85.

Fong, Vanessa L. 2004. *Only Hope: Coming of Age under China's One-Child Policy*. Stanford, CA: Stanford University Press.

———. 2011. *Paradise Redefined: Transnational Chinese Students and the Quest for Flexible Citizenship in the Developed World*. Stanford, CA: Stanford University Press.

Fortes, Meyer. 1949. *The Web of Kinship among the Tallensi: The Second Part of An Analysis of the Social Structure of A Trans-Volta Tribe*. London: Oxford University Press.

Freedman, Maurice. 1958. *Lineage Organisation in Southeastern China*. London: Athlone Press.

———. 1966. *Chinese Lineage and Society: Fukien and Kwangtung*. London: Athlone Press.

Freeman, Caren. 2011. *Making and Faking Kinship: Marriage and Labor Migration between China and South Korea*. Ithaca, NY: Cornell University Press.

Friedman, Sara L. 2010a. 'Determining "Truth" at the Border: Immigration Interviews, Chinese Marital Migrants, and Taiwan's Sovereignty Dilemmas', *Citizenship Studies* 14(2): 167–83.

———. 2010b. 'Marital Immigration and Graduated Citizenship: Post-Naturalization Restrictions on Mainland Chinese Spouses in Taiwan', *Pacific Affairs* 83(1): 73–93.

———. 2015. *Exceptional States: Chinese Immigrants and Taiwanese Sovereignty*. Oakland, CA: University of California Press.

Fwu, Bi-Jen. 1999. 'Who Became Teachers? – Changes in the Composition of Taiwanese Teachers', *Proceedings of the National Science Council: Part C, Humanities and Social Sciences* 9(3): 377–97.

Gaetano, Arianne. 2014. '"Leftover Women": Postponing Marriage and Renegotiating Womanhood in Urban China', *Journal of Research in Gender Studies* 4(2): 124–49.

Gallin, Bernard. 1967. 'Emerging Individualism in Changing Rural Taiwan', *Journal of the China Society* 5: 3–8.

Gallin, S. Rita. 1984. 'The Entry of Chinese Women into the Rural Labor Force: A Case Study from Taiwan', *Signs: Journal of Women in Culture and Society* 9(3): 383–98.

———. 1986. 'Mothers-in-Law and Daughters-in-Law: Intergenerational Relations Within the Chinese Family in Taiwan', *Journal of Cross-Cultural Gerontology* 1: 31–49.

Gell, Alfred. 1988. 'Technology and Magic', *Anthropology Today* 4(2): 6–9.

Giddens, Anthony. 1992. *The Transformation of Intimacy: Sexuality, Love and Eroticism in Modern Societies*. Cambridge: Polity Press.

———. 1998. *The Third Way: The Renewal of Social Democracy*. Cambridge: Polity Press.

Glosser, Susan. 2003. *Chinese Visions of Family and State, 1915–1953*. Berkeley, CA: University of California Press.

Godley, Michael R. 1981. *The Mandarin-Capitalists from Nanyang: Overseas Chinese Enterprise in the Modernisation of China, 1893–1911*. Cambridge: Cambridge University Press.

Gold, Thomas B. 1986. *State and Society in the Taiwan Miracle*. Armonk, NY: M.E. Sharpe.

Goodkind, Daniel. 1997. 'The Vietnamese Double Marriage Squeeze', *International Migration Review* 31(1): 108–27.

Graeber, David. 2013. 'It Is Value that Brings Universes into Being', *HAU: Journal of Ethnographic Theory* 3(2): 219–43.

Guo, Dinh-Yin. 1997. 'The Social Mobility of the Students in Teachers College', *Proceedings of the National Science Council: Part C, Humanities and Social Sciences* 7(2): 181–97.

Han-Yu. 2012. *Bansheng Rongma zai Kinmen: Lao Rongmin de Gushi* [The Stories of Veterans in Kinmen]. Kinmen: Kinmen xian wenhuaju.

Hirsch, Jennifer S. and Holly Wardlow (eds). 2006. *Modern Loves: The Anthropology of Romantic Courtship and Companionate Marriage*. Ann Arbor: University of Michigan Press.

Ho, Ming-sho. 2019. 'Taiwan's Road to Marriage Equality: Politics of Legalizing Same-Sex Marriage', *China Quarterly* 238: 482–503.

———. 2020. 'The Religion-Based Conservative Countermovement in Taiwan: Origin, Tactics and Impacts', in David Chiavacci, Simona Grano and Julia Obinger (eds), *Civil Society and the State in Democratic East Asia*. Amsterdam: Amsterdam University Press, pp. 141–65.

Hom, Marlon K. 2010. 'Voices of Resistance and Subversion: Folksongs on Emigration and Family in the Pearl River Delta', *Overseas Chinese History Studies* 4: 31–44.

Hong Fincher, Leta. 2014. *Leftover Women: The Resurgence of Gender Inequality in China*. London; New York: Zed.

Hong, Yuru. 2017. *Jindai Taiwan Nuxing Shi: Rizhi Shiqi Xing Nuxin de Dansheng* [The History of Women in Modern Taiwan: The Birth of New Women in the Period of Japanese Governance]. Taipei: National Taiwan University Press.

Howlett, Zachary M. 2020. 'Tactics of Marriage Delay in China: Education, Rural-to-Urban Migration, and "Leftover Women"', in Marcia C. Inhorn and Nancy J. Smith-Hefner (eds), *Waithood: Gender, Education, and Global Delays in Marriage and Childbearing*. New York; Oxford: Berghahn Books, pp. 177–209.

Hsia, Hsiao-Chuan. 2007. 'Imaged and Imagined Threat to the Nation: The Media Construction of the "Foreign Brides' Phenomenon" As Social Problems in Taiwan', *Inter-Asia Cultural Studies* 8(1): 55–85.

Hsiau, A-chin. 2005. 'Generational Identity and Historical Narrative: The Emergence of the "Back-to-Reality" Generation in 1970s Taiwan', *Taiwanese Sociology* 9: 1–58.

Hsu, Francis L.K. 1948. *Under the Ancestors' Shadow: Chinese Culture and Personality*. New York: Columbia University Press.

Hsu, Hui-Chi. 2005. 'Guo Xin Shenghuo Zuo Xin Nüxing: Xunzheng Shiqi Guomin Zhengfu dui Shidai Nüxing Xingxiang de Suzao' [Living New Life, Being New Woman: The Image-making of Modern Ideal Woman by KMT Government in the Nanjing Decade], *Humanitas Taiwanica* 62: 277–320.

Hsu, Madeline. 2000. *Dreaming of Gold, Dreaming of Home: Transnationalism and Migration between the United States and South China, 1882–1943*. Stanford, CA: Stanford University Press.

Hsu, Mei, Yih-Chyi Chuang and Yen-Ling Chen. 2015. 'Preliminary Analysis of the Sources of Household Income Inequality in Taiwan', *Review of Social Sciences* 9(1): 1–31.

Hsu, Mei-Yu. 2009. *Qianxian Nüxing zai Baodao: Yonghe Diqu Kinmen Funü Shenghuo Yanjiu, 1949–2001* [Women From the Battlefield to Taiwan: Life Stories of Women from Kinmen and Living in Yonghe, 1949–2001]. Kinmen: Kinmen xian wenhuaju.

Hu, Shu and Zheng Mu. 2021. 'Extended Gender Inequality? Intergenerational Coresidence and Division of Household Labor', *Social Science Research* 93: 102497.

Hu, Tai-li. 1999. 'Taros and Sweet Potatoes: Ethnic Relations and Identities of "Glorious Citizens" (Veteran-mainlanders) in Taiwan', *Bulletin of the Institute of Ethnology, Academia Sinica* 69: 107–32.

Hu, Yu-Ying. 2017. 'Cong "Xianshen" dao "Guanxi": Taiwan Xingbie Shehui Bianqian yu Nütongzhi Qinzi Xieshang' [From Visibility to Relationality: Changing Socio-gender Structure and Lesbian Parent-child Negotiation in Contemporary Taiwan], *Journal of Women's and Gender Studies* 40: 107–51.

———. 2018. 'He yi wei "Jia"? Kuer Quanqiuhua zhong de Tongzhi yu Jiating' [How to Make a "Family"? LGBT and the Family in the Era of Queer Globalization], in Mei-Hua Chen, Hsiu-Yun Wang and Yu-Ling Huang (eds), *Yuwangxing Gongmin: Tongxing Qinmi Gongminquan Duben* [Citizens with Desires: A Collection of Essays about LGBTQ Intimate Citizenship]. Kaohsiung: Chuliu, pp. 59–78.

Huang, Deng-Shing. 2015. 'On the Wage Stagnation of Taiwan: Trade and FDI Partners under Globalization', *Review of Social Sciences* 9(1): 33–58.

Huang, Jia-Li. 2019. 'A Historical Approach on the Government-Funded System for Teacher Preparation', *Journal of Research in Education Sciences* 64(2): 99–129.

Huang, Lang-Wen Wendy. 2013. 'The Transition Tempo and Life Course Orientation of Young Adults in Taiwan', *Annals of the American Academy of Political and Social Science* 646: 69–85.

Ikels, Charlotte (ed.). 2004. *Filial Piety: Practice and Discourse in Contemporary East Asia*. Palo Alto, CA: Stanford University Press.

Inhorn, Marcia C. 2020. 'The Egg Freezing Revolution? Gender, Education, and Reproductive Waithood in the United States', in Marcia C. Inhorn and Nancy J. Smith-Hefner (eds), *Waithood: Gender, Education, and Global Delays in Marriage and Childbearing*. New York; Oxford: Berghahn Books, pp. 362–90.
Inhorn, Marcia C. and Nancy J. Smith-Hefner (eds). 2020. *Waithood: Gender, Education, and Global Delays in Marriage and Childbearing*. New York; Oxford: Berghahn Books.
Ishikawa, Yoshitaka. 2010. 'Role of Matchmaking Agencies for International Marriage in Contemporary Japan', *Geographical Review of Japan Series* B 83(1): 1–14.
Johnson, C. et al. 2011. 'Interventions on Rethinking "the Broder" in Border Studies', *Political Geography* 30: 61–69.
Johnston, James. 2013. 'Filial Paths and the Ordinary Ethics of Movement', in Charles Stafford (ed.), *Ordinary Ethics in China*. London; New York: Berg, pp. 45–65.
Jones, Gavin W. and Bina Gubhaju. 2009. 'Factors Influencing Changes in Mean Age at First Marriage and Proportions Never Marrying in the Low Fertility Countries of East and Southeast Asia', *Asian Population Studies* 5(3): 237–65.
Juan, Kuanying. 2003. 'Kuajie Dixia Jingji: Kinmen Xiao Maoyi zhi Shehui Fenxi [The Cross-border Informal Economy: A Study of Small Trades in Kinmen]', Master's dissertation. Taipei: National Taiwan University.
Judd, Ellen. 1989. 'Niangjia: Chinese Women and Their Natal Families', *The Journal of Asian Studies* 48(3): 525–44.
———. 2009. '"Families We Create": Women's Kinship in Rural China As Spatialized Practice', in Susanne Brandstädter and Gonçalo D. Santos (eds), *Chinese Kinship: Contemporary Anthropological Perspectives*. London: Routledge, pp. 29–47.
Kandiyoti, Deniz. 1988. 'Bargaining with Patriarchy', *Gender and Society* 2(3): 274–90.
Kao, Ming-Tse. 2014. *Taiwan Diming Ci Shu, Juan 24, Kinmen Xian* [Encyclopedia of Names of Places in Taiwan, Vol. 24, Kinmen County]. Nantou: Guoshiguan Taiwan wenxian guan.
Kim, Minjeong. 2013. 'Citizenship Projects for Marriage Migrants in South Korea: Intersecting Motherhood with Ethnicity and Class', *Social Politics* 20(4): 455–81.
Kinmen xian wenxian weiyuanhui (ed.). 1968. *Kinmen Xian Zhi* [The Gazetteer of Kinmen County]. Kinmen: Kinmen xian zhengfu.
Kipnis, Andrew B. 2009. 'Education and the Governing of Child-Centred Relatedness', in Susanne Brandstädter and Gonçalo D. Santos (eds), *Chinese Kinship: Contemporary Anthropological Perspectives*. London: Routledge, pp. 204–22.
———. 2011. *Governing Educational Desire: Culture, Politics, and Schooling in China*. Chicago: University of Chicago Press.
Knight, Daniel M. 2018. 'The Desire for Disinheritance in Austerity Greece', *Focaal–Journal of Global and Historical Anthropology* 80: 30–42.
Kuhn, Philip A. 2008. *Chinese among Others: Emigration in Modern Times*. Lanham, MD: Rowman and Littlefield.
Kulp, Daniel H. 1925. *Country Life in South China*. New York: Teachers College, Columbia University.
Kung, Hsiang-Ming. 2019. 'Persistence and Change in the Comparative Status of Mothers-in-Law and Daughters-in-Law in Taiwanese Families: 1979 to 2016', *Journal of Family Issues* 40(14): 1937–62.
Kung, Lydia. 1983. *Factory Women in Taiwan*. Ann Arbor, MI: UMI Research Press.
Kunreuther, Laura. 2009. 'Between Love and Property: Voice, Sentiment, and Subjectivity in the Reform of Daughter's Inheritance in Nepal', *American Ethnologist* 36(3): 545–62.

Kwon, Heonik. 2010. *The Other Cold War*. New York: Columbia University Press.
Lamb, Sarah. 2018. 'Being Single in India: Gendered Identities, Class Mobilities, and Personhoods in Flux', *Ethos* 46(1): 49–69.
Lambek, Michael. 2011. 'Kinship As Gift and Theft: Acts of Succession in Mayotte and Ancient Israel', *American Ethnologist* 38(1): 2–16.
Lan, Pei-Chia. 2008. 'Migrant Women's Bodies As Boundary Markers: Reproductive Crisis and Sexual Control in the Ethnic Frontiers of Taiwan', *Signs: Journal of Women in Culture and Society* 33(4): 833–61.
———. 2018. *Raising Global Families: Parenting, Immigration, and Class in Taiwan and the US*. Stanford, CA: Stanford University Press.
Lang, Olga. 1946. *Chinese Family and Society*. New Haven, CT: Yale University Press.
Lee, Anru. 2004a. *In the Name of Harmony and Prosperity: Labor and Gender Politics in Taiwan's Economic Restructuring*. Albany, NY: State University of New York.
———. 2004b. 'Between Filial Daughter and Loyal Sister: Global Economy and Family Politics in Taiwan', in: Catherine S. Farris, Anru Lee and Murray A. Rubinstein (eds), *Women in the New Taiwan: Gender Roles and Gender Consciousness in A Changing Society*. Armonk, NY: M.E. Sharpe, pp. 101–19.
Lee, Cheng-En. 2018. 'Kinmen Nan Tongzhi de Rentong Licheng' [The Sexual Orientation Identity Formation Process of Kinmenese Gays], Master's dissertation. Changhua: National Changhua University of Education.
Lee, Hyunok, Lindy Williams and Florio Arguillas. 2016. 'Adapting to Marriage Markets: International Marriage Migration from Vietnam to South Korea', *Journal of Comparative Family Studies* 47(2): 267–88.
Lee, Mei-Lin and Te-Hsiung Sun. 1995. 'The Family and Demography in Contemporary Taiwan', *Journal of Comparative Families Studies* 26(1): 101–15.
Lee, Zong-Rong and Thung-Hong Lin (eds). 2017. *Weijing de Qiji: Zhuanxing zhong de Taiwan Jingji yu Shehui* [Unfinished Miracle: Taiwan's Economy and Society in Transition]. Taipei: Sociology Institute of Sociology, Academia Sinica.
Lévi-Strauss, Claude. 1969 [1949]. *The Elementary Structures of Kinship*, trans. James Harle Bell, John Richard von Sturmer and Rodney Needham. Boston, MA: Beacon Press.
Li, Cheng-Chi and Yu-Lin Lee (eds). 2015. *The Empires on Taiwan: Time, Space, Knowledge, and Sentiment of Colonial Taiwan*. Taipei: National Taiwan University Press.
Li, Chi-ping. 1998. '"Yu Bing yu Nong" de Dongbu Tuifu Laobing: Yige Tunken de Huo Lishi' [The Old Veterans as Farmers in East Taiwan: A Living History of Farming and Settling], Master's dissertation. Hualien: National Dong Hwa University.
Li, Shide (ed.) 2009. *Kinmen Xian Zhi* [The Gazetteer of Kinmen County]. Kinmen: Kinmen xianzhengfu.
Liang, Hui-Ling. 2018. 'Kinmen Xian Changzhu Renkou Tuigu zhi Tantao' [The Study of Calculating the Number of Resident Population in Kinmen County], *Zhuji Yuekan* 756: 38–44.
Liao, Ping-hui and David Der-wei Wang. 2006. *Taiwan under Japanese Colonial Rule, 1895–1945: History, Culture, Memory*. New York: Columbia University Press.
Lin, Ju-Ping and Chin-Chun Yi. 2013. 'A Comparative Analysis of Intergenerational Relations in East Asia', *International Sociology* 28(3): 297–315.
Lin, Kunhuang. 1993 [1882]. *Kinmen Zhi* [The Gazetteer of Kinmen County]. Nantou: Taiwan sheng wenxian weiyuanhui.
Lin, Tung-Fa. 2009. *1949 Da Chetui* [The Great Retreat in 1949]. Taipei: Linking Publishing.

Lin, Wei-Ping. 2021. *Island Fantasia: Imagining Subjects on the Military Frontline between China and Taiwan.* Cambridge; New York: Cambridge University Press.

Lin, Wen-Ling. 2014. 'Kua Xingbie Zhe de Chengjia zhi Dao' [The Ways in Which Transgender People Create their Families], in Ying-Kuei Huang (ed.), *21 Shiji de Jia: Taiwan de Jia He Qu He Cong?* [Family in the Twenty-First Century: Where is the Taiwanese Family Headed?]. New Taipei City: Socio Publishing, pp. 169–200.

Liou, Liang-ya. 2005. 'Queer Theory and Politics in Taiwan: The Cultural Translation of (Re) Production of Queerness in and beyond Taiwan Lesbian/Gay/ Queer Activism', *NTU Studies in Language and Literature* 14: 123–54.

Liu, Fengshu. 2008. 'Negotiating the Filial Self: Young-Adult Only-Children and Intergenerational Relationships in China', *Young* 16(4): 409–30.

Liu, Hsiang-Chin. 2006. 'Fuhui Qiaojuan Funü de Shenghuo Tuxiang: Tantao Kinmen Diqu 1930–1950 Qiaojuan Jiating Funü de Jiaose yu Gongneng' [The Depiction of the Lives of the Wives of Overseas Chinese Migrants from Kinmen: Exploring their Role and Function in their Homeland, Kinmen, 1930–1950], Master's dissertation. Taipei: Ming Chuan University.

Liu, Jieyu. 2004. 'Holding Up the Sky? Reflections on Marriage in Contemporary China', *Feminism & Psychology* 14(1): 195–202.

Liu, Jin (ed.). 1958 [1921]. *Kinmen Xian Zhi* [The Gazetteer of Kinmen County]. Kinmen: Kinmen xian wenxian weiyuanhui.

Lu, Hsin-Yi. 2014. 'Difang Wenhua de Zai Chuangzao: Cong Shequ Zongti Yingzao dao Wenhua Chanye' [The Re-creation of Local Cultures: From Community Empowerment to Cultural Industries], in Shu-Rong Lin, Zhong-Min Chen and Maa-Ling Chen (eds), *Chongdu Taiwan: Renleixue de Shiye* [Anthropological Study of Taiwan over the Last Century: Accomplishment and Prospects]. Xinzhu: National Tsing Hua University, pp. 151–89.

Lu, Jennifer. 2020. 'Shifting Public Opinion in Different Cultural Contexts: Marriage Equality in Taiwan', *Georgetown Journal of International Affairs* XXI: 209–15.

Lu, Melody Chia-Wen. 2005. 'Commercially Arranged Marriage Migration: Case Studies of Cross-Border Marriage in Taiwan', *Indian Journal of Gender Studies* 12(2&3): 275–303.

———. 2008. 'Gender, Marriage and Migration: Contemporary Marriages between Mainland China and Taiwan', PhD dissertation. Leiden: Leiden University.

Lu, Weijing. 2008. *True to Her Word: The Faithful Maiden Cult in Late Imperial China.* Stanford, CA: Stanford University Press.

Magee, Siobhan. 2021. '"You Can Learn to Do it Right, or You Can Learn to Do it Wrong": Marriage Counselling, Togetherness and Creative Conservatism in Lynchburg, Virginia', in Janet Carsten et al. (eds), *Marriage in Past, Present, and Future Tense.* London: UCL Press, pp. 54–75.

Mann, Susan. 1991. 'Grooming A Daughter for Marriage: Brides and Wives in the Mid-Ching Period', in Rubie Watson and Patricia Buckley Ebrey (eds), *Marriage and Inequality in Chinese Society.* Berkeley, CA: University of California Press, pp. 204–30.

———. 2011. *Gender and Sexuality in Modern Chinese History.* New York: Cambridge University Press.

Maqsood, Ammara. 2021a. 'Love As Understanding: Marriage, Aspiration, and the Joint Family in Middle-Class Pakistan', *American Ethnologist* 48(1): 93–104.

———. 2021b. 'Love in Liminality: The Modes and Spaces of Intimacy in Middle-Class Pakistan', *South Asian History and Culture* 12(2–3): 261–77.

Masuda, Hajimu. 2015. *Cold War Crucible: The Korean Conflict and the Postwar World*. Cambridge, MA: Harvard University Press.

Mazumdar, Sucheta. 2003. 'What Happened to the Women? Chinese and Indian Male Migration to the United States in Global Perspective', in Shirley Hune and Gail Nomura (eds), *Asia/Pacific Islander American Women: A Historical Anthology*. New York: New York University Press, pp. 58–74.

McKeown, Adam. 2001. *Chinese Migrant Networks and Cultural Change: Peru, Chicago, Hawaii, 1900–1936*. Chicago: University of Chicago Press.

McKinnon, Susan. 2013. 'Kinship within and beyond the "Movement of Progressive Societies"', in Susan McKinnon and Fenella Cannell (eds), *Vital Relations: Modernity and the Persistent Life of Kinship*. Santa Fe, NM: SAR Press, pp. 39–62.

McKinnon, Susan and Fenella Cannell. 2013. 'The Difference Kinship Makes', in Susan McKinnon and Fenella Cannell (eds), *Vital Relations: Modernity and the Persistent Life of Kinship*. Santa Fe, NM: SAR Press, pp. 3–38.

Momesso, Lara and Isabelle Cheng. 2017. 'A Team Player Pursuing Its Own Dreams: Rights-Claim Campaign of Chinese Migrant Spouses in the Migrant Movement before and after 2008', in Dafydd Fell (ed.), *Taiwan's Social Movements under Ma Ying-jeou: From the Wild Strawberries to the Sunflowers*. Abingdon: Routledge, pp. 219–35.

Nakano, Lynne. 2016. 'Single Women and the Transition to Marriage in Hong Kong, Shanghai and Tokyo', *Asian Journal of Social Science* 44: 363–90.

Newman, David. 2006. 'The Lines That Continue to Separate Us: Borders in Our "Borderless" World', *Progress in Human Geography* 31(2): 143–61.

Obendiek, Helena. 2016. 'Rural Family Backgrounds, Higher Education, and Marriage Negotiations in Northwest China', *Modern Asian Studies* 50(4): 1250–76.

Ochiai, Emiko. 2011. 'Unsustainable Societies: The Failure of Familialism in East Asia's Compressed Modernity', *Historical Social Research* 36(2): 219–45.

Ochiai, Emiko and Leo Aoi Hosoya (eds). 2014. *Transformation of the Intimate and the Public in Asian Modernity*. Leiden: Brill.

Oxfeld, Ellen. 1993. *Blood, Sweat and Mahjong: Family and Enterprise in an Overseas Chinese Community*. Ithaca, NY: Cornell University Press.

———. 2005. 'Cross-Border Hypergamy? Marriage Exchanges in A Transnational Hakka Community', in Nicole Constable (ed.), *Cross-Border Marriages: Gender and Mobility in Transnational Asia*. Philadelphia: University of Pennsylvania Press, pp. 17–33.

Paasi, Anssi et al. (eds). 2018. *Borderless Worlds for Whom? Ethics, Moralities and Mobilities*. London: Routledge.

Pai, Iris Erh-Ya. 2017. *Sexual Identity and Lesbian Family Life: Lesbianism, Patriarchalism and the Asian Family in Taiwan*. Singapore: Palgrave Macmillan.

Papadaki, Eirini. 2021. 'Marriage, Time, Affect and the Politics of Compromise in Athens', in Janet Carsten et al. (eds), *Marriage in Past, Present, and Future Tense*. London: UCL Press, pp. 76–94.

Pasternak, Burton. 1972. *Kinship and Community in Two Chinese Villages*. Stanford, CA: Stanford University Press.

Peletz, Michael G. 2001. 'Ambivalence in Kinship Since the 1940s', in Sarah Franklin and Susan McKinnon (eds), *Relative Values: Reconfiguring Kinship Studies*. Durham, NC: Duke University Press, pp. 413–44.

Radcliffe Brown, A.R. and Daryll Ford (eds). 1950. *African Systems of Kinship and Marriage*. London: Oxford University Press.

Raymo, James M. et al. 2015. 'Marriage and Family in East Asia: Continuity and Change', *The Annual Review of Sociology* 41: 471–92.

Rofel, Lisa and Sylvia Yanagisako. 2019. *Fabricating Transnational Capitalism: A Collaborative Ethnography of Italian-Chinese Global Fashion*. Durham, NC: Duke University Press.
San Román, Beatriz. 2020. 'Waiting Too Long to Mother: Involuntary Childlessness and Assisted Reproduction in Contemporary Spain', in Marcia C. Inhorn and Nancy J. Smith-Hefner (eds), *Waithood: Gender, Education, and Global Delays in Marriage and Childbearing*. New York; Oxford: Berghahn Books, pp. 339–61.
Sangren, P. Steven. 2000. *Chinese Sociologics: An Anthropological Account of the Role of Alienation in Social Reproduction*. London: The Athlone Press.
Santos, Gonçalo D. 2006. 'The Anthropology of Chinese Kinship: A Critical Overview', *European Journal of East Asian Studies* 5(2): 275–333.
———. 2021. *Chinese Village Life Today: Building Families in An Age of Transition*. Seattle: University of Washington Press.
Santos, Gonçalo D. and Stevan Harrell. 2017. 'Introduction', in Gonçalo D. Santos and Stevan Harrell (eds), *Transforming Patriarchy: Chinese Families in the Twenty-First Century*. Seattle: University of Washington Press, pp. 3–36.
Schubert, Gunter. 2016. *Routledge Handbook of Contemporary Taiwan*. London; New York: Routledge, Taylor & Francis Group.
Schwarcz, Vera. 1986. *The Chinese Enlightenment: Intellectuals and the Legacy of the May Fourth Movement of 1919*. Berkeley, CA: University of California Press.
Shen, Huifen. 2012. *China's Left-Behind Wives: Families of Migrants from Fujian to Southeast Asia, 1930s-1950s*. Hong Kong: Hong Kong University Press.
Shih, Kristy Y. and Karen Pyke. 2009. 'Power, Resistance, and Emotional Economies in Women's Relationships with Mothers-in-Law in Chinese Immigrant Families', *Journal of Family Issues* 31(3): 333–57.
Shih, Shu-mei. 1998. 'Gender and A New Geopolitics of Desire: The Seduction of Mainland Women in Taiwan and Hong Kong Media', *Signs: Journal of Women in Culture and Society* 23(2): 287–319.
Singerman, Diane. 2007. 'The Economic Imperatives of Marriage: Emerging Practices and Identities among Youth in the Middle East', *Middle East Youth Initiative*, Working Paper No. 6, September, The Brookings Institution, Wolfensohn Center for Development, Washington, DC.
———. 2013. 'Youth, Gender, and Dignity in the Egyptian Uprising', *Journal of Middle East Women's Studies* 9(3): 1–27.
Smith-Hefner Nancy J. and Marcia C. Inhorn. 2020. 'Introduction', in Marcia C. Inhorn and Nancy J. Smith-Hefner (eds), *Waithood: Gender, Education, and Global Delays in Marriage and Childbearing*. New York; Oxford: Berghahn Books, pp. 1–28.
So, Alvin Y. 2003. 'Cross-Border Families in Hong Kong: The Role of Social Class and Politics', *Critical Asian Studies* 35(4): 515–34.
Sommer, Matthew H. 2000. *Sex, Law, and Society in Late Imperial China*. Stanford, CA: Stanford University Press.
———. 2002. 'Dangerous Males, Vulnerable Males, and Polluted Males: The Regulation of Masculinity in Qing Dynasty Law', in Susan Brownell and Jeffrey Wasserstrom (eds), *Chinese Femininities/Chinese Masculinities: A Reader*. Berkeley, CA; London: University of California Press, pp. 67–88.
Sor, Chunghee Sarah. 2000. 'From Imperial Gifts to Sex Slaves: Theorizing Symbolic Representations of the "Comfort Women"', *Social Science Japan Journal* 3(1): 59–76.
Stafford, Charles. 1995. *The Roads of Chinese Childhood: Learning and Identification in Angang*. Cambridge: Cambridge University Press.

———. 2000a. 'Chinese Patriliny and the Cycles of Yang and Laiwang', in Janet Carsten (ed.), *Cultures of Relatedness*. Cambridge: Cambridge University Press, pp. 37–54.

———. 2000b. *Separation and Reunion in Modern China*. Cambridge: Cambridge University Press.

———. 2009. 'Actually Existing Chinese Matriarchy', in Susanne Brandtstädter and Gonçalo D. Santos (eds), *Chinese Kinship: Contemporary Anthropological Perspectives*. Milton Park, Abingdon, Oxon: Routledge, pp. 137–53.

Stockman, Norman, Bonny Norman and Xuewen Sheng. 1995. *Women's Work in East and West: The Dual Burden of Employment and Family Life*. London: UCL Press.

Szonyi, Michael. 2005. 'Mothers, Sons and Lovers: Fidelity and Frugality in the Overseas Chinese Divided Family Before 1949', *Journal of Chinese Overseas* 1(1): 43–64.

———. 2008. *Cold War Island: Quemoy on the Front Line*. Cambridge: Cambridge University Press.

Tai, Pao-Tsun. 2007. *The Concise History of Taiwan* (Chinese-English bilingual edition). Taipei: Taiwan Historica.

The Executive Yuan of the Republic of China. 2013. 'Population Policy White Paper: Fewer Children, Population Aging and Immigration'. Taipei.

Thomas, Todne, Asiya Malik and Rose Wellman. 2017. 'Re-Sacralizing the Social: Spiritual Kinship at the Crossroads of the Abrahamic Religions', in Todne Thomas, Asiya Malik and Rose Wellman (eds), *New Directions in Spiritual Kinship: Sacred Ties Across the Abrahamiic Religions*. London: Palgrave, pp. 1–28.

Thornton, Arland and Hui-Sheng Lin. 1994. *Social Change and the Family in Taiwan*. Chicago, IL: University of Chicago Press.

To, Sandy. 2015. *China's Leftover Women: Late Marriage among Professional Women and Its Consequences*. London; New York: Routledge.

Tsai, Pan-Long. 1999. 'Explaining Taiwan's Economic Miracle: Are the Revisionists Right?', *Agenda: A Journal of Policy Analysis and Reform* 6(1): 69–82.

Tsai, Wen-Qi and Jin-Su Lee. 2016. 'How Do the Children of the Working Class Become Teachers of the Small Country: Taking the Teachers of the Pingtung Area As An Example', in Guang-Zheng Zeng and Yu-Zun Lin (eds), *Change and Consolidation: The Development Crisis, Transformation and Rebirth of South Taiwan*. Pingtung, Taiwan: National Pingtung University, pp. 121–48.

Tseng, Hsun-Hui. 2015. 'Gender and Power Dynamics in Transnational Marriage Brokerage: The Ban on Commercial Matchmaking in Taiwan Reconsidered', *Cross-Currents: East Asian History and Culture Review* 15: 108–32.

———. 2016. 'Racialization of Foreign Women in the Transnational Marriage Market of Taiwan', in Tiantian Zheng (ed.), *Cultural Politics of Gender and Sexuality in Contemporary Asia*. Honolulu: University of Hawaii Press, pp. 205–21.

Tseng, Yen-Jung. 2018. 'Shei shi Gouge Jiating? Nütongzhi Jiating Qinzi Shizuo' [What is Qualified Family? Lesbian Parenthood], in Mei-Hua Chen, Hsiu-Yun Wang and Yu-Ling Huang (eds), *Yuwangxing Gongmin: Tongxing Qinmi Gongminquan Duben* [Citizens with Desires: A Collection of Essays about LGBTQ Intimate Citizenship]. Kaohsiung: Chuliu, pp. 333–56.

Turner, Terence. 2008. 'Marxian Value Theory: An Anthropological Perspective', *Anthropological Theory* 8(1): 43–56.

Vialle, Manon. 2020. 'Blamed for Delay: French Norms and Practices of ART in the Context of Increasing Age-Related Female Infertility', in Marcia C. Inhorn and Nancy J. Smith-Hefner (eds), *Waithood: Gender, Education, and Global Delays in Marriage and Childbearing*. New York; Oxford: Berghahn Books, pp. 317–38.

Vlahoutsikou, Christina. 1997. 'Mothers-in-Law and Daughters-in-Law: Politicizing Confrontations', *Journal of Modern Greek Studies* 15(2): 283–302.

Wakabayashi, Masahiro and Micha Wu (eds). 2000. *Taiwan Chongceng Jindaihua Lunwenji* [Collection on Taiwan's Multi-layered Modernization]. Taipei: Bozhong zhe youxian gongsi.

Wang, Gungwu. 1991. *China and the Chinese Overseas*. Singapore: Times Academic Press.

Watson, James L. 1975. *Emigration and the Chinese Lineage: The Mans in Hong Kong and London*. Berkeley, CA: University of California Press.

———. 1982. 'Chinese Kinship Reconsidered: Anthropological Perspectives on Historical Research', *China Quarterly* 92: 589–622.

Wilson, Thomas M. and Hastings Donnan (eds). 2012. *A Companion to Border Studies*. Hoboken, NJ: Wiley Blackwell.

Wolf, Margery. 1972. *Women and the Family in Rural Taiwan*. Stanford, CA: Stanford University Press.

———. 1985. *Revolution Postponed: Women in Contemporary China*. Stanford, CA: Stanford University Press.

Wong, Magdalena. 2020. *Everyday Masculinities in 21st-Century China: The Making of Able-Responsible Men*. Hong Kong: Hong Kong University Press.

Wu, Ming-Chi. 2001. 'Shiluo de Huayu: Hualien Waisheng Laobing de Liuwang Chujing ji Qi Lunshu' [The Losing Words: Experiences of Diaspora and Discourses of Old Veterans from the Chinese Mainland in Hualien], Master's dissertation. Hualien: National Dong Hwa University.

Xianying [Shining]. 2006 (Reprinted). Kinmen: National Kinmen Institute of Technology and Jushan Xue's Association.

Xie, Kailing. 2021. *Embodying Middle Class Gender Aspirations: Perspectives from China's Privileged Young Women*. Singapore: Springer Singapore Pte. Limited.

Yamaura, Chigusa. 2015a. 'From Manchukuo to Marriage: Localizing Contemporary Cross-Border Marriages between Japan and Northeast China', *The Journal of Asian Studies* 74(3): 565–88.

———. 2015b. 'Marrying Transnational, Desiring Local: Making "Marriageable Others" in Japanese-Chinese Cross-Border Matchmaking', *Anthropological Quarterly* 88(4): 1029–58.

Yan, Yunxiang. 2003. *Private Life under Socialism: Love, Intimacy, and Family Change in a Chinese Village, 1949–1999*. Stanford, CA: Stanford University Press.

———. 2006. 'Girl Power: Young Women and the Waning of Patriarchy in Rural North China', *Ethnology* 45(2): 105–23.

———. 2009. *The Individualization of Chinese Society*. Oxford: Berg.

———. 2016. 'Intergenerational Intimacy and Descending Familism in Rural North China', *American Anthropologist* 118(2): 244–57.

———. 2021. 'Introduction: The Inverted Family, Post-Patriarchal Intergenerationality and Neo-Familism', in Yunxiang Yan (ed.), *Chinese Families Upside Down: Intergenerational Dynamics and Neo-Familism in the Early 21st Century*. Leiden; Boston: Brill, pp. 1–30.

Yanagisako, Sylvia. 2002. *Producing Culture and Capital: Family Firms in Italy*. Princeton, NJ: Princeton University Press.

———. 2013. 'Transnational Family Capitalism', in Susan McKinnon and Fenella Cannell (eds), *Vital Relations: Modernity and the Persistent Life of Kinship*. Santa Fe, NM: SAR Press, pp. 74–95.

———. 2019. 'On Generation', in Lisa Rofel and Sylvia Yanagisako, *Fabricating Transnational Capitalism: A Collaborative Ethnography of Italian-Chinese Global Fashion*. Durham, NC: Duke University Press, pp. 228–63.
Yang, Shu-Qing. 2011. *Jun zi Guxiang Lai: Yixie Kinmen Ren, Kinmen Shi* [Coming from the Homeland: Stories of Kinmen and its People]. Taipei: Showwe.
Yang, Tian-Hou and Li-Kuan Lin. 1997. *Kinmen Hun Jia Lisu* [Marital Rites in Kinmen]. Taipei: Daotian.
Yang, Tsui. 1993. *Riju Shiqi Taiwan Funu Jiefang Yundong: Yi Taiwan Minbao wei fenxi changyu, 1920–1932* [Women's Liberalization Movement in Taiwan under Japanese Occupation: An Analysis Focusing on *Taiwan Minbao*, 1920–1932]. Taipei: Shibao.
Yang, Wen-Shan and Pei-Chih Yen. 2011. 'A Comparative Study of Marital Dissolution in East Asian Societies: Gender Attitudes and Social Expectations towards Marriage in Taiwan, Korea and Japan', *Asian Journal of Social Science* 39: 751–75.
Yang, Wen-Shan and Ying-ying T. Liu. 2013. 'Gender Imbalances and the Twisted Marriage Market in Taiwan', in Dudley L. Poston, Wen San Yang and D. Nicole Farris (eds), *The Family and Social Change in Chinese Societies*. Dordrecht: Springer Netherlands, pp. 117–30.
Yao, Huei-Yao. 2019. 'Zhanhou Taiwan "Jun Zhong Le Yuan" Yanjiu, 1951–1992' [Study on the Postwar Taiwan's 'Military Paradise', 1951–1992], Master's dissertation. Taipei: National Taiwan Normal University.
Yeh, Kuang-Hui and Olwen Benford. 2004. 'Filial Belief and Parent-Child Conflict', *International Journal of Psychology* 39(2): 132–44.
Yi, Chin-Chun and Ying-Hwa Chang (eds). 2012. *Taiwan de Shehui Bianqian, 1985–2005: Jiating yu Hunyin* [Social Change in Taiwan, 1985–2005: Family and Marriage]. Taipei: Institute of Sociology, Academia Sinica.
Yin, A. Chien-chung. 1981. 'Voluntary Associations and Rural-Urban Migration', in Emily Martin Ahern and Hill Gates (eds), *The Anthropology of Taiwanese Society*. Stanford, CA: Stanford University Press, pp. 319–37.
Yu, Ruoh-Rong and I-Chia Huang. 2018. 'Jiating Dongtai Diaocha: Yangben Jiegou, Wenjuan Neirong, Ziliao Waishi yu Yingyong' [The Panel Study of Family Dynamics: Samples, Questionnaires, Data Dissemination and Applications], *Journal of the Chinese Statistical Association* 56(4): 98–115.
Yu, Sojin. 2020. 'Gendered Nationalism in Practice: An Intersectional Analysis of Migrant Integration Policy in South Korea', *Gender & Society* 34(6): 976–1004.
Yu, Wei-hsin. 2009. *Gendered Trajectories: Women, Work, and Social Change in Japan and Taiwan*. Stanford, CA: Stanford University Press.
Zavoretti, Roberta. 2017. 'Being the Right Woman for "Mr. Right": Marriage and Household Politics in Present-Day Nanjing', in Gonçalo D. Santos and Stevan Harrell (eds), *Transforming Patriarchy: Chinese Families in the Twenty-First Century*. Seattle: University of Washington Press, pp. 129–45.
Zhang, Hong. 2017. 'Recalibrating Filial Piety: Realigning the State, Family, and Market Interests in China', in Gonçalo D. Santos and Stevan Harrell (eds), *Transforming Patriarchy: Chinese Families in the Twenty-First Century*. Seattle: University of Washington Press, pp. 234–50.
Zhang, Jun and Peidong Sun. 2014. '"When Are You Going to Get Married?" Parental Matchmaking and Middle-Class Women in Contemporary Urban China', in Deborah S. Davis and Sara L. Friedman (eds), *Wives, Husbands, and Lovers: Marriage and Sexuality in Hong Kong, Taiwan, and Urban China*. Stanford, CA: Stanford University Press, pp. 118–44.

Zhang, Yi. 2016. 'Practising and Displaying Xiao – Young Mothers' Negotiations of Obligations to Elders', *The Journal of Chinese Sociology* 3: 27.

Zheng, Yangwen, Hong Liu and Michael Szonyi (eds). 2010. *The Cold War in Asia: The Battle for Hearts and Minds*. Leiden; Boston: Brill.

Zuo, Jiping. 2016. *Work and Family in Urban China: Women's Changing Experience Since Mao*. New York: Palgrave Macmillan.

Index

adulthood, 90, 95, 100, 105n1
AGATM, 11, 22n8
a-ping-ko business, 6, 47, 54, 56–60, 71, 72–73, 83
   family business, 57, 59
   female entrepreneurs and labour of, 47, 54, 56–60, 72–73, 149–50
   maximization of family labour, 72

Beck, Ulrich, 14, 129
   and Beck-Gernsheim, 14
border, 9, 108–109, 111, 123–24
   conceptualization of, 113
   control of, 109, 112–13, 124–25, 151–52 (*see also* sovereignty)
   porous and permeable, 109, 111
   practices of bordering, 113–14, 124–25
   studies of, 113
borderland, 20, 108–110, 111, 113, 119, 124–25, 127, 152. *See also* Kinmen
boundary
   Barth's theory of ethnicity, 113
   'boundary work', 113, 124
   bureaucratic and discursive boundaries, 111, 124
   concept of, 113
   regarding sex and gender, 11, 16, 28–29, 56, 63
   regarding territory, 109
   social boundaries, 111, 119
Brainer, Amy, 16, 153–55. *See also* LGBT

Carsten, Janet, 142. *See also* new kinship studies
Chan, Shelly, 24–25. *See also* diaspora
Chao, Antonia Yen-Ning, 52. *See also* cross-border marriage; 'mainland soldiers': intimate relationships of
chastity
   chaste widowhood, 27–29, 39–40, 43
   faithful maiden (*zhennü*), 29–30, 40, 44nn2–3 (*see also* Lu, Weijing)
   faithful woman (*jienü*), 29, 30, 39
   fidelity, 26–27, 38–39, 41, 53
   grass widow, 37, 39
   martyred woman (*lienü*), 29
   memorial arches of chastity (*zhenjie paifang*), 24, 28–29, 39
   value or virtue of, 26, 28, 29, 42
   womanly work, 28–29, 44n3
Chen, Changching, 50. *See also* military brothel
Chen, Da, 31. *See also qiaoxiang*
child
   child betrothal, 30
   childbearing, 17, 46, 53, 64, 90, 97, 98–99, 100–101, 104, 108, 120, 124, 125, 135–36, 146n5, 151
   childbirth out of wedlock, 87, 101, 105
   childcare and rearing, 18, 41, 43, 46, 63, 65n3, 87, 99, 100, 108, 118, 120, 125, 129, 136, 139–40, 154

One-Child policy (China), 14–15, 84
policies of childcare, 46, 84
queer, 155
China. *See* People's Republic of China
Chinese Civil War, 1–2, 25, 100, 149
Chinese Communist Party (CCP), 2, 6, 45–46, 48–50, 53–54, 65n3, 78, 127n3. *See also* People's Republic of China
Chinese female spouses, 107–11, 112, 115–27
  cultural similarities, 115–18
  discourses around, 108, 110, 119, 124
  vs. female spouses from Southeast Asia, 109–10, 116, 120
  kin and social networks, 114–18, 125
  in patrilocal joint households, 118–24, 125–26 (*see also* in-laws)
  regulation of (Taiwan), 113–14, 119–20, 123–24 (*see also* citizenship)
  work and economic independence of, 119–22, 123–24, 125
  as *xin zhumin* (Taiwan), 110
citizenship, 16, 109, 113–14, 120, 123–24, 151–52. *See also* sovereignty
civilians (Kinmen)
  lives during the Cold War, 6, 41, 45–46, 64, 80
  relations with soldiers, 41, 45–47, 50–51, 52–53, 64–65 (*see also a-ping-ko* business; 'mainland soldiers')
class, 8, 30, 113, 141
  middle class, 8, 91, 128, 131, 143
  middle-class lifestyle, 8, 143, 150
  reproduction of, 69, 75, 92
  working class, 8, 73, 108, 151 (*see also gongren* status)
Cold War
  context of, 2, 7, 11, 45, 63–65, 70, 91, 149, 157
  framework of bipolar politics, 6, 45–46, 65n1
  military strife between Taiwan and China, 6, 45–46, 65n2
  post-Cold War context, 3, 110, 125
commodity, 20, 70, 82, 84, 88
  commodification of sex and marriage, 16, 17, 109, 114, 116, 125, 151

consumption, 14, 82, 84, 132, 143, 150
  as medium for objectifying desires and emotions, 82, 84, 132, 143
  See also marketization
Confucianism
  Confucian heritages and traditions, 14, 26, 30, 32, 42, 46, 69
  Confucian scholars and officials, 4, 26
  Confucian teachings, 26, 29, 41
  criticism of, 26, 32 (*see also* New Culture Movement)
  Neo-Confucianism, 26, 65n3
conjugality, 78, 129, 131
  conjugal bonds and intimacy, 19, 82, 84, 126, 128–30, 131–33, 140–41, 143–44
  conjugal interest, 84, 118, 126, 142
  conjugal or nuclear family, 26, 65n3, 132–34, 138–40, 144–45, 145n4, 152, 158
  See also under intimacy
'creative conservatism', 67–68, 83. *See also* Magee, Siobhan
cross-border marriage, 16, 151
  'fake marriage', 113
  in Hong Kong, 109, 116, 126–27
  in Kinmen, 8, 11, 92, 107–127, 127n1, 145n1, 151
  parental intervention in, 114–15, 119, 122
  in Taiwan, 107, 109, 127n1
  See also Chinese female spouses; matchmaking
Cruz, Resto, 69–70. *See also* education: as inheritance; inheritance
'the cycle of *laiwang*', 78. *See also* Stafford, Charles
'the cycle of *yang*', 69, 77, 78, 130
  fengyang (respectful care), 69, 138 (*see also* elderly care and support)
  yang (to care for), 69, 75, 77, 79, 130
  See also Stafford, Charles

Dadeng, island, 112, 127n3
Das, Veena, 27, 39–40, 42, 43, 138. *See also* 'ordinary ethics'
diaspora, 25
  time (Kinmen, 1920–1949), 25–27, 37, 42

See also Chan, Shelly; migration
Democratic Progressive Party (DPP), 7, 22n5. *See also* Taiwan
democratization, 2, 7, 20, 68, 104, 148, 150, 153–58. *See also* Taiwan

East Asia
  'compressed modernity', 3
  studies of family change in, 13, 17–18, 23n10, 101, 128–29, 143, 147
  transnational marriage in, 107–08, 116, 151–52
  trends of later and less marriage in, 87
economy (Kinmen)
  development, 6–9, 47, 68, 70, 91
  economic ties with China, 111–12, 114, 123–24
  household, 12, 13, 70–71, 73, 149
  relating to labour migration, 6, 24–26, 37–38, 42, 56 (*see also* remittance)
  See also a-ping-ko business; Kinmen; tourism
education, 20, 68–70
  educational level, 8, 88, 91, 100
  as inheritance, 69–70, 73 (*see also* Cruz, Resto)
  mandatory, 55, 73
  modernization of, 6, 13, 32
  parental investment in children's, 16–17, 55–56, 71–74, 75–76, 150–51
  relating to housing, 75
  relating to marriage, 84–84, 88–89, 91–92, 100, 103, 104, 105n2
  upward mobility, 15, 64, 71
  Western education, 27, 32, 34, 42, 149 (*see also* New Culture Movement; *Xianying*)
  women's access to, 27, 33, 43, 55–57, 59, 71–75, 83–84, 150
elderly care and support, 14, 84, 87, 103, 136–38. *See also* 'the cycle of *yang*': *fengyang*

family
  conjugal or nuclear, 26–27, 65n3, 132–34, 138–40, 142, 144–45, 145n4, 152, 158
  divided, 38

  extended family, 13, 31, 38, 47, 64, 122, 126, 129–31, 143
  familism, 22n10
  family change, 3–4, 12–13, 16, 19, 22n10, 23n11, 101, 110
  Italian family firms, 35
  model of corporate family, 12–14, 38, 43, 64, 147
  property of, 12, 38, 75–77, 103, 118, 123, 126, 128, 132, 150, 154 (*see also* inheritance)
  queer or non-normative, 16
  single-parent families, 101
  'traditional Chinese family', 12, 22n9, 33, 35, 43
Fan, Yu-Wen, 49. *See also* 'mainland soldiers'
filial piety (*xiaoshun*), 14, 40, 56, 69, 80, 84, 126, 131
  filial duties and obligations, 20, 29, 38, 39–40, 58, 73, 84, 90, 94, 100, 101–103, 105, 128–29, 134–35, 142–43
  See also Stafford, Charles; 'the cycle of *yang*'
Friedman, Sara L., 17, 113. *See also* cross-border marriage
Fujian (province), 4–6, 31, 114. *See also* Minnan; *qiaoxiang*

Gell, Alfred, 59. *See also* kinship
gender, 2, 11, 18–19, 47, 58–59, 63, 70–75, 92, 103, 104, 113, 148, 150, 157–58
  as analytical lens, 18–19, 148
  equality, 6, 13, 21n2, 33, 63, 84, 146n5
  gendered boundary, 16
  gendered expectations and roles, 12–13, 16, 22n9, 39, 47, 60, 65, 103, 118, 125, 135, 142, 147
  gendered transmission of family property, 12, 16, 69–70, 75–77, 83 (*see also* inheritance)
  inequality, 12, 16, 36, 39, 42–43, 69–70, 75–77, 126, 130, 149, 154
  performance of, 16, 18, 21n2
  political attitudes towards (Taiwan), 46, 64, 65n3
  sex-gender norms, 18, 22n9, 28, 128, 149

stereotypes, 18, 70, 84, 145
transgender, 16, 155
generation
  as analytical lens, 18–19, 148
  as 'creation', 35 (see Yanagisako, Sylvia)
  generational differences, 8, 14, 67–69, 83, 101, 132, 150
  generational hierarchy, 2, 12, 16–17, 22n9, 58, 63, 78, 105, 118, 125–26, 149
  intergenerational interaction and relations, 2, 14–15, 58, 69, 78, 81–82, 83–85, 105, 118, 155, 158 (see also under intimacy)
  intergenerational transmission, 12, 16, 68–70, 71, 75–77, 83, 150, 158 (see also inheritance)
gongren status, 92. See also class: working class
gossip, 39, 56, 93–94, 95, 153
Guangdong (province), 5, 6, 31, 53. See also *qiaoxiang*

Han-Yu, 48, 52–53. See also 'mainland soldiers'
housing, 14, 68–70, 75, 83, 106, 123, 132, 150, 154
  purchase of, 8, 75–76, 128, 132, 145n2
  real estate market, 72, 114, 125, 128
  See also generation: intergenerational transmission; inheritance

imaginings, 14, 15, 18, 19, 31, 37, 64–65, 90, 100, 104–105, 116, 149, 151, 153–58
  imaginative work incited by marriage, 18, 90, 100, 148, 151
in-laws
  interaction within patrilocal households, 38–39, 118–26, 129, 131, 137–38
  relations between daughter- and mother-in-law, 40, 71, 73, 118–26, 129–31, 133–40, 143–44, 145n4, 146n6
  See also 'the work of marriage'; 'uterine family'
individual

autonomy, 12, 17, 27, 34, 54, 58–60, 65n3, 84, 89–90, 92, 101, 103, 105, 111, 121–22, 126, 131, 143, 147, 151
desires, 13–15, 17, 43, 60, 64–65, 76, 81, 84, 90, 94, 97, 100, 101–104, 105, 116, 118, 128, 131, 133, 141–42, 143–44, 148, 150, 158
emotions, 13–15, 43, 64, 82, 104, 121, 143, 148
privacy, 14, 92–94, 132, 143, 150
See also individualism; individualization
individualism, 4, 83, 128, 141. See also individual; individualization
individualization, 14, 84. See also Beck, Ulrich; individual; individualism; Yan Yunxiang
Indonesia, 5, 24, 103, 110, 127n1. See also cross-border marriage; migration; Southeast Asia
inheritance, 69–70, 73, 75–77, 103. See also Cruz, Resto; family: property of; gender: gendered transmission of family property; generation: intergenerational transmission
intimacy
  between generations, 2, 15, 69–70, 82, 84–85, 118, 140 (see also parent-child ties)
  conjugal intimacy and affective ties, 82, 84, 126, 128, 131–33, 143–44, 152 (see also conjugality)
  heterosexual intimate or romantic relationship, 17, 47–48, 51–53, 54, 55, 61, 63, 92–94, 98–99, 105, 125–26, 130, 131–32

Japan, 17, 22n10, 107, 124
  anti-Japanese activities, 25, 36, 44n7
  colonizing Taiwan (1895–1945), 21n2
  First Sino-Japanese War, 2
  invading China (1937–1945), 6, 65n3
  occupying Kinmen (1937–1945), 6, 35, 44n4

Kinmen (islands)
  as anti-communist frontline during the Cold War, 2

benefits and social welfare in, 7–8, 21n4, 117
description of, 2–3, 4–9
landscape of, 2–3, 9, 24–25, 118
location of, 2–3
sorghum and liquor industry, 6, 7–8, 21n4, 47, 71, 91–92, 107, 122
See also civilians; militarization; Minnan
kinship
constitutive power of, 2, 13, 26, 30, 42–43, 85, 147–48
labour of, 80, 82, 85
LGBT kinship practices, 16 (*see also* LGBT)
positive and negative effects of, 16, 42, 59, 63, 129, 148, 152
processual and performative aspects of, 15, 69, 142, 148
reproductive aspects of, 12, 36, 47, 59, 63, 65, 104, 108, 124–25, 148
social networks based on, 10, 15, 17, 35, 37, 42, 58, 78, 80, 82, 88, 93, 102, 114, 116, 126, 139, 140, 142, 149, 152
studies of Chinese kinship, 12–13, 14–15, 16, 43, 147–48
transformative capacities of, 12–13, 17, 27, 34–36, 42, 55, 68, 70, 111, 131, 148–49, 153–54
Kuomintang (KMT), 2, 6–7, 36, 45–46, 47–50, 52–53, 55, 63–64, 65n3, 78, 159n12
Chinese Cultural Renaissance Movement, 46

LGBT
families, 16
Loving Parents of LGBT Taiwan, 155
Pride parade, 155, 157
rights campaigns, 7, 16, 21, 153, 155–58
Taiwan Equality Campaign (TEC), 156
Taiwan Tongzhi (LGBTQ+) Hotline Association, 153
See also same-sex marriage
Lin Ma-Teng, 31, 37, 54
Liu, Hsiang-Chin, 27
Lu, Weijing, 30, 40. *See also* chastity

Magee, Siobhan, 67–68, 141. *See also* 'creative conservatism'
'mainland soldiers', 47, 48–53, 57, 63, 64
intimate relationships of, 47, 52–53, 63 (*see also* Chao, Antonia Yen-Ning; Han-Yu)
legal regulation of their marriages, 46, 48–49, 51–52
military morale of, 48–50
'snatched' by the KMT's army, 52, 53
vs. Taiwanese soldiers, 51
transgression of the marriage law, 49, 51, 53, 63
veterans, 47, 48, 52
Malaysia, 5, 10, 24, 38. *See also* migration; Southeast Asia
Mann, Susan, 28
marital options
constrained, 48, 52, 64, 89, 90, 104, 105n1
diversified, 47, 54, 61, 64, 83, 101
marital reform, 2, 19, 33, 42
reform of marital rites, 78–79
reformers, 1–2, 21n2, 26–27, 33, 34, 43, 65n3
See also New Culture Movement
marketization, 5, 14–15, 84, 118, 143, 148. *See also* commodity; neoliberalism
marriage
age at first marriage, 88
arranged, 30, 35, 42, 58, 61, 101
by choice, 6, 13, 15, 26, 33–34, 131, 145n1
deferral of, 74, 83, 89–91, 94, 103, 104, 105n1, 151
future-making aspect of, 1, 19, 83, 89, 116, 129, 141, 144, 148
market of, 31–33, 47, 60, 91–92, 104, 151
marriageability, 89, 91, 92 (*see also* social status)
relational aspect of, 1, 84, 89, 116, 129, 141, 144, 147–48, 152
remarriage, 38–39, 41, 43, 54, 122
tongju (form of marriage), 34, 42
tongyangxi (form of marriage), 30, 31
visions of, 1, 4, 26–27, 32–33, 34, 42–43, 91, 126, 149

martial law, 7, 45, 68, 150
matchmaking, 31, 87, 112
  commercialized, 114, 116, 151
  cross-border, 110–11, 114, 125, 151 (*see also* cross-border marriage)
  'matchmaking corner' (Shanghai), 15
  through on-line dating, 92
  tours of, 114, 120, 122
  See also marital options; *meiren*
meiren
  as marriage ritual facilitator, 78, 80 (*see also* ritual; wedding)
  as matchmaker, 30, 32, 67, 112, 114–15, 117 (*see also* matchmaking)
migration, 24, 113
  migrant economy, 6, 19, 24, 25, 42 (*see also* remittance)
  transnational labour migration, 5–6, 24–25, 26, 30, 31, 42, 149 (*see also* diaspora)
  See also cross-border marriage; mobility
militarization, 6, 10, 45, 47, 54, 60, 64
  ad hoc, 45
  demilitarization, 7, 9, 10, 72, 111
  military mobilization, 50, 63, 64
  militia and training, 6, 46, 52, 56, 62
  See also Cold War; *Zhandi Zhengwu*
military brothel, 46, 48–50
  '831', 50
  military prostitution, 50
  prostitutes or sex workers, 46, 47
  See also 'mainland soldiers'; militarization
Minnan, 4, 34, 114, 116, 117, 118, 120, 125
  architectural style, 5, 9
  Hokkien (dialect), 4, 114, 116, 156
mobility, 10, 55, 92, 103, 104, 108, 112
  physically transnational, 6, 25, 92 (*see also* migration)
  socially upward mobility, 7, 8, 15, 27, 36, 37, 42, 55, 59, 64, 69–71, 75, 92, 116, 129, 143, 148, 150 (*see also* class; education)
modernity, 1, 6, 17, 21n2, 24, 39, 42, 43, 148, 149
  capitalist, 80, 83, 85
  militarized, 6
  multiple forms or conditions of, 3, 4, 19, 148

  regimes of, 2, 12
  theories of, 3, 13, 17, 147
  Western, 12, 32
modernization, 1, 3, 13, 21n2, 64, 147
  alongside democratization and expansive neoliberalism, 7
  under militarization, 6, 47, 149
  in *qiaoxiang*, 6, 26, 32, 34, 35, 53, 149
  theories of, 13, 83

neo-familism, 15, 85. *See* Yan, Yunxiang
neoliberalism, 3, 7, 82
  neoliberal economy, 70, 92, 143 (*see also* marketization)
  neoliberal governance, 85, 143
New Culture Movement, 6, 21n2, 26–27, 33, 42, 43n1, 65n3
May Fourth movement, 43n1
new kinship studies, 13, 15, 16, 18, 47, 69, 129–30, 147–48

'ordinary ethics', 27, 39–40, 43, 138
  empathy, 40, 41, 43
  ethical judgements, 18, 43, 90
  ethical striving and struggles, 43, 60, 64–65, 130, 136–38, 140, 144, 146n6
  moral subjectivities, 39, 41
  See also Das, Veena

parent-child ties, 14, 18, 68, 70, 84, 129, 145
  father-daughter ties, 77, 83, 150
  father-son filiation, 12, 22n9, 77, 83, 150 (*see also* patriliny)
  mother-daughter ties, 55, 83, 150
  mother-son ties, 70, 130, 131, 135 (*see also* 'uterine family')
  See also generation; intimacy: between generations
patriarchy
  Chinese patriarchy, 15, 18, 24, 40, 47, 81, 129, 145, 150
  generational and gender hierarchies, 2, 12, 13, 16, 18, 19, 22n9, 58, 63, 65, 69, 125, 126, 148–49
  patriarchal norms, 18, 39, 58, 87, 111, 128, 142, 147
  patriarchal ordering, 9, 63, 64

'transforming patriarchy', 18
patriliny
  ancestral hall, 4, 5, 24, 32, 78, 79
  continue family or patrilineal lines, 12, 29, 38, 53, 58, 67, 88, 100, 139
  patrilineage, 5, 10, 24, 78, 134, 148, 149
  patrilineal settlements or villages, 5, 9, 12, 36, 78, 129, 139
  written genealogy (*zupu*), 4, 5, 112
People's Republic of China (PRC), 1, 45
  collectivization, 14, 84
  Cultural Revolution, 46
  One-Child policy, 14, 15, 84
  post-reform, 14, 82, 117, 118, 126, 132
  See also Chinese Communist Party
personhood, 11, 69, 74, 77, 78, 80, 83, 84, 104, 143. *See also* kinship; relatedness
public employment, 74, 96
  civil servants, 75, 91, 96
  civil service examination, 73, 96
  school teachers, 71, 75, 91–92, 134
  See also class; social status

qiaoxiang, 6, 31, 32, 37. *See also* Fujian; Guangdong; Kinmen; migration; remittance

relatedness, 1, 18, 21, 69, 78, 82, 90, 130, 138, 142, 144. *See also* kinship; new kinship studies; personhood
remittance, 6, 26, 31, 33, 34, 37, 38, 53, 55, 56, 149. *See also* migration; *qiaoxiang*; Southeast Asia
Republic of China (ROC). *See* Taiwan
Republican era (1912–1949), 3, 26, 27, 39, 42
ritual
  ancestor worship, 4, 10, 22n7, 58, 118, 123, 125, 134
  based on kinship and patriliny, 9, 10, 13, 58, 85, 88, 118, 125, 132
  continuities of, 5, 11, 13, 46, 88, 150
  novel rites of celebration, 78, 82
  rites of *yingqu*, 78, 81 (*see also* wedding)
  sociality within, 10, 69, 85 (*see also* 'the cycle of *laiwang*')
  traditional marital rites, 33, 34, 77–78, 80, 81, 82, 84, 85n2, 150 (*see also* wedding)

same-sex marriage (Taiwan)
  campaigns supporting, 155–57
  conservative groups and campaigns against, 155–57
  constitutional court's ruling on, 153, 155
  legalization of, 104, 153, 155–57, 159n5
  referendum, 104, 155–56, 158n3, 159n6, 159n11
  See also LGBT
siblings
  difficult or negative feelings between, 64
  inequality between heterosexual siblings, 70, 76
  ties and support between, 55, 56, 59, 63–64, 70, 73, 102, 150
Singapore, 5, 24, 26, 31, 32, 34, 36, 39. *See also* migration; Southeast Asia
single person
  interaction with families, 74, 90, 101–103
  'leftover women" (China), 92, 103
  'loneliness', 103
  matchmaking activities for, 87
  See also 'waithood'
smuggling (*zousi*), 111, 112, 113
social status, 28, 35, 42, 52, 89, 91, 92, 94. *See also* class; education
Sommer, Matthew H., 28
Southeast Asia
  as bride-sending countries, 107, 109, 116
  as destinations of Kinmen migrants, 5, 33, 37, 38
  See also cross-border marriage; Indonesia; Malaysia; migration; Singapore
sovereignty
  performance of, 113
  Taiwan, 16, 109, 113
  See also border; citizenship; cross-border marriage
Stafford, Charles, 69, 78, 130. *See also* new kinship studies; 'the cycle of *laiwang*'; 'the cycle of *yang*'

Sun Yat-sen, 6, 25
Szonyi, Michael, 6, 45–47, 60, 65n4

Taiwan
  description of, 2, 6–7, 45, 68
  economic development, 6–7, 68
  economic recession and wage
    stagnation, 71, 74, 85n1, 91
  international status, 7, 68
  social movements, 7, 68, 150
  See also democratization; Japan;
    Kuomintang; sovereignty
temporality
  as analytical lens, 18–19, 90, 100, 142,
    148
  in migration studies, 24–25 (*see also*
    Chan, Shelly; diaspora)
  personal and familial experiences,
    24, 25–26, 31, 42–43, 100–101,
    140–43, 151
  social and political times, 3, 12, 19, 42
  'the work of time', 142
tourism (Kinmen), 7, 9, 91, 116, 123, 124
  featured by tax-free shopping, 8, 91, 121
  tourists from China, 8, 22n5, 121, 123,
    152
  See also cross-border marriage; *Xiao
    San Tong*

'uterine family', 70, 130–31, 138–39, 143.
  See also Wolf, Margery

'waithood', 90, 105n1
wedding
  biscuits and cakes (*xibing*), 79, 80, 85n3
  bridal photography, 78, 81–82
  bridewealth (*pinjin*), 33, 60, 79, 86n4,
    91, 104, 115
  dowry (*jiazhuang*), 70, 76, 83
  feast or banquet (*xiyan*), 67, 77, 78, 80,
    81, 85n3

jituan jiehun (group wedding
  ceremony), 80
parental intervention in children's, 8,
  77–80
planning of, 7, 77, 81
sociality within, 35, 58, 80, 82 (*see also*
  'the cycle of *laiwang*')
as way of intergenerational
  transmission, 68–70 (*see also*
  inheritance)
as way of making intergenerational
  bonds, 70, 79, 82, 84 (*see also*
  parent-child ties)
See also ritual
Wolf, Margery, 130–31, 135, 138, 139,
  143–44. *See also* in-laws; 'uterine
  family'
'the work of marriage', 130–31, 134, 138,
  139, 142, 144

Xiamen, 5–6, 8, 34, 111, 114, 116, 117,
  122, 127n3, 128. *See also* Minnan;
  Xiao San Tong
Xianying (*Shinging*), 31–35, 44nn4–5. *See
  also* migration; *qiaoxiang*
Xiao San Tong (ferry service), 8, 111, 113,
  114, 123–24, 125. *See also* Kinmen;
  tourism; Xiamen

Yan, Yunxiang, 14–15, 84–85, 126, 141.
  See also neo-familism
Yanagisako, Sylvia, 35. *See also* family;
  generation: as 'creation'
yanglou, 24–25, 32. *See also* Kinmen;
  migration; remittance

Zhandi Zhengwu, 45
  system of military rule, 2, 62, 68
  See also Kinmen; militarization

www.ingramcontent.com/pod-product-compliance
Lightning Source LLC
Chambersburg PA
CBHW051547020426
42333CB00016B/2142